The Apostolic Church Order

Early Christian Studies 10

The Apostolic Church Order
The Greek Text with Introduction, Translation and Annotation

by

Alistair Stewart-Sykes

The Apostolic Church Order: The Greek Text with introduction, translation and annotation.
by Alistair Stewart-Sykes

First published in Australia in October 2006 by
ST PAULS PUBLICATIONS
Society of St Paul
60-70 Broughton Road
P O Box 906
Strathfield, NSW 2135
Australia

in association with the

Centre for Early Christian Studies
Australian Catholic University
1100 Nudgee Road
Banyo, QLD 4014
Australia
http://www.cecs.acu.edu.au

National Library of Australia Cataloguing-in-publication data:

The Apostolic Church Order: The Greek Text with introduction, translation and annotation.
Bibliography. Includes index.

1. Canon law – Early church, ca. 30-600. 2. Christian life – Early works to 1800. 3. Church history – Primitive and early church, ca. 30-600 – Sources. 4. Church orders, Ancient. I. Stewart-Sykes, Alistair. II. Australian Catholic University. Centre for Early Christian Studies (Series: Early Christian Studies).

270.1

Printed and bound by:
Watson Ferguson & Company
Moorooka, Brisbane

ISBN 0 9752138 4 9 (pbk.).

Preface

I was first introduced to this work by Fr Austin Milner, of Jamaica, in a conversation in Barbados concerning the state of study of the church orders generally. I am not ashamed to admit that at the time I had never come across the work owing to the neglect which it suffered for the greater part of the last century, but being interested in Christian prophecy, and female prophecy in particular, I was intrigued at Fr Milner's description of a church which supported two widows who had revelations. It seemed to me that some publication should reawaken study of this text.

Although the seed of the work was found in the Caribbean it was not possible to plant it there; I had hoped to begin the work after moving to the USA but events conspired to prevent this happening and so the present work was grown entirely in Dorset soil and is the product of a country parson's leisure, therefore coming forth over ten years after its first inception.

The purpose of this work is an attempt to bring this church order to renewed scholarly attention. As such I feel that no particular apology is required, for as Faivre, one of the few scholars to have paid any serious attention to this work, remarks: "Depuis sa dernière édition... son abandon est quasi-total." (Faivre, "Apostolicité", 22). A context for this remark may be provided by the observation that this last edition was published in 1914. Others have likewise lamented the neglect of this church order and so, even should my conclusions in the introduction, in which I essay a date rather earlier than that usually offered, a *Sitz im Leben* for the redaction of the text, and an exploration of the sources employed, be found entirely wanting by the scholarly community, and even should the text I have produced be utterly scorned, I would claim nonetheless to have done a service by rescuing this church order from undeserved obscurity.

An apologia, however, needs to preface the text. Indeed, this is the eighth edition of the Greek text, the text having previously been edited by Bickell, Pitra, Lagarde, Hilgenfeld, Funk, Harnack and Schermann, as well as receiving attention from Wilamowitz-Moellendorff and Hennecke. I am therefore moving somewhat hubristically in exalted company. The Greek text is extant in its entirety in but one MS; in addition there are MSS of the Epitome, a work related to the Apostolic Church Order, and another abbreviated version of the two ways section in a further MS. Beyond this there are versions of the whole in Syriac, Sahidic, Arabic and Ethiopic and a substantial fragment in Latin, which are of varying value in determining the Greek text.

Thus when I come to present the text, not every variation between the versions is given, as at some points the text is clear, and at others the versions diverge so widely from the Greek that they are clearly attempts to impose a meaning comprehensible to the reader upon an obscure text; as such they are interesting for the *Nachleben* of this living literature, but not useful for the exercise of establishing the original. Likewise not every suggested emendation from the editors is listed, nor every obvious error in the Greek MSS, the sole criterion being worth of due consideration in the reconstruction of the Greek text.

Because of the complexity of the task I have employed annotation rather than a conventional apparatus, thereby attempting to show the rationale by which I have concluded each disputed point so that others may more readily disagree, especially as I am by no means convinced of the correctness of every reading printed.

Besides a text and an introduction I have also provided an English translation for the convenience of readers. As far as I can tell this is the first time that a translation of the entire Greek text into a modern language has been published. Readers are nonetheless warned that the translation is made on the basis of the text presented here, which diverges significantly at several points from earlier texts, and may therefore be entirely misleading, as much depends on conjecture. I have, however, signalled some of the more radical points of departure from the received text. Annotation beyond this has been fairly minimal because most points of particular interest are covered in the introduction and since much of the material is parallel to the Didache, on which many excellent commentaries are already available, and is therefore left without comment to avoid duplication of what is already available.

The most pleasant duty, however, is the acknowledgement of those who have assisted me in this task. First mention must of course be given to Fr Milner; however special thanks must be accorded to Philip Purchase, once of my parish but now a classicist in far-off places, Allen Brent, and Wendy Mayer, each of whom have read the MS and suggested corrections and improvements. Subsequently Gilles Dorival most graciously made me welcome in Aix en Provence and gave me access to the papers of the late Pierre Nautin; there, on the feast of Saints Timothy and Titus this year, I thought that the work had been completed. However, Allie Ernst subsequently gave me cause to reconsider many points, though here I may state that I have not accepted all the suggestions that I have received and must be held responsible at the last for any error. In the closing stages of the work, Christine Trevett was gracious in sharing material and ideas with me, and finally David Luckensmeyer and Dinah Joesoef at the Centre for Early Christian Studies brought order to unruly tables and apparatūs.

The dedication is to a fine priest, a former student, and true friend; that he hardly embodies the characteristics demanded in this text of a presbyter, but rather those of bishop and deacon, says more about the history of the text than about his exercise of his sacred office.

Sturminster Marshall Vicarage:
St John`s day, 2005

Abbreviations

H.E.	*Historia Ecclesiastica*
HThR	*Harvard Theological Review*
JECS	*Journal of Early Christian Studies*
JEH	*Journal of Ecclesiastical History*
JSNT	*Journal for the Study of the New Testament*
JTS	*Journal of Theological Studies*
RevScRel	*Revue des Sciences Religieuses*
SBL	*Society for Biblical Literature*
ThQ	*Theologische Quartalschrift*
TU	Texte und Untersuchungen
TWT	Two Ways Tradition
VigChr	*Vigiliae Christianae*
WUNT	Wissenschaftliche Untersuchungen zum Neuen Testament
ZNW	*Zeitschrift für die Neutestamentliche Wissenschaft*

To my friend and brother presbyter
Noel Burke
Canon of the Cathedral of St Michael
in the island Diocese of Barbados

Table of Contents

The Apostolic Church-order

This church-order was first published in Greek in 1843 by Bickell under the name of *Die apostolische Kirchenordnung.*[1] Although it has received a variety of names, that given by Bickell is as good as any, and is employed here in its accepted English translation. This is abbreviated to K, for *Kirchenordnung*, following Schermann, whose system of abbreviation is largely followed.[2]

Although several editions were published in the nineteenth century, K was eclipsed in scholarly attention by the discovery of the *Didache*.[3] It was in his monograph on the *Didache* that Harnack determined that K was a late and secondary work, the product of Egypt in the fourth century and, although he recognised that ancient sources lay behind the church-order, it is his conclusion on date and provenance that is remembered. Harnack's work thus concluded the process of investigation, and ushered in the virtual end of the serious study of K.

Although Harnack's conclusion that K was a late and secondary work is that which is remembered, Harnack did make some effort to determine the redactional history of the church-order and to determine older sources that lay behind it. Since we may now see church-orders as "living literature" we may study both the sources and the manner of their redaction in evaluating the historical value of the work and so give attention once again to the ancient sources lying behind the work, as well as revisiting Harnack's conclusions. Such is the purpose of this introduction.

The work is clearly composite. After an epistolary opening describing the gathering of the apostles there follows an ethical section consisting of the two-ways material, similar to that found in the *Didache*, in which different sections of the material are attributed to different apostles. After this there is

---

[1] In his *Geschichte des Kirchenrechts* I (Giessen 1843). This was the first edition of the Greek text, though the Ethiopic version was published with a Latin translation by J. Ludolfus (Leutholf) in his *Iobi Ludolfi alias Leutholf dicti ad suam Historiam Aethiopicam antehac commentarius* (Frankfurt am Main 1691) 304-314.

[2] T. Schermann, *Eine Elfapostelmoral oder die x-Rezension der "beiden Wege"* (Veröffentlichungen aus dem Kirchenhistorischen Seminar München 2.2; Munich 1903).

[3] For further introductory comments regarding the discussion before Harnack, see A. Harnack, *Die Lehre der zwölf Apostel nebst Untersuchungen zur ältesten Geschichte der Kirchenverfassung und des Kirchenrechts* (TU 2.1; Leipzig 1886) 193-209, and B. Steimer, *Vertex Traditionis* (Berlin 1992) 60-63. However, particular mention must be made of A. Krawutzcky, "Über das altkirchliche Unterrichtsbuch 'Die zwei Wege oder die Entscheidung des Petrus'", *ThQ* 64 (1882) 359-445, to which Harnack was particularly indebted.

a section concerning ministries, beginning with directions for the election of a bishop, and then a discussion of the ministries of women, which follows dialogically from the discussion of ministries more generally. Lemoine thus sees the work built up of different sections, and suggests that the work was extended in sections in different centuries: the first being the dialogical construction of the TWT in the second century; the second, the discussion of ministries and the elaboration of a threefold order which excludes women (in the third); and finally, the redaction of the introductory material later in the third century.[4] Frankly this is too simple; within the sections there are signs of expansion and the composite nature of the completed work indicates that the sections had independent life before their redactional juncture. The starting point for the discussion is therefore that of Harnack, who assumes that the document was built up redactionally from distinct and ancient sources and who went on to reconstruct and to discuss these sources.

Harnack determined that there were three main sources employed by the redactor: a document of the TWT type, which he first identified as the *Didache*,[5] and subsequently as a prior edition of the TWT material used by the didachist,[6] and two ancient sources on office and ordination. Beyond that he suggested that the redactor had an apostle list of some antiquity and the *Epistle of Barnabas*, which he employed in the construction of the TWT section of K.[7] Although we will discover some differences with Harnack, his discussion provides a useful starting point. However, in determining the complex redactional history of K we may well begin with the TWT material, in that there are other versions of the material, which, once the order of relationships is established, can be employed as comparative material to enable us to discern the hand of various redactors.

1: The TWT section

The first section of K is taken up with the ethical discourse which is known as the TWT. This same discourse is also found in the *Didache* (henceforth D), in a Latin translation known as the *Doctrina apostolorum* (henceforth L) and in the *Epistle of Barnabas* (henceforth B). The origin of this discourse in Jewish ethical discourse is widely recognised. Thus, as examples, we may

---

[4] B. Lemoine, "Étude de la notice sur l'évêque dans la 'Constitution ecclésiastique des apôtres (C.E.A.)'", *Questions liturgiques* 80 (1999) 5-23. This conclusion is provisionally stated at 12, and subsequently elaborated.

[5] Harnack, *Lehre*, 210-211.

[6] A. Harnack, *The Sources of the Apostolic Canons* (Eng. trans; London 1895) 1.

[7] Harnack, *Lehre*, 210-215.

observe *Testament of Levi* 19: "Choose for yourself light or darkness", and the statement of ethical dualism which states the existence of two ways, which God has granted, in *Testament of Asher* 1.[8] Most pressing of the parallels, however, is that noted by Audet between the Christian TWT and that of the Qumran *Community Rule*.[9] The TWT material of K thus has a long ancestry, but we need to determine the extent of that ancestry and its history.

1.1: The TWT section of K and E

As already noted, TWT material is found in D and B as well as in K. The first issue, therefore, which this section of K throws up, is the literary relationships between these various versions. Before this set of relationships can be discussed, however, it is necessary to determine the relationship between K itself and a further version, which is found in three MSS and which describes itself as the epitome of the canons of the apostles (E).[10] This is the closest version of TWT to K, in that the material is divided in the same way between the same eleven apostles. As Wengst points out, a literary relationship is evident not simply in that both contain the way of life divided among the same eleven apostles in the same manner, but in view of their agreements against D.[11] Among them we may note:

D	K	E
ἡ μὲν οὖν ὁδὸς τῆς ζωῆς ἐστιν αὕτη· πρῶτον ἀγαπήσεις τὸν θεὸν τὸν ποιήσαντά σε,	ἡ μὲν γὰρ ὁδὸς τῆς ζωῆς ἐστιν αὕτη· πρῶτον ἀγαπήσεις τὸν θεὸν τὸν ποιήσαντά σε **ἐξ ὅλης τῆς καρδίας** σου	ἡ οὖν τῆς ζωῆς ἐστιν αὕτη· πρῶτον ἀγαπήσεις τὸν θεὸν τὸν ποιήσαντά σε **ἐξ ὅλης σου καρδίας·**

[8] Note the discussions of K. Niederwimmer, *Die Didache* (Göttingen 1993²) 57-58, 84-87; W. Rordorf and A. Tuilier, *La doctrine des douze apôtres* (Paris 1998) 24; H. van de Sandt and D. Flusser, *The Didache: Its Jewish Sources and Its Place in Early Judaism and Christianity* (Assen 2002) 57-58.

[9] J.-P. Audet, "Affinités littéraires et doctrinales du 'Manuel de discipline'", *Revue Biblique* 59 (1952) 219-238.

[10] Ἐπιτομὴ ὅρων τῶν ἁγίων ἀποστόλων.

[11] K. Wengst, *Schriften des Urchristentums* 2 (Darmstadt 1984) 7-8.

οὐ ποιήσεις σχίσμα, εἰρηνεύσεις δὲ μαχομένους, κρινεῖς δικαίως, οὐ λήψη πρόσωπον ἐλέγξαι ἐπὶ παραπτώμασιν.	Κηφᾶς εἶπεν· οὐ ποιήσεις σχίσματα, εἰρηνεύσεις δὲ μαχομένους, κρινεῖς δικαίως, οὐ λήψη πρόσωπον ἐλέγξαι **τινὰ** ἐπὶ **παραπτώματι**, οὐ γὰρ ἰσχύει πλοῦτος παρὰ κυρίῳ· οὐ γὰρ ἀξία προσκρίνει οὐδὲ κάλλος ὠφελεῖ, ἀλλ' **ἰσότης ἐστι** πάντων **παρ**' αὐτῷ.	Κηφᾶς εἶπεν· οὐ ποιήσεις σχίσμα, εἰρηνεύσεις δὲ μαχομένους, κρινεῖς δικαίως, οὐ λήψη πρόσωπον ἐλέγξαι **τινὰ** ἐπὶ **παραπτώματι**, **ἰσότης** γὰρ **ἐστι** **παρὰ** θεῷ·

Whereas Harnack suggested that E was an abbreviation of K,[12] Schermann argued that E was not derived from K but actually a source of K, interpreting the title, namely *ἐπιτομὴ ὅρων τῶν ἁγίων ἀποστόλων καθολικῆς παραδόσεως*, as stating that E was a compendium of apostolic teaching, rather than an abbreviation of the apostolic canons (namely K).[13] Further to this, he points out that the apostle lists of E and K are different, in that K includes Jude the son of James, who is added to this list in order to make up the number of twelve, whereas there is no part for him in the TWT material. He therefore suggests that the list of eleven apostles to whom the material is attributed is the more original, as one would expect a later correction to make twelve.[14] The list preceding K must therefore be secondary, and on this basis he suggested that E was one of the sources of K. The text of E is reprinted as appendix A, and a synopsis of K, D, and E is to be found at appendix B.

There are certain factors which speak in favour of seeing E as a source of K. For instance, there are several points at which K is more extensive in its treatment than the corresponding point in E, and this may readily be seen as an expansion of an earlier source; in this light Wengst suggests that such material, had it been available to E, would not have been omitted.[15] Although this is possible, it is not a secure argument; if E is seen as an abbreviation

[12] Harnack, *Lehre,* 204.
[13] Schermann, *Elfapostelmoral*, 19-20.
[14] Schermann, *Elfapostelmoral*, 21-22.
[15] Wengst, *Schriften*, 8.

there is no reason why the omission of this secondary material might not be seen as part of the abbreviating technique. Wengst further argues that at several points when K follows D, E appears to preserve a more original reading.[16] As an example we may take:

D	K	E
ὁδοὶ δύο εἰσί, μία τῆς ζωῆς καὶ μία τοῦ θανάτου, διαφορὰ δὲ πολλὴ μεταξὺ τῶν δύο ὁδῶν.	ὁδοὶ δύο εἰσί, μία τῆς ζωῆς καὶ μία τοῦ θανάτου, διαφορὰ δὲ πολλὴ μεταξὺ τῶν δύο ὁδῶν.	ὁδοὶ δύο εἰσί, μία τῆς ζωῆς καὶ μία τοῦ θανάτου, **καὶ διαφορὰ πολλὴ τῶν δύο.**

With this one exception, however, all of Wengst's more original readings are absences from E of material which is in D, which, once again, may be seen as the result of the process of abbreviation. However, the concluding speech, that of Bartholomew, which in E is a *Haustafel* parallel to D, is entirely different in K, which has a concluding eschatological exhortation with a close relationship to B. The text of this eschatological conclusion is shown at appendix C in a synoptic arrangement with the parallel B material.

Given the significant departure here, were E derived from K as Harnack and the majority of scholars have assumed, then it would have to be assumed that E had determined to leave K at this point and to follow D, which seems improbable given the otherwise close reliance on K. If E is directly dependent upon D, however, and K, in turn, on E, then there is no difficulty in accepting that K, which expands material elsewhere, has determined at this point to follow another source. This may be classed as a major agreement of D and E against K. There are, moreover, other minor agreements of D and E against K, which would suggest that E, and not K, is the document directly derived from D, and that K is derived from E.

First is that occurring in Nathanael's speech:

[16] Wengst, *Schriften*, 9.

D	K	E
Οὐχ ὑψώσεις σεαυτόν, οὐδὲ δώσεις τῇ ψυχῇ σου **θράσος**. οὐ **κολληθήσεται** ἡ ψυχή σου μετὰ ὑψηλῶν, ἀλλὰ μετὰ δικαίων καὶ ταπεινῶν ἀναστραφήσῃ.	Οὐχ ὑψώσεις σεαυτόν, οὐδὲ δώσεις τὴν ψυχήν σου μετὰ ὑψηλῶν ἀλλὰ μετὰ δικαίων καὶ ταπεινῶν ἀναστραφήσῃ.	Οὐχ ὑψώσεις σεαυτόν, οὐ δώσεις τῇ ψυχῇ σου **θράσος**, οὐδὲ **κολληθήσῃ** τῇ ψυχῇ σου μετὰ ὑψηλῶν· ἀλλὰ μετὰ δικαίων καὶ ταπεινῶν

Here E is much closer to D than to K; against K, both D and E contain the statement *οὐ δώσεις τῇ ψυχῇ σου θράσος* and include the verb *κολληθήσεται*.

In Thomas` speech we read:

D	K	E
μνησθήσῃ **νυκτὸς καὶ ἡμέρας**, τιμήσεις **δὲ** αὐτὸν ὡς κύριον.	μνησθήσῃ αὐτοῦ νύκτα καὶ ἡμέραν, τιμήσεις αὐτὸν ὡς τὸν κύριον.	μνησθήσῃ αὐτοῦ **νυκτὸς καὶ ἡμέρας**, τιμήσεις **δὲ** αὐτὸν ὡς κύριον,

D and E have *νυκτὸς καὶ ἡμέρας*, as opposed to K's *νύκτα καὶ ἡμέραν*, and both, moreover, contain the statement *τιμήσεις δὲ αὐτὸν ὡς κύριον* as opposed to K`s *τιμήσεις αὐτὸν ὡς τὸν κύριον*.

Next, close to the beginning of TWT, we may note:

D	K	E
ἡ μὲν **οὖν** ὁδὸς τῆς ζωῆς ἐστιν αὕτη·	ἡ μὲν γὰρ ὁδὸς τῆς ζωῆς ἐστιν αὕτη·	ἡ **οὖν** τῆς ζωῆς ἐστιν αὕτη·

οὖν is present in D and E, but not K. Harnack and Schermann, however, read *οὖν* here, without MS evidence for K and against the versions.[17] Part of the problem with assessing the extent of agreement between K, D and E is the problem of text, and the extent to which E should be counted as a textual witness for K.

Another is thus less textually secure:

[17] See the textual commentary ad loc.

D	K	E
δεύτερον τὸν πλησίον σου ὡς σεαυτόν	δευτέρα δὲ· ἀγαπήσεις τὸν πλησίον σου ὡς ἑαυτόν,	**δεύτερον** ἀγαπήσεις τὸν πλησίον σου ὡς ἑαυτόν.

Although the text is not secure, again it seems that editors, wishing to read *δεύτερον* against the *δευτέρα* of the MSS,[18] are attempting to conform K to D and E.

Finally we may note in Kephas' speech:

D	K	E
οὐ ποιήσεις **σχίσμα**,	Κηφᾶς εἶπεν· οὐ ποιήσεις σχίσματα,	Κηφᾶς εἶπεν· οὐ ποιήσεις **σχίσμα**,

Against these minor agreements, however, must be set the many agreements both of E and K against D, and D and K against E, which imply that K, and not E, is the middle term. As an example we may take Nathanael's speech in which minor agreements of D and E against K occur: words appearing in boldface are instances where K agrees with D or E against the other. Clearly these vastly outnumber the minor agreements; in addition there are several omissions of words in K, where a word appears either in D or in E but not in both; these are likewise agreements in which K is the middle term, though they cannot readily be marked as such.

D	K	E
τέκνον μου, μὴ γίνου ψεύστης, ἐπειδὴ ὁδηγεῖ τὸ ψεῦσμα εἰς τὴν κλοπήν, μηδὲ φιλάργυρος, μηδὲ κενόδοξος· ἐκ γὰρ τούτων ἁπάντων κλοπαὶ γεννῶνται.	Ναθαναὴλ εἶπεν· **τέκνον μου,** μὴ γίνου ψεύστης, **ἐπειδὴ ὁδηγεῖ τὸ ψεῦσμα** ἐπὶ **τὴν κλοπήν,** μηδὲ φιλάργυρος, μηδὲ κενόδοξος· ἐκ τούτων ἁπάντων κλοπαὶ **γεννῶνται.**	Ναθαναὴλ εἶπεν· μὴ γίνου ψεύστης, μηδὲ φιλάργυρος, μηδὲ κενόδοξος· ἐκ τούτων ἁπάντων κλοπαὶ γίνονται·

[18] See the textual commentary ad loc.

Τέκνον μου, μὴ γίνου γόγγυσος, ἐπειδὴ ὁδηγεῖ εἰς τὴν βλασφημίαν, μηδὲ αὐθάδης, μηδὲ πονηρόφρων· ἐκ γὰρ τούτων ἁπάντων βλασφημίαι γεννῶνται. Ἴσθι δὲ πραΰς, ἐπεὶ οἱ πραεῖς κληρονομήσουσι τὴν γῆν. Γίνου μακρόθυμος, ἐλεήμων καὶ ἄκακος καὶ ἡσύχιος καὶ ἀγαθός καὶ τρέμων τοὺς λόγους διὰ παντός οὓς ἤκουσας. Οὐχ ὑψώσεις σεαυτόν, οὐδὲ δώσεις τῇ ψυχῇ σου θράσος. οὐ κολληθήσεται ἡ ψυχή σου μετὰ ὑψηλῶν, ἀλλὰ μετὰ δικαίων καὶ ταπεινῶν ἀναστραφήσῃ. Τὰ δὲ συμβαίνοντά σοι ἐνεργήματα ὡς ἀγαθὰ προσδέξῃ, εἰδὼς ὅτι ἄτερ θεοῦ οὐδὲν γίνεται.	**Τέκνον,** μὴ γίνου γόγγυσος, **ἐπειδὴ** ἄγει πρὸς **τὴν βλασφημίαν, μηδὲ** αὐθάδης, **μηδὲ** πονηρόφρων· ἐκ γὰρ τούτων ἁπάντων βλασφημίαι **γεννῶνται.** Ἴσθι δὲ πραΰς, **ἐπειδὴ** πραεῖς κληρονομήσουσι **τὴν βασιλείαν** τῶν οὐρανῶν. Γίνου μακρόθυμος, ἐλεήμων, **εἰρηνοποιός, καθαρὸς τῇ καρδίᾳ** ἀπὸ παντὸς κακοῦ, ἄκακος **καὶ ἡσύχιος,** ἀγαθός καὶ **φυλάσσων** καὶ τρέμων τοὺς λόγους **οὓς ἤκουσας.** Οὐχ ὑψώσεις σεαυτόν, **οὐδὲ** δώσεις τὴν ψυχήν σου μετὰ ὑψηλῶν ἀλλὰ μετὰ δικαίων καὶ ταπεινῶν ἀναστραφήσῃ. Τὰ **δὲ** συμβαίνοντά σοι ἐνεργήματα ὡς ἀγαθὰ **προσδέξῃ,** εἰδὼς ὅτι ἄτερ θεοῦ οὐδὲν γίνεται.	μὴ γίνου γόγγυσος, μὴ θυμώδης, μὴ αὐθάδης, μήτε πονηρόφρων· ἐκ γὰρ τούτων ἁπάντων βλασφημίαι γίνονται. Ἴσθι δὲ πραΰς, ἐπειδὴ πραεῖς κληρονομήσουσι τὴν βασιλείαν τοῦ θεοῦ. Γίνου μακρόθυμος, ἐλεήμων, εἰρηνοποιός, καθαρὸς τὴν καρδίαν, ἄκακος, ἥσυχος, ἀγαθός, φυλάσσων καὶ τρέμων τοὺς λόγους τοῦ θεοῦ. Οὐχ ὑψώσεις σεαυτόν, οὐ δώσεις τῇ ψυχῇ σου θράσος, οὐδὲ κολληθήσῃ τῇ ψυχῇ σου μετὰ ὑψηλῶν· ἀλλὰ μετὰ δικαίων καὶ ταπεινῶν. Τὰ συμβαίνοντά σοι ἐνεργήματα ὡς ἀγαθὰ προσδέξαι, εἰδὼς ὅτι ἄτερ τοῦ θεοῦ οὐδὲν γίνεται.

Schermann explains K as a middle term by suggesting that E is an independent derivative from TWT, independent, that is, from D. But in this case he has to explain the absence of so much TWT material from E. Because of the presence in K of the material that is absent from E, he has to assume that D, as well as E, is a source of K, thus making K the middle term in the way that Mark is the middle term in the Griesbach hypothesis.

There are, moreover, several points at which K and D agree against E, where K and D clearly preserve the more original reading. For Wengst this is compelling evidence that E is not the immediate source of K. These are as follows:

D	K	E
Ὅθεν γὰρ **ἡ κυριότης** λαλεῖται, ἐκεῖ κύριός ἐστιν.	Ὅθεν γὰρ **ἡ κυριότης** λαλεῖται, ἐκεῖ κύριός ἐστιν.	ὅθεν γὰρ Ἰησοῦς Χριστὸς λαλεῖται, ἐκεῖ κύριός ἐστιν.
Ἐὰν ἔχῃς διὰ τῶν χειρῶν σου, δώσεις **λύτρωσιν** ἁμαρτιῶν σου.	Ἐὰν ἔχῃς διὰ τῶν χειρῶν σου, δώσεις **λύτρωσιν** τῶν ἁμαρτιῶν σου.	Ἐὰν ἔσται ἔχειν σε ἀπὸ τῶν χειρῶν σου, δὸς εἰς ἄφεσιν ἁμαρτιῶν σου.
Δευτέρα δὲ ἐντολὴ τῆς διδαχῆς· οὐ φονεύσεις, **οὐ μοιχεύσεις,** **οὐ παιδοφθορήσεις, οὐ πορνεύσεις,** οὐ κλέψεις, οὐ μαγεύσεις, οὐ φαρμακεύσεις, οὐ φονεύσεις τέκνον ἐν φθορᾷ οὐδὲ γεννηθὲν ἀποκτενεῖς,	Πέτρος εἶπεν· οὐ φονεύσεις, **οὐ μοιχεύσεις, οὐ πορνεύσεις, οὐ παιδοφθορήσεις,** οὐ κλέψεις, οὐ μαγεύσεις, οὐ φαρμακεύσεις, οὐ φονεύσεις τέκνον ἐν φθορᾷ οὐδὲ γεννηθὲν ἀποκτενεῖς	Πέτρος εἶπεν· οὐ φονεύσεις, οὐ ποιήσεις ἁμαρτίαν τινὰ τῇ σαρκί σου, οὐ κλέψεις, οὐ μαγεύσεις, οὐ φαρμακεύσεις,

Wengst suggests that it is possible that D was the basis of the appearance of these phrases in K; but rightly notes that, if K is following E, it would be hard to explain a sudden reversion to D.[19]

---

[19] Wengst, *Schriften*, 9.

Finally, and perhaps most critically, if E is an independent document, as Schermann's theory must suppose, then the rationale for the apostolic speeches is entirely absent, for as it stands E makes no sense. Were K the source of E then E can be seen as an abbreviation of K, in which the apostolic speeches are part of an organised fiction by which the apostles are directing the church, but a presentation of the TWT material shared out between apostles, with no prior account of a meeting of the apostles, is inconceivable. Thus, E is not a source of K, as it is unlikely ever to have been a freestanding document; rather, like the version of K found in Codex Mosquensis 125,[20] it is a summary abbreviation.

However, the problems posed by the final chapter, by the expansion of the apostle list in K and by the minor agreements remain. If E is derived from K, then E must have turned to D for the final section. If we reject the simultaneous redaction of two documents by K we must do the same for E.

This impasse may be solved by suggesting that E does not derive from K as it stands, but must derive from an earlier recension of K, which we may call *κ*. A similar suggestion is made by Wengst, though on different grounds,[21] and Niederwimmer likewise describes the relationship between K and E as dependent upon a common original.[22] The alternative explanation is that E is an abbreviation of K, but that it is in some way contaminated through the memory, or through the oral transmission, of TWT closer to D than to K. This, however, still does not explain the final chapter of E, with the replacement of K's eschatological conclusion with the *Haustafel* found in D. Although the existence of *κ* is inevitably hypothetical, there is some evidence that such a recension of TWT existed as Rufinus refers to a work which he calls "duae viae vel iudicium Petri".[23] Neither K nor E can be called *duae viae* as only one way is described in each, but the inclusion of Peter`s name indicates that some apostolic attribution was made, which excludes any other version of TWT beyond the branch represented by K and E; thus a document attributing elements of the TWT to different apostles which is not presently extant must have existed. This may well have been *κ*.

If we accept the possibility of a *κ*-redaction, then we may suggest that *κ* contained a final chapter close to that of D, which K has altered. The same

---

[20] The version of K in this codex may be found in O. Gebhardt et al. (eds), *Patrum apostolicorum opera* 1.2 (Leipzig 1878) xxix-xxxi. The very existence of this peculiar version indicates that the material continued to be rewritten.

[21] Wengst, *Schriften*, 10.

[22] Niederwimmer, *Didache*, 63. See 1.2.2.2 below for further discussion of Niederwimmer's genealogy of TWT.

[23] Ruf., *Exp. sym.*, 38.

explanation may be used to account for the minor agreements noted above. For instance, whereas there is no obvious reason why K should choose to recast the speech in the mouth of Nathanael, it may readily be seen as a recasting, and the minor agreements attributed to such an editorial process. In support of this we may note that the phrase *οὐ δώσεις τῇ ψυχῇ σου θράσος*, which was recast in K but is intact in D and E, also appears in B, and therefore stood somewhere in TWT; thus the recasting of the phrase must be the work of K. The minor agreement in Thomas' speech in which the article is included may be read as a strengthening of the precept, in that the teacher is not to be obeyed simply as a master but as the Lord, in the context of a strong statement concerning the place of leadership in the church, which may be assigned, as will be argued in more detail below, to the K redactor. Finally we may readily see that, as Schermann suspected, the list of twelve apostles is secondary and does not belong to the speeches by eleven of them, but that K has made the list of eleven into a list of twelve.

There are thus two possible explanations of the relationship of K and E. That of Schermann is as follows :

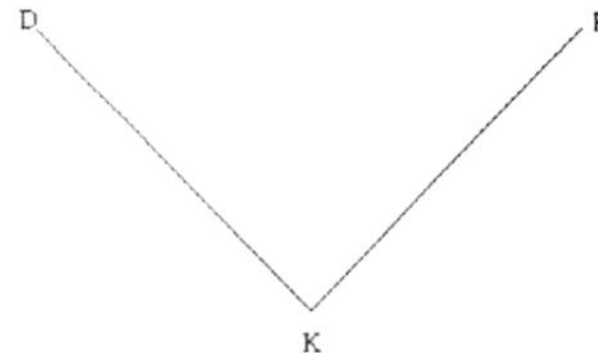

Whereas this is possible, it is difficult to envisage, in part because it assumes a complex redactional effort by K, and in part because the independent existence of E is unlikely; it makes no sense as a document.

The relationship suggested instead is:

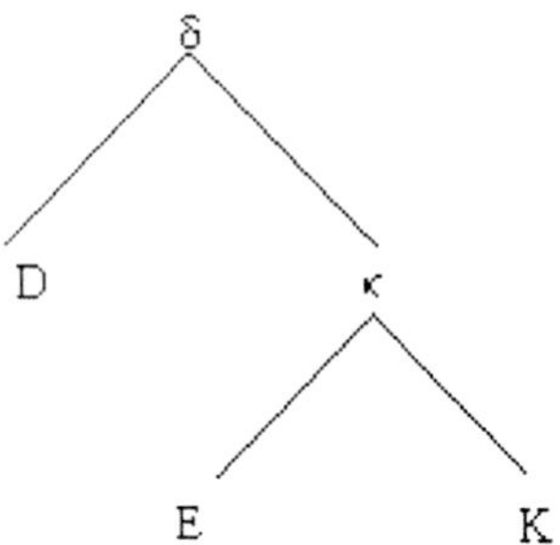

Here δ signifies not the extant D but the version of the TWT which was incorporated into D. The rationale for this will be given below.

Although we have argued against his reconstruction, we should nonetheless note the suggestion of Wengst.[24]

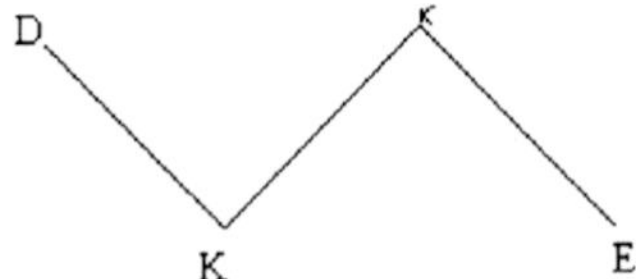

Although this is conceivable, it assumes a complex redactional task on the part of K which is unnecessary if we postulate a reception of the δ tradition. It does not, moreover, explain the presence of B parallels in K, to which we will turn presently, and assumes a proximity of κ to E.[25] One of the objections to the priority of E was that it would make no sense as a document in itself as it gives no rationale to the apostolic attribution of the commandments; the list should stand independently of the attribution of different speeches. The same objection must be raised to any view of κ as proximate to E in this regard.

What positively has been gained is that when there is disagreement between E and K in content it is possible to see that E is reflecting κ more closely than K; where there is agreement, then we can be assured that this material was present in κ.

1.2: The relationship between K, D and B

Using K, rather than E, as the base, we can now go on to explore the relationship of K with the other documents containing the TWT. In this introduction we are solely concerned with K, rather than the whole history of TWT, and will in particular not give consideration to the precise relationship between L and D. It is quite possible that L reflects δ very closely,[26] but in that case need not detain us further.

---

[24] Wengst, *Schriften*, 22.

[25] As is explicitly stated by Wengst, *Schriften*, 10.

[26] So E.J. Goodspeed, "The Didache, Barnabas and the Doctrina", *Anglican Theological Review* 27 (1945) 228-247, at 228-237; van de Sandt and Flusser, *Didache*, 61-63; E. Hennecke, "Die Grundschrift der Didache und ihre Recensionen", *ZNW* 2 (1901) 58-72.

A synoptic arrangement of D, K and B is found at appendix D. A glance at this synopsis reveals the following salient features:

- There is material in D that does not appear in any other version.
- B is independent of the other three documents, as the order of material is entirely different, whereas D and K, whatever their other divergences, contain substantially the same material, and this material is arranged in the same order in both documents. There is, moreover, a large block of material in both D and K which is not present in B.
- As already noted, there is a significant diversion between K and D (and E) at the conclusion of the TWT material; an eschatological conclusion is found instead of the *Haustafel.*
- There is substantial material in K which does not appear in the other versions.

We must explore the implications of each of these features in turn.

1.2.1: The additional material in D

As has been observed there is a substantial section of D which does not appear in K or B. This means either that D has inserted this into its source, or that the other versions have consciously omitted it. Harnack at first believed that this material was deliberately omitted by K, but subsequently changed his mind. The overwhelming consensus, given the absence of this material in L, is that this is an insertion in the tradition,[27] which means that K (and L) are not directly dependent on D but on an earlier version of the material, which was subsequently redacted by the didachist.[28] This we have labelled δ.

1.2.2: The relationship between B and D

As has already been suggested, K is in a literary relationship with D, but on the basis of the different order of material, B is not in the same relationship. On the basis of its order, B is

---

[27] According to F.X. Funk, *Doctrina duodecim apostolorum* (Tübingen 1887) xxix, Massebieau was first to suggest this, in *Revue d'histoire des religions* (1884) 168. It could be seen as the consensus by Harnack, *Apostellehre*, 26 by 1886! Most recently see van de Sandt and Flusser, *Didache*, 62.

[28] Van de Sandt and Flusser, *Didache*, 65.

- a deliberate re-arrangement of the TWT as received by D, or
- the form of TWT as received by D, which D has reordered, or
- a different and independent form of TWT.

We consider each of these possibilities in turn.

1.2.2.1: B as reordering of D

That B is a reordering of D was suggested by Goodspeed, and has received recent support from van de Sandt and Flusser, as well as being cautiously suggested by Draper.

Goodspeed's argument centres on seeing B as an improvement on D. In observing the omission of material in B he suggests:

> ...a closer examination of Barnabas' great omission...shows that much of it – murder, lust, enchantment, magic, lying, avarice, grumbling, – are covered elsewhere in Barnabas...mostly in *positive* command, adjusted to a loftier plane of Christian living....Anger, murder, enchantment, magic and grumbling are covered either generally or specifically in Barn. 19:3-11. It is a mistake to suppose Didache superior to Barnabas in its presentation of the TWT material; Didache is in fact inferior, for it contains some repetitions which Barnabas strips off...Moreover Barnabas presents not so much vices to be shunned as virtues to be cultivated...The average Christian then as now does not so much need to be told not to murder...as to be kind, generous, pure and true.[29]

Attractive as this argument is, it does not really hold up. If this is B's plan it is not applied consistently, for not only does B positively assert that Christians are not to fornicate, but many of the D passages that do not appear in B are warnings that lesser foibles may turn to greater sins.

Whereas Goodspeed's argument is based on seeing B as an improvement on D, the argument of van de Sandt and Flusser derives from a view of B as inferior! Their argument is the essentially negative one that it is hard to imagine how the ordered form of D (and L, which they see as an even more primitive form of TWT than D) might emerge from B. B is "chaotic", and so the ordered form of paraenesis in D can hardly have been created by unravelling the form in B.[30] In answer we might say that, if D is such a reasonable and rational presentation, it is even harder to see why B should wish to confuse it.

---

[29] Goodspeed, "The Didache, Barnabas and the Doctrina", 235-236.

[30] Van de Sandt and Flusser, *Didache*, 60.

Something of an answer to this is offered by Draper, who suggests that B is a hostile witness to D, and that B is an ironic presentation of the catechetical material of the D community. D is essentially still Jewish-Christian, whereas B is virulently anti-Jewish.[31] Even if this were demonstrable,[32] it would explain only why the TWT is relegated to an appendix in B, but would not explain the distinct order of presentation.

However, an interesting point in Draper's study, which will prove pertinent to the use of TWT by K, is the suggestion that TWT is transformed by B from a baptismal catechesis to advanced teaching. That D uses TWT in a manner which conforms to its original generation, in which it is found in *Community Rule*, is confirmed by the instruction to baptise following the presentation of TWT, but B presents this teaching as for the advanced. To an extent it might be suggested that literary documents present material only to those who are literate and, moreover, that D is addressed to those who are advanced, in that it is addressed to those who are to undertake the baptism of those who are catechised using TWT. But it remains the case that this material, albeit mediated, is addressed to catechumens, whereas B presents this material as additional to the substantive teaching which has already been given. So, in comparison to K, we may note that there is a difference in the address of the eschatological conclusion which in K is addressed to "brothers" but in B is addressed to those in positions of leadership. This is a clear indication that B has removed the material from its catechetical frame, as Draper suggested. There may be, moreover, some truth in Draper's contention that this relates to the divergent attitudes of D and B towards Judaism, but this is not germane to the present study. What is germane is that there is no proof here that B reorders D as, even if there is a relationship, the reordering of the material is not what distinguishes the uses to which it is put.

Critical for anyone wishing to argue for B as a rearrangement of D is the "great omission" to which Goodspeed refers. Kraft and Niederwimmer explain the presence of material which is present in both D and K but not B, namely the *teknon* sayings, by suggesting that they were added as a group either by D or at an earlier level of redaction of D which we may term δ.[33]

---

[31] J.A. Draper, "Barnabas and the Riddle of the Didache Revisited", *JSNT* 58 (1995) 89-113.

[32] For a brief critique of Draper, which suggests that Draper does not demonstrate what he has set out to prove, see J. Carleton Paget, *The Epistle of Barnabas: Outlook and Background* (WUNT 2.64; Tübingen 1994) 50-51. C. Bestmann, *Geschichte der christlichen Sitte* 2 (Nördlinger 1885) 136-153, suggested, on similar lines to Draper, that B is a gentile response to the Jewish-Christian D.

[33] Niederwimmer, *Didache*, 63; R.A. Kraft, *The Apostolic Fathers 3: Barnabas and the Didache* (New York 1965) 146.

This means that, unless we were to postulate an even earlier version of δ, we cannot know that the order found by B was anything like D. By contrast, Van de Sandt and Flusser suggest that it is equally possible that B omitted the block;[34] this would in turn imply that the block was established as a block prior to δ in TWT, and requires anyone wishing to argue that B rearranged TWT material found in an order proximate to that of D to explain the rearrangement as a whole, including the deliberate omission of this block.

In conclusion, therefore, it is hard to justify seeing B as a rearrangement of D.

1.2.2.2: D as reordering of TWT preserved by B

That D is a re-ordering of B was extensively argued in the twentieth century, but these arguments largely derived from the rather eccentric view that D was a late fiction, intended to create a primitive past to the apostolic church. We will not consider these arguments, based as they are upon a view of D which is entirely discredited, but should give serious consideration to the arguments of Niederwimmer. He does not actually argue that D is directly based on B, but places them both in a single stream of tradition, and suggests that B represents a more primitive stratum.

He diagrammatises his hypothesis thus:[35]

[34] Van de Sandt and Flusser, *Didache*, 73-74. In view of the linkage between these sayings and Jewish tradition observed by Kraft, *Apostolic Fathers*, 146, it is more likely than not that this material was part of TWT before its Christian adoption. Kraft, however, believes that the material was joined to the tradition before the β branch diverged.

[35] Diagram at Niederwimmer, *Didache*, 62.

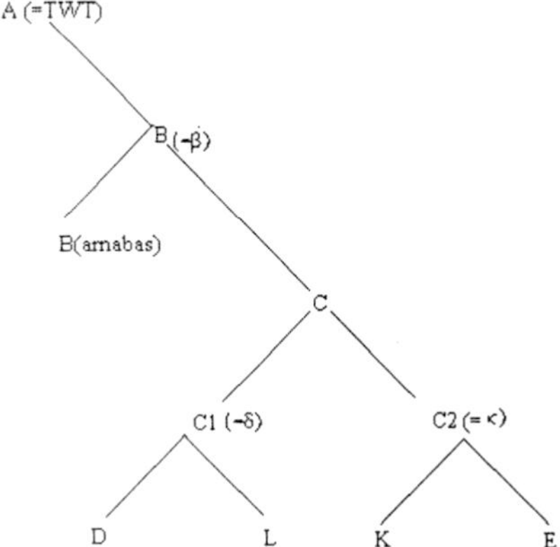

At the earliest stage lies a loose collection of Jewish material. This material is lightly Christianised (b) and in this guise is a source of B. At this point the original eschatological conclusion is Christianised, and this Christianised eschatological conclusion appears in part in B21. He does suggest, however, that B uses this source very carelessly, and suggests that much of D had already attained a recognisable shape at this stage, which B disrupts. At the C stage the *teknon* sayings are added, as is the double-love commandment, which is absent in B and absent therefore in B's source (which we may label *β*). This version in turn forms the archetype for D and L, which drop the eschatological conclusion. C2, however, which is equivalent to our *κ*, retains it, for which reason it is found in K14.

There is much to commend in Niederwimmer`s reconstruction. He does not satisfactorily explain B's order, but this is not his concern, and neither is it ours. A minor criticism may, however, be levelled at Niederwimmer's treatment of the absence of the double love commandment from B. Its form may suggest a Christianisation of TWT, and so its absence in B may indeed point to a form of TWT closer to a Jewish original, as he suggests. Van de Sandt and Flusser, however, point out that the form of the commandment as found in D is not exactly synoptic, and is therefore not derived from the Gospels but from an independent tradition which, given that the linkage of love of God and neighbour is not exclusively Christian, might even be Jewish.[36] The absence of this commandment in B does not therefore

[36] Van de Sandt and Flusser, *Didache*, 73.

necessarily mean that B is earlier, but is further evidence nonetheless for its independence.[37]

What is most critical however, for a study of K, is the fate of the eschatological conclusion; here we must part company entirely with Niederwimmer. Whereas Niederwimmer suggests that it was included at his C2 stage of development (roughly equivalent to κ) and was omitted by the C1 strand (roughly equivalent to δ), it cannot have been present in κ (= C2), because it is not in E. E, in common with δ, has the *Haustafel*, which K replaces with the eschatological conclusion, and so the *Haustafel* must have been present in κ, whereas the eschatological conclusion was not. Since the *Haustafel* is present in D in the same position as in κ/E, whereas the eschatological conclusion is not, it is hardly likely that the conclusion was present in δ, for if it were we would have to assume that two redactors independently determined to omit identical material whilst otherwise following the same source closely. K must have the conclusion from elsewhere; the source of this we must determine at a later stage, but for the moment we must conclude that, as the *Haustafel* was present in κ, the eschatological conclusion was not, and since it was not in δ either, there is not the single stream of tradition which Niederwimmer perceives, but either that the eschatological conclusion dropped out early in the stream of tradition or that there are two streams. Otherwise, however, our conclusions concerning the relationship of K/E to D are in rough conformity with those of Niederwimmer. Niederwimmer's diagram is more complex than ours because he wishes to account for the presence of the eschatological conclusion in K whilst recognising its relationship with D; when we realise that it had come to K from a separate source then the diagram can be simplified in the manner presented above. But since B contains the eschatological conclusion as well as the *Haustafel* it must be in a distinct strand. As such, β was not simply the TWT as received by δ, though it is fair to say that it is at least possible that δ has extensively reworked the tradition which may well have been closer to B (β) than to D in its original form.

1.2.2.3: D and B as independent variants of TWT

Since our concern is purely with K we need not be overlong detained on the details of the relationship of B and D; the study thus far has suggested that

---

[37] B.C. Butler, "The 'Two Ways' in the Didache", *JTS* 12 (1961) 27-38, similarly suggests that TWT in B has undergone less Christianisation than the version found in D, and therefore that B represents earlier tradition.

whereas they are each formed out of a loose compilation of positive and negative commands in a dualistic context that had existence in Judaism, they are not in a single stream of tradition but independent offshoots from TWT. We may accept this without commitment to any particular rationale for the difference in shape between B and δ.

However, the study has alerted us to the distinct use of TWT in B and D. Whereas D clearly preserves the function of TWT in catechesis, this is not the case in B. Niederwimmer therefore questions the common characterisation of TWT as catechetical, suggesting instead (following Wengst), a school-setting.[38] This may be the setting for B, but B might, as Draper suggests, have altered the context of TWT through the inclusion of this traditional material into his discourse, and in particular by including it as an appendix. Niederwimmer's observation that ritual prescription is absent in the material, from which he concludes that it is unrelated to any liturgy of initiation, does nothing to support his argument, as, in keeping with the prescriptions of BT *Yebamoth* 47A-B, one would expect ritual prescription to *follow* the catechism, and therefore to have no place in the catechetical material itself. Rather, the independent forms of TWT in B and D imply that TWT might have readily moved outside of a catechetical frame. We may bear this in mind in examining K's use of the tradition. In particular we may be aware of the possibility that instruction continued after baptism; instruction in ritual is commonplace in later centuries, and, in the light of Jewish practice and in the light of D, which follows catechetical ethical instruction with instruction concerning the eucharist, this may be rooted in earlier practice. Thus if Hermas' *Mandates* are, as Henne has argued,[39] intended for a baptised audience, we may note that the first mandate begins with a basic article of faith, the oneness of God, which one might expect in catechesis itself. In spite of its basic nature one may see this as part of post-baptismal paraenesis.

1.2.3: The replacement of the Haustafel *in K*

In exploring the relationship between K and E it was observed above that the *Haustafel*, which is replaced in K, appears in E. From this, and from other considerations, it was deduced that K had employed an earlier redaction of the church-order which we have labelled κ. It is probably not possible to go beyond stating that the *Haustafel* was omitted in order to make room for the eschatological conclusion. However, it will be suggested below that K has so

---

[38] Niederwimmer, *Didache*, 37-38.

[39] P. Henne, *L'unité du Pasteur d'Hermas* (Paris 1992).

adopted the TWT that its provisions are directions aimed at clergy rather than catechumens; K's preference, moreover, is that clergy should be celibate, and so directions for the ordering of clergy families are largely redundant! Harnack, moreover, notes that the omission of the *Haustafel* material is implicitly recognised by the redactor who, in ch. 15, has Peter state that the Scriptures are sufficient to teach other directions.[40]

An account alternative to the replacement of the *Haustafel* is offered by Hennecke.[41] According to Hennecke, K is derived from a variant of TWT, identical to that from which B derived, the major reworking being on the part of B. Here is a simplified version of his diagram:

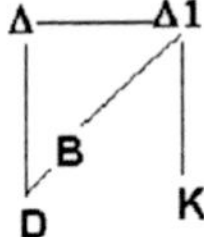

What K and B have in common, apart from some stray traditions, is an eschatological conclusion and an epistolary opening. Hennecke would seem to see Δ1 as a version of TWT with such an opening and conclusion. Thus, he would not say that K has replaced the *Haustafel*, but rather that the *Haustafel* was never in the TWT received by K. We argue at 2.2 below that the opening is taken from elsewhere in the tradition, and so that this cannot be a defining element in TWT as received by K. More significantly, Hennecke does not deal with E; it is the presence of the *Haustafel* there which is the clue to the existence of *κ*, and which tends to discount his hypothesis. However, there is some merit in his suggestion that there was a version of TWT which had an eschatological conclusion, and that this is reflected more closely in K than in B.

1.2.4: The additional material in K

In discussing the relationship between K and the other manifestations of the TWT it was determined that K is dependent on δ, whereas B is independently derived from TWT. The following stemma thus results:

[40] Harnack, *Lehre*, 211 n. 35.

[41] Hennecke, "Grundschrift", 58-72.

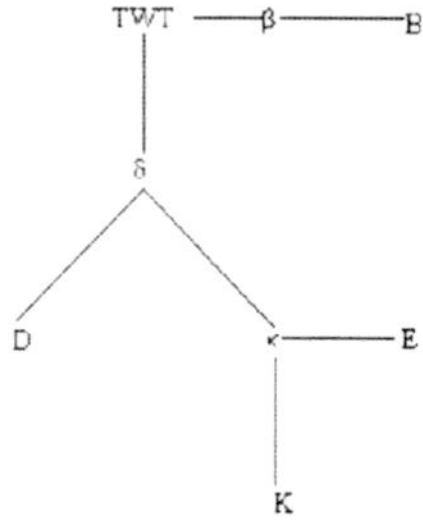

However, there is a confusion in this simple picture. Namely, although K is dependent on the same branch of tradition as D, there are several agreements of B and K against D, as well as material which uniquely appears in K. We deal first with the material which is parallel between K and B.

1.2.4.1: K material with B parallels

In discussing the parallels between K and B a particular issue is whether K is directly and literarily dependent on B; this was the conclusion reached by Krawutzcky and Harnack, subsequently followed by Barnard.[42] The pattern of relationships expressed in the diagram above is essentially the same as that of Harnack,[43] and it is the need to explain these B parallels which led to Harnack's assumption that K had employed B. Before discussing the implications of these parallels, however, we need to examine them. They are as follow:

- The opening greeting in K, which is similar to that in B but has no parallel in D. We shall examine this point to section 2 of this introduction, where it will be argued that the greeting, together with the apostle list, comes from a different source altogether, and not from B.
- In the statement of the love commandment K diverges from the version of D, the K version being comparable to the different version in B.

---

[42] L.W. Barnard, "The Dead Sea scrolls, Barnabas, the Didache and the later history of the 'two ways'", in *Studies in the Apostolic Fathers and Their Background* (Oxford 1966) 87-107 at 102-103.

[43] Thus note the diagram at A. Harnack, *Die Apostellehre und die jüdischen beiden Wege* (Lepizig 1886) 32. The main difference (apart from the fact that we take no account of L here) is that Harnack does not reckon with the existence of *κ* as a first edition of TWT as found in K.

- At K12 the commandment to treasure one`s teacher is expanded in a manner with proximity to a similar statement at B19.9.
- As has already been noted, there is a significant difference between K and D in the conclusion, for whereas D has a *Haustafel*, K has an eschatological conclusion with similarities with B. Again, this is shown in appendix C.

We deal with these latter three in turn, reserving discussion of the first parallel, which is not part of the TWT material.

1.2.4.1.1: The commandment to love God

The different versions of this commandment are as follow:

D	K	B
πρῶτον ἀγαπήσεις τὸν θεὸν τὸν ποιήσαντά σε	πρῶτον ἀγαπήσεις τὸν θεὸν τὸν ποιήσαντά σε ἐξ ὅλης τῆς καρδίας σου καὶ δοξάσεις τὸν λυτρωσάμενόν σε ἐκ θανάτου	ἀγαπήσεις τὸν ποιήσαντά σε, φοβηθήσῃ τόν σε πλάσαντα, δοξάσεις τόν σε λυτρωσάμενον ἐκ θανάτου·

Whereas D simply contains the command to love God the creator, this is expanded in K to love for creator and redeemer. The parallel with B is not exact, as B has a triple version as well as minor divergences, such as the position of the pronoun σέ, which tend to discount reliance upon B unless no other explanation is feasible. It should, moreover, be noted here that *κ* follows neither D nor B in that the statement that love should be wholehearted is added to the love-commandment in K and E alike, conforming the saying better to scripture. Given that they are present in each of these witnesses we must assume that they were present in κ, their common archetype, and that *κ* therefore is following a tradition independent of B. However, the critical words *καὶ δοξάσεις τὸν λυτρωσάμενόν σε ἐκ θανάτου* are not present in E. E is certainly an abbreviation of *κ*, as may be seen where K and D are in parallel and E does not follow them, and so it is quite possible that they were in *κ*, and that E has let them drop. However, we do not know this, and must keep an open mind whether they derive from *κ* or K.

Although K and B are close, this parallel is simply one example of a host of such formulae. One may note, in particular, Hermas, *Mand.* 1.1:

Πρῶτον πάντων πίστευσον, ὅτι εἷς ἐστὶν ὁ θέος, ὁ τὰ πάντα κτίσας καὶ καταρτίσας καὶ ποιήσας ἐκ τοῦ μὴ ὄντος εἰς τὸ εἶναι... πίστευσον οὖν αὐτῷ καὶ φοβήθητι αὐτόν... This is a particularly significant parallel because of its proximity to B, though not to D or K. Yet, because *Mandates* 1 does not appear in a context of TWT there is no suggestion of any literary relationship between Hermas and B. This is recognised by Dibelius as a statement of traditional material of Jewish origin,[44] and, we may suggest, following Henne, is from the context of post-baptismal paraenesis. This is adduced not simply to illustrate the wide distribution of this material and the multiple forms that it could take, though this is itself significant, as such a wide distribution implies that B is not necessarily the source for the material here, but also because this is further illustration of a background in Jewish paraenesis and Christian catechesis. Nonetheless, what is unique in K and B is the instruction to glorify Christ as the one who ransomed the hearer. Prostmeier suggests that the triple formula is a production of B, on the grounds that B is fond of such formulae,[45] but this could be a more widespread addition to the standard formula on the basis of the employment in catechesis or post-baptismal paraenesis. Thus Prostmeier notes that the reference in B is baptismal. Since the formula is found in this context, it is entirely feasible that the same tradition reached K (or possibly *κ*) independently. Whilst this cannot be proved, given the wide divergence between K and B, it is no less likely than dependence on B.

What is notable about the formula is that it seems to express a functional binitarianism of God the Father and Christ the redeemer. This is not a theological binitarianism, though the unreflective christological monotheism of Melito, in particular, comes close to this, but is a traditional statement reminiscent of other passages which seem to reflect traditional credal formulae such as 1 Cor 8:6 and 1 Tim 2:5-6.[46] Thus, given the extensive use of formulae like this it seems more probable that the tradition, rather than literary dependence upon B, is the source of this particular parallel, and, moreover, that the source of this tradition, like the TWT material in which this tradition is set, is catechetical or post-baptismal instruction.

1.2.4.1.2: Loving one's teacher as the apple of an eye

The different versions of this commandment are as follow:

---

[44] M. Dibelius, *Der Hirt des Hermas* (Tübingen 1923) 497.

[45] F.R. Prostmeier, *Der Barnabasbrief* (Göttingen 1999) 537.

[46] See the discussion in J.N.D. Kelly, *Early Christian Creeds* (London 1950) 19-22.

D	K	B
τέκνον μου, τοῦ λαλοῦντός σοι τὸν λόγον τοῦ θεοῦ	Θωμᾶς εἶπεν· τέκνον, τὸν λαλοῦντά σοι τὸν λόγον τοῦ θεοῦ καὶ παραίτιόν σοι γινόμενον τῆς ζωῆς καὶ δόντα σοι τὴν ἐν κυρίῳ σφραγῖδα ἀγαπήσεις ὡς κόρην ὀφθαλμοῦ σου,	ἀγαπήσεις ὡς κόρην τοῦ ὀφθαλμοῦ σου πάντα τὸν λαλοῦντά σοι τὸν λόγον κυρίου.
μνησθήσῃ	μνησθήσῃ αὐτοῦ	μνησθήσῃ ἡμέραν κρίσεως
νυκτὸς καὶ ἡμέρας,	νύκτα καὶ ἡμέραν,	νυκτὸς καὶ ἡμέρας,

Firstly, however, it must be noted that, whereas there is a clear parallel between B and K, the parallel is also present between B and E:

B	E
ἀγαπήσεις ὡς κόρην τοῦ ὀφθαλμοῦ σου πάντα τὸν λαλοῦντα σοι τὸν λόγον κυρίου.	Θωμᾶς εἶπεν· τὸν λαλοῦντα σοι τὸν λόγον τοῦ θεοῦ καὶ παραίτιόν σοι γινόμενον τῆς ζωῆς καὶ δόντα σοι τὴν ἐν κυρίῳ σφραγῖδα ἀγαπήσεις αὐτὸν ὡς κόρην ὀφθαλμοῦ σου,
μνησθήσῃ ἡμέραν κρίσεως νυκτὸς καὶ ἡμέρας, καὶ	μνησθήσῃ αὐτοῦ νυκτὸς καὶ ἡμέρας, τιμήσεις δὲ αὐτὸν ὡς κύριον, ὅθεν γὰρ Ἰησοῦς Χριστὸς λαλεῖται, ἐκεῖ κύριός ἐστιν.
ἐκζητήσεις καθ' ἑκάστην ἡμέραν τὰ πρόσωπα τῶν ἁγίων, ἢ διὰ λόγου κοπιῶν καὶ πορευόμενος εἰς τὸ παρακαλέσαι καὶ μελετῶν εἰς τὸ σῶσαι ψυχὴν τῷ λόγῳ...	Ἐκζητήσεις δὲ αὐτὸν καὶ τοὺς λοιποὺς ἁγίους, ἵνα ἐπαναπαυσθῇς τοῖς λόγοις αὐτῶν· κολλώμενος γὰρ ἁγίους ἅγιος ἁγιασθήσεται.

Since the material appears in E as well as K we may deduce that the material appeared in κ. Proponents of a dependence upon B must therefore also argue that κ, as well as K, had knowledge of B and that both employed it in different ways! The appearance of this parallel in κ, which is in turn literarily dependent upon δ (since it is an expansion of δ material), therefore indicates that this parallel at least derives from the tradition and not from the use of any literary source. The assumption that the one who teaches is the same who baptises the candidate is yet another indication that the locus for the transmission of the material is catechetical, and that it is catechetical speaks further against B as a source. A final indication of catechetical origin is the saying that sanctification accrues to the one who adheres to the saints. This appears at *1 Clem.* 46:2, cited as scripture. Obviously κ is not the source, but it likewise unnecessary to assume that κ derived it from 1 Clement, as otherwise there is no particular parallel.[47] Most probably it is a saying transmitted as part of catechesis.

Also speaking to the catechetical origin of the saying is the debt to Prov 7:2. Here the teachings, rather than the teacher, are to be valued, but a transference of honour from teachings to teacher may readily come about in a catechetical context. What is most interesting, and indicative that this clause is the product of a relatively early stage in the Christian tradition, is the assumption that the teacher is also the baptiser. In the early third century we find that baptism is normally performed by the bishop, regardless of who had prepared the candidate. In an earlier period we must assume that this was not the case, but that independent teachers baptised their own candidates as they saw fit, and constructed the sort of patronal relationship that is envisaged and described here. Thus, this B parallel is, once again, not derived from B, but from independent tradition, which is of a similar date to B.

Finally, we may note that there are echoes of this passage in the Syrian *Didascalia*. Of the support of the bishop the didascalist writes: "He it is who ministers the word to you and is your mediator, your teacher, and, after God, is your father who has regenerated you through the water. He is your chief, he is your master, he your powerful king."[48] And a little later, in stating that none should insult the bishop, he describes him as the one " through whom you have learned the word and come to know God, and through whom you have been made known to God, through whom you were sealed, and through

[47] Cf. Funk, *Doctrina*, 57. There are some possible parallels with *1 Clem.* further below in K, but these are not from κ material.

[48] *Didascalia* 2.26.4.

whom you have become sons of light".[49] Connolly notes the parallels with K,[50] but we may suggest that if the didascalist has received this from a written source then that source is catechetical. Given, however, that a few lines before the earlier citation there is an echo of D it seems likely that elements from the tradition are being freely employed.

1.2.4.1.3: The eschatological conclusion

We have already suggested that κ had the same *Haustafel* as D, and that K had altered the conclusion by omitting the *Haustafel* and replacing it with an eschatological conclusion. We have also noted that the same eschatological conclusion is present in part in B. A synoptic table of the eschatological conclusions is found in appendix C to this introduction. There are several possible explanations of this phenomenon.

1.2.4.1.3.1: K revised in the light of B

One possible understanding of the relationship is that of Harnack, followed by Funk, that K also knew B, and revised the TWT section, taken from δ, in the light of B.[51] This would give a stemma thus:

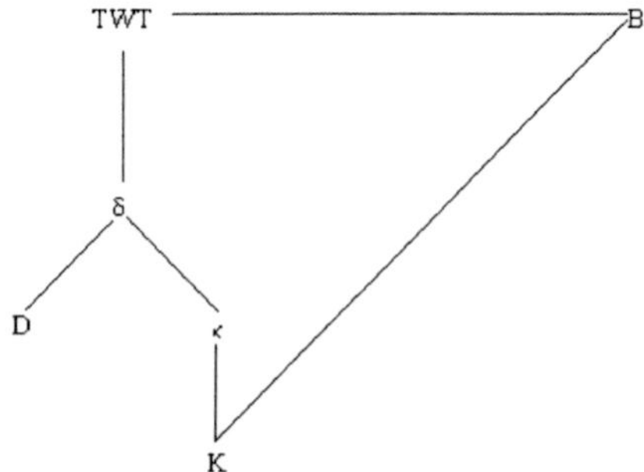

Although this is possible, there are two objections:

- It is strange that K should follow δ so closely, and yet then undertake the complex literary task of comparing the text to another document

---

[49] *Didascalia* 2.32.3.

[50] R.H. Connolly, *Didascalia apostolorum* (Oxford 1929) 87, 93.

[51] Harnack, *Lehre*, 211; Funk, *Doctrina*, 58-59.

in order to include a few stray points not picked up in the main source, whilst omitting the *Haustafel.*

- It is particularly strange that a redactor employing B should not include the material which is found in B (as in L) stating that angels are set over the TWT. As we shall see below, K has a cosmologically dualist view, and so it is particularly odd that material consonant with this outlook should be omitted.

1.2.4.1.3.2: The eschatological conclusion as inherent in TWT

The position that the eschatological material was in the TWT as received by K, is that adopted by Niederwimmer. We have already criticised this view at 1.2.2.2 above and need not repeat the critique here.

1.2.4.1.3.3: K as having a source independent of B

The possibility should be considered that K was aware of this material from a source other than B, whether oral or written. Whereas the *literary* relationship of K to D is that of joint dependence on δ, and whereas B represents an independent branch of the tradition, there may be elements of free-floating tradition besides, which were known independently to B and K alike, or else K was aware of the literary source employed by B.

A related position is espoused by van de Sandt and Flusser and by Hennecke[52] namely, that B and K draw upon the same literary source. For Hennecke this is true of the whole of TWT. Whereas this is possible, one would anticipate that the statement that angelic beings are set over the TWT is part of the Jewish original, as indeed van de Sandt and Flusser argue, and so part of the common source of B and K. Again, it is hard to explain this omission were this the sole source. Nonetheless, it would be possible were we to suggest that K, in revising *κ*, was aware of the material independently of *κ*, and that K conformed this material to the apostolic shape given by *κ*, only preferring his own version of the material when it did not coincide with the source before him. The other areas of common material between K and B have been identified as catechetical, and whereas there is nothing in the eschatological material which is self-evidently of a catechetical origin, there is likewise nothing which is inconsistent with such an origin. In this instance it is possible to see why the angelic powers over the TWT do not appear in

[52] Hennecke, "Grundschrift", 65; van de Sandt and Flusser, *Didache*, 75.

K, namely because they were not present in *κ*, which at this point is close to D/*δ*, and that the reworking required would be too extensive.

Hennecke, in suggesting that the same literary source is employed, further suggests that K is closer to the origin than B, on the grounds of B's repetitions (of ἐρωτῶ and συναπολεῖται) and on the grounds that the introduction is more expansive.[53] Certainly this points to B`s reworking of his source, and moreover indicates that K`s fidelity to what the two have in common is greater. In turning to the parallels between B and K in the eschatological section we may observe that they are not all that extensive. On the basis of his use of *κ*, we may note that K is generally a conservative redactor, but the looseness of the parallels with B may be explained along the lines suggested by Hennecke that K has indeed used this source conservatively, whereas all the reworking is on the part of B. What K and B hold in common is that each is an eschatological warning in conclusion to TWT material, which indicates, if K is not dependent on B, that both knew a version of TWT which concluded with an eschatological warning. Such is far from impossible, as the version of the Qumran *Community Rule*, to which B is particularly close, has precisely such a conclusion. Whether the source was oral or literary may remain an open question. There are two small points, however, albeit points at which the text of K is not absolutely secure, that also indicate a certain degree of tradition in common between B and K, and which indicate that, whether *β* was oral or written, K is citing from memory. Both occur in K13.

D	E	K	B
συγκοινωνήσεις δὲ πάντα τῷ ἀδελφῷ σου καὶ οὐκ ἐρεῖς ἴδια εἶναι· εἰ γὰρ ἐν τῷ ἀθανάτῳ κοινωνοί ἐστε, πόσῳ μᾶλλον ἐν τοῖς **θνητοῖς.**	**συγκοινωνήσεις** δὲ πάντα τοῖς ἀδελφοῖς σου καὶ οὐκ ἐρεῖς ἴδια εἶναι· εἰ γὰρ ἐν τῷ θανάτῳ κοινωνοί ἐστε, πόσῳ μᾶλλον ἐν τοῖς **θνητοῖς.**	**κοινωνήσεις** δὲ ἁπάντων τῷ ἀδελφῷ σου καὶ οὐκ ἐρεῖς ἴδια εἶναι· εἰ γὰρ ἐν τῷ ἀθανάτῳ κοινωνοί ἐστε, πόσῳ μᾶλλον ἐν τοῖς **φθαρτοῖς;**	**κοινωνήσεις** ἐν πᾶσιν τῷ πλησίον σου καὶ οὐκ ἐρεῖς ἴδια εἶναι· εἰ γὰρ ἐν τῷ αφθάρτῳ κοινωνοί ἐστε, πόσῳ μᾶλλον ἐν τοῖς **φθαρτοῖς.**

[53] Hennecke, "Grundschrift", 65.

The extent to which E conforms to D at these points indicates that this was the reading of *κ*, which K has recast, and has thus brought it into closer conformity with B. Otherwise we would have to imagine that E had independently recast the sayings and coincidentally produced the same reading as D. But the conformity with B in the recasting by K is likewise unlikely to be coincidental. An indication that the recasting is not made directly from a written source is the lack of balance in the last clause in K, in which *ἀθανάτῳ* is contrasted to *φθαρτοῖς*, rather than the *θνητοῖς*, which we might otherwise expect. Had K been using a written source close to B, however, then one would expect that the earlier *ἀθανάτῳ* would have been replaced with *ἀφθάρτῳ*, in accordance with B. This not only indicates that *β* is oral, but the very proximity of K and B at this point, as contrasted to D and E, indicates K's access to a stream of tradition distinct from *κ*.

1.2.5: Some conclusions on the relationship between B, D and K

The stemma resulting from the conclusions reached above is:

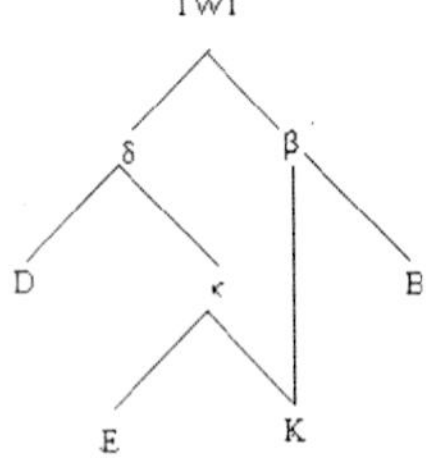

The significance of this lies not simply in ironing out the literary relationships between the various documents, but gives us the following information regarding the redactors of *κ* and K:

- *κ* had a copy of *δ*.
- *κ* functioned in the same area of tradition as *β*.
- K had a copy of *κ*.
- Because K was aware of a version of TWT proximate to that deriving from the Essenes with an eschatological conclusion (*β*), K either functioned in the same area of tradition as *β* or, if *β* is a document, had a copy of *β*.

The dating of δ is largely dependent on the dating of D, which used δ as a source; however, a dating at the turn of the second century is entirely reasonable. Its geographical location is similarly dependent on a positioning of D; however the consensus is that D is Syrian, and this would be consistent with the probability that TWT originated in Palestine. Thus Syria or Palestine is the original locus of δ, which was in turn employed by κ.

The dating of β is similarly dependent on the dating of B. However, a time early in the second century would again not be ridiculous. As to the geographical location of this material, there is less certainty. The consensus is that B is Alexandrian. This has recently been ably defended by Carleton Paget,[54] but this does not mean that the sources employed are all from this milieu. In particular it is possible that β had come to Alexandria from elsewhere, in that the TWT is found as an appendix to the body of B. Thus the question remains open, but since the use of B was a central plank in Harnack`s argument for an Alexandrian origin to K this is significant nonetheless, as Syria or Palestine are more probable loci than Alexandria for κ and K alike.

1.3: TWT material in K which is not found elsewhere

Three salient features were identified above as emerging from a first glance at a synoptic arrangement of the TWT. There is also a fourth, not mentioned above, which is the inclusion in K of material which is without parallel in the other versions. Since we have determined that K is not the earliest exemplar of the TWT we may safely determine that these are either growths within the tradition or redactional additions. We should therefore determine their purpose and place within the redactional history of K.

1.3.1: Gendered demons

The first is the ethical expansion, which states that anger is a male demon and lust a female demon, which conspire to lead people to their destruction.

There is much here that breathes the atmosphere of early Judaism and its ethical discourse. Thus *Testament of Reuben* speaks of seven spirits that conspire against people and lead them to destruction[55] and *Testament of Dan* speaks specifically of the spirit of anger that co-operates with Satan.[56] The

[54] Carleton Paget, *Barnabas*, 30-42.
[55] *T. Reu.* 3.
[56] *T. Dan.* 2-3

gendering of these demons is also consonant with early Judaism; the *Testament of Solomon*, with its complex demonology, alludes to the existence of female demons,[57] and 4Q560, an incantation against demons, whilst fragmentary, seems to envisage male and female demons which attack men and women in divergent ways. We may also be reminded of the syzygies of the pseudo-Clementine literature, again deriving from Jewish Christianity within Syria, and deriving from a context in which there is conflict with gnosticism.[58] The statement at K8.2 regarding the entry of a demon into the soul is also very proximate to the discussion of a similar phenomenon at ps-Clement, *Hom.* 9.9. The closest parallel, however, is found in Clement of Alexandria. He is discussing a statement, possibly found within a gnostic work, in which Christ refers to a time when "you have trampled on the garment of shame, and when the two become one and the male with the female is neither male nor female". Clement attributes this statement to *Gospel of the Egyptians*, but goes on to comment: "He (Cassianus, whose theories Clement is opposing) seems to me to fail to recognize that by the male impulse is meant wrath and by the female lust."[59] The manner in which this is stated sounds as though it is considered common knowledge, and part of the catechetical tradition; elsewhere Clement makes passing reference to lust as female.[60]

Thus, although the appearance of gendered demons at this point is a literary addition in the redaction of TWT the appearance of the statement in a catechetical context and as the basis of ethical exhortation is an indication that the redactor who added this material is close to the root of the tradition, and expands it here in a manner not alien to the milieu in which the tradition grew up and was fostered. Whereas it is possible that this is a free-floating piece of tradition that has survived and has been attached to the TWT by K, the very fact that that the tradition has been passed on through ethical paraenesis, and is found still in that context, indicates that the redactor understood the material with which he was dealing, and that the circle in which the tradition was passed on was a circle derived from the same early Jewish group in which the TWT was originated.

As such it is impossible to determine whether this was *κ* or K, and whether this was therefore a natural growth within the tradition or a deliberate redactional expansion. There is, however, one small indication that the expansion is the work of K. *Gospel of Philip* 61a states that "among the

---

[57] *T. Sol.* 1.7; 4.1.

[58] The significance of this conflict with gnosticism will emerge in 3.4.2 below.

[59] Clem., *Strom.* 3.91.

[60] Clem., *Strom.* 3.63.

forms of the unclean spirit there are male and female". On the basis that male spirits attack women, and female spirits attack men, it explains the apotropaic power of the rite of the bridechamber. This gospel is a compilation of other material, but it is notable that Mary Magdalene has a prominence among the disciples. We note below that one of K's sources is likewise a gospel in which an (unidentified) Mary is prominent, and we must ask whether K is privy to a similar selection of sources. This, however, is far from being a safe argument, as the tradition of *Gospel of Philip* may likewise be derived from the Jewish tradition. Nonetheless, since K, like Clement, is, as we suggest below, operating in an ambit in which Christian gnosticism is prominent, it is also possible that he is heir to the same tradition of interpretation, which is both shared and disputed between Christians of gnostic and anti-gnostic bent.

1.3.2: The support of teachers

In 1.2.4.1.2 above it was observed that the instruction that a teacher should be honoured was derived from the tradition and not from B. The direction continues:

> You shall honour him as much as you are able from your sweat and from the labour of your hands. If the Lord through him has made you worthy to be given spiritual food and drink and eternal life, much the more should you bring him corruptible and temporary food. "For the workman is worthy of his hire" and "You shall not muzzle a threshing ox" and "Nobody plants a vine and does not eat the fruit of it."

This is therefore a continuation of the direction that the teacher should be honoured, which was part of *κ*. Whether this is likewise part of *κ* or an expansion of K alone is hard to determine. However, if, as we intend to argue below, the qualifications of TWT are being read by K as no longer catechetical but as preliminary to the selection of bishops, then this is far from being an appropriate expansion, and may well be part of the original.

There is more that points in the direction of the earlier redactional level, in the significance of the patronal relationship here established. Paul (1 Cor 1:12-17) implies that a particular relationship might come about between baptised and baptiser. Theissen suggests that this relationship issued in hospitality offered to the baptiser,[61] who at this time would be an itinerant apostle, which in turn might be a means by which the baptised gained status in the community. The baptised thus becomes a patron of the baptiser. Although hospitality would no longer be necessary if the baptiser was no longer itinerant, it remains a possibility that those baptised might offer patronage to those who baptised them as a means of gaining status within the Christian community. This casts light on Ignatius' instruction that no baptism or *agapē* take place without the consent of the bishop.[62] As I have argued elsewhere,[63] the reason for this prohibition is that these two events are rituals which construct patronage, an *agapē* through the sharing of food, which may be construed as a patronal act, and baptism as the means by which the newly baptised might become a patron (or client) of the baptiser. Ignatius thus seizes upon them as events that are not to take place without the bishop`s consent, since by this means the bishop would be able to control patronage networks. There is, however, no trace of such a relationship in a later period. Baptism is certainly tied up to patronage in third-century Africa, but in this event the baptiser, who is normally the bishop, becomes the patron, rather than the client. We must also note that these directions continue to tie TWT to pre-baptismal catechesis rather than to any other locus of instruction. We must therefore conclude that this is a natural growth within TWT, and is more probably from the *κ* redaction than from K, even though we may yet be open about the date of K.

1.4: Conclusions on the TWT in K

There is some evidence that K has reworked the TWT as found in *κ*, *κ* in turn being a derivation of δ distinct from D. The date of the reworking is uncertain, as is the location. The source, however, is ancient. The other stream of tradition which may be recognised in the material is likewise ancient. Finally, there are some independent streams redacted by K, but likewise showing signs of antiquity. Fundamentally the K version of TWT reflects second-century traditions. We may therefore go on to examine the other sources to determine whether they likewise are sources of antiquity.

---

[61] G. Theissen, *The Social Setting of Pauline Christianity* (Philadelphia 1982) 54-56.

[62] Ign., *Smyrn.* 8.2.

[63] A. Stewart-Sykes, *The Life of Polycarp: An Anonymous vita from Third-Century Smyrna* (Early Christian Studies 4; Sydney 2002) 70.

2: The epistolary opening and apostle list

2.1: The apostle list

We have already observed that whereas twelve apostles appear in the prescript to K, only eleven speak. We therefore agreed with Schermann that the list implied by E is more original and that the presence of Jude the son of James was a rationalising addition, though without accepting his hypothesis that K was directly derived from E. Part of the reason for not accepting his hypothesis was that without the fiction of an apostolic gathering the presence of the apostles and the attribution of speeches to them made no sense. The apostles and their presence are intimately bound up to the material which is found in their mouths in this recension.

To turn to the list of eleven certain peculiarities are obvious, namely the duplication of Peter and Kephas and the duplication of Nathanael and Bartholomew. Although, according to Harnack and Schermann,[64] the duplication of Peter and Kephas points to an Alexandrian origin, as the same peculiarity is found in Clement,[65] this argument is far from secure as Clement was not a native Alexandrian, nor did he spend his entire career in Alexandria. Rather, as Schmidt suggests, the list is far closer to that of *Epistula apostolorum*,[66] and may indeed be derived from this document. Both are lists of eleven and both locate the gathering of the disciples after the resurrection.[67] The main difference between the two lists is that Matthew is moved higher up the list in *κ*;[68] we may accept Harnack's suggestion here that the redactor wishes to bring to prominence those apostles who had produced gospels but should observe that the basis of the list, including the presence of John at the head, is best ascribed either to *Epistula apostolorum* or to a common source.[69]

[64] Harnack, *Lehre*, 217 n.; Schermann, *Elfapostelmoral*, 22; A. Baumstark, "Alte und neue Spuren eines ausserkanonischen Evangeliums", *ZNW* 14 (1913) 232-247, at 237.

[65] Cited by Eus., *H.E.* 1.12.

[66] C. Schmidt, *Gespräche Jesu mit seinen Jüngern nach der Auferstehung* (TU 43; Leipzig 1919) 242-243.

[67] S. Giet, "La Didache: enseignement des douze apôtres?" *Melto* 3 (1967) 223-236 also contains some discussion of the apostle list in E and K.

[68] This movement of Matthew's name may be deduced as the work of κ rather than of K because of the prominent position (second after John) of Matthew's speech in E and K alike.

[69] It is taken as axiomatic that the list is derived from a source and is not the independent composition of *κ* because of the improbability that *Epistula apostolorum* and *κ* would produce two lists with the same peculiarities unless these lists were founded in some

In answering the question whether K is directly dependent on *Epistula apostolorum* or whether the apostle lists derive from a common source we should note that not only do the documents share a list of apostles and a fictive setting but that their basic literary form is likewise the same; as we shall observe below, *κ*, like *Epistula apostolorum*, is a *Sendschreibe*. On the basis of this concatenation of similarities Schmidt suggests that the relationship is one of direct literary dependence. For Schmidt the relationship has to be dependence on the part of K on *Epistula apostolorum*, on the assumption that K is later than *Epistula apostolorum*.[70] Since we are dealing with an earlier redaction which was employed by K it is theoretically possible that the direct relationship works the other way, and that *Epistula apostolorum* has derived its list from *κ*. However, the editorial hand of *κ* is nonetheless clear in the movement of Matthew and since it is more likely that Matthew would be moved up the list than down priority has to be given to *Epistula apostolorum*. Nonetheless, there is not enough here to claim direct dependence, for Schmidt was assuming that K was an Egyptian work of the fourth century, whereas if *κ* is earlier then it may still be in direct contact with the same tradition that produced the apostle list of *Epistula apostolorum*.

Whether the redactor of *κ* was in possession of *Epistula apostolorum* or whether the two simply draw on a common tradition, in either case *κ* derives from a very similar circle. Although an Egyptian provenance has often been suggested for *Epistula apostolorum* an Asian provenance is far more likely.[71] Even so, if the apostle list is a direct derivation from *Epistula apostolorum* it may be suggested that the provenance of the *Epistula* does not affect greatly the discussion of the origin of *κ*, as once produced it is quite easy for *Epistula apostolorum* to travel. But we may note that the *Gospel of the Ebionites* similarly adds Matthew to an essentially Johannine list of apostles, no doubt because of the attribution of a gospel to Matthew and since this is an Asian document of the second century, the suspicion, though not proof, that *κ* is likewise Asian, is raised.[72] Thus far we have suggested that *κ* was in a circle of Syrian influence on the basis of the version of TWT which it

---

tradition (contra Funk, *Doctrina*, 50-51 who cannot see why the list should not have been the author's composition).

[70] Schmidt. *Gespräche Jesu*, 245.

[71] So A. Stewart-Sykes, "The Asian origin of *Epistula apostolorum* and of the new prophecy", *VigChr* 51 (1997) 416-438, and C.E. Hill, "The *Epistula apostolorum*: an Asian tract from the time of Polycarp", *JECS* 7 (1999) 1-53.

[72] A.J. Maclean, *The Ancient Church Orders* (Cambridge 1910) 68, similarly suggests an Asian origin for K on the basis of the pre-eminence of John in the list of apostles.

employed; but TWT might likewise be a mobile tradition. The apostle list belongs with the TWT material, as it is to the apostles which are listed that TWT is attributed, but the combination may be secondary. But since the apostle list and the TWT were both combined in κ (we may deduce that κ was prefaced by some kind of list, since otherwise its apostolic attribution would have no meaning or context) it seems more likely that the combination was made at the source of both elements, rather than that each should independently travel to some other part of the Christian world there to be joined. Thus we are pointed, once again, in the direction of Asia, Syria, or perhaps Cilicia or Cappadocia.

2.2: The epistolary opening

If the context and the apostle list are derived from the same circle as *Epistula apostolorum*, an important consequence derives from this. For whereas Harnack, Funk and Goodspeed[73] determined that the epistolary greeting, χαίρετε, and the address to sons and daughters, were derived from B, and Hennecke that it derived from Δ1 (which is equivalent to our β)[74] we may now, in keeping with the argument above that there was no direct literary relationship between κ and B, see that this greeting is likewise derived from the context. *Epistula apostolorum* is intended as a *Sendschreibe* from the apostles to the church across the world,[75] as, it would appear, was κ. Such a form was known in second-century Asia,[76] and thus this may be taken as further evidence that κ is likewise to be attributed to that century. Although *Epistula apostolorum* is not unique in this form it shares with κ a fictive setting not of secret teaching before the resurrection, nor of prophetic revelation, but of apostolic directions given after the resurrection.[77] Again this does not oblige us to accept literary dependence, but certainly points to the same context.

However, before reaching any final conclusions on the opening, we need to determine how much of the opening of the extant K is κ and what is

---

[73] Goodspeed, "Barnabas", 232; Funk, *Doctrina*, 50.

[74] Hennecke, "Grundschrift", 65-66.

[75] So Hennecke, "Grundschrift", 66 correctly notes, though ascribing this to β on the basis that B is likewise a *Sendschreibe* with the same greeting.

[76] So, apart from *Epistula apostolorum* itself, and possibly some exemplars in the New Testament, note the activity of Themiso in sending a general epistle, according to Apollonius at Eus., *H.E.* 5.18.5: μιμούμενος τὸν ἀποστόλον. For discussion see Stewart-Sykes, "Asian context", 425-426.

[77] Schmidt, *Gespräche Jesu*, 244-245.

to be attributed to the K redaction. At a literary level it may be observed that the greater part of K1 is redundant. The redundant passage is bracketed in the excerpt below:

> Greetings, sons and daughters, in the name of the Lord Jesus Christ. John and Matthew and Peter and Andrew and Philip and Simon and James and Nathanael and Thomas and Kephas and Bartholomew and Jude the son of James.
>
> In accordance with the command of Our Lord Jesus Christ the Saviour we gathered ourselves together, as he laid down: [Before you determine the eparchies, calculate the numbers of the places, the rewards of bishops, the seats of presbyters, the assistance offered by deacons, the understanding of readers, the blamelessness of widows and whatever is necessary for the foundation of the church, so that knowing the type of those things which are heavenly, they should guard themselves against every fault, seeing that, in the great day of judgement, they should give an account of those who heard and did not keep. And he ordered us to send these words out to the whole inhabited world.]
>
> It seemed to us, [therefore,] that we should command you as an admonition of brotherhood and an exhortation, so that you might be mindful through the writing of what the Lord revealed to each of us in accordance with the will of God through the Holy Spirit.

If this literary instinct is correct, we may secondly note that the description of the contents which is bracketed is not what follows immediately. K2, however, with its description of admonition and exhortation, may readily be applied to TWT. If this is the case then it is entirely possible that this is derived from *κ*, and accompanied the original apostle list and the TWT.

What then of the greater part of K1 bracketed above? Although K has joined this to *κ* in order to bolster the apostolic sanction to the church-order which follows TWT, and thus supplied the apostolic attribution to the sections of the church-order, nonetheless we may suggest that this passage is not the production of K, but was derived from that very church-order which, as we shall see, is employed as a source for K16-21 and 23. This introduction has been placed by K at the beginning of the overall work, conceivably with minor amendments to fit it to the context, (including, possibly, the addition of the final statement that the Lord had ordered the apostles to publish the order to the whole earth)[78] and certainly adding the *οὖν* at the beginning of the next clause, in order to smooth the transition between the two sources.

---

[78] A similar suggestion is made by L. Duchesne, untitled review of Harnack, *Quellen*, in *Bulletin Critique* 7 (1886) 361-370 at 362-363.

The reason for this attribution is that the church-order is concerned to align the service of presbyters and laypersons on earth with that of angels in heaven, which is precisely what K1 states is the intention of the directions that are to be given. This church-order, with which K concludes, is a separate source, and so before finally determining the extent of K's redactional work, and thus the date of K as it has been received, we need to examine the extent of this source. Nonetheless, before moving to that section, we may suggest that *κ* is Asian, or from an adjacent area, and that it is a product of the second century.

2.3: Conclusions on the opening of K

Although both B and *Epistula apostolorum* have been suggested as sources for the opening of K, it is equally likely that this is an independent product, though one deriving from the same Asian circle as *Epistula apostolorum*. The TWT material has been joined to the apostle list by *κ*. Another redactor, however, has supplied the greater part of K1. Nonetheless, although the position of this material is redactional, and probably has been placed in this position in the work overall by K, it is itself derived from a source, since it has a great similarity of outlook to the church-order with which K concludes.

The other significant point that is to be gathered from the introduction is that *κ* had the recognisable genre of a *Sendschreibe*. As a means of propagating prophetic literature this was known in second-century Asia. The dialogic form is secondary, but, as in *Epistula apostolorum*, may find its place within a *Sendschreibe*. The classification of K as a church-order thus blinds us to its true genre. The church-order content is secondary, as the *Sendschreibe* originally extended only to TWT, but the inclusion of this material by K has thus altered the work overall.

It is to this church-order that our attention may now be turned.

3: The sources and redaction of the church-order of K

3.1: Harnack's two ancient sources

Once again we may begin with Harnack, who distinguished two ancient sources lying behind the church-order. First is that now found in K16-21, which he named *κατάστασις τοῦ κλήρου*, the second that beginning in K22, which he termed *κατάστασις τῆς ἐκκλησίας*. In what follows we retain

Harnack's name for the first hypothetical source, abbreviating it, for convenience, to κκ.

The reason for Harnack's division of K is that K22 is a doublet of K20, and, we may note, in different grammatical form.[79] Having legislated for the appointment of deacons, and gone on to discuss widows, the subject then turns back to the duties of deacons. Harnack thus suggested that K22, together with what follows, was excerpted from a different source than K16-21. The first source, Harnack considered, could hardly be later than the first third of the third century,[80] the second he placed earlier, in the second century.[81] We will examine the dating of K's sources below but for the moment may note, with Harnack, that the doublet is clumsy as well as repetitive, and is indicative therefore of some redactional activity. This, however, is not the only peculiarity about the chapters. When John suggests that two presbyters should be appointed, he is contradicted by the other apostles, who demand three; again, this appears to be a redactional intervention.[82] Beyond this the discussion of the qualifications for a presbyter is not only more extensive than might be expected, but contradicts the statement about bishops in that whereas married bishops are allowed, though unmarried bishops are preferred, presbyters are simply to have had no congress with women. However, before tracing all the peculiarities of the church-order we should examine Harnack's discussion of his two sources in more detail.

As we have seen, fundamental for Harnack's hypothesis is the doublet at K20 and K22, which led to his suggestion that K22, together with what follows, is the tail-end of a separate church-order which had already dealt with bishops and deacons, and now goes on to laymen at K23. However, it is to be noted that K23 compares the place of a layman with the conduct of an angel, which is the same imagery employed of the presbyters at K18. Moreover K23 is not a statement of appointment, as are K16-21; laymen as such are not appointed, and so this statement could well follow on from K21 as the final statement in a series extending from K16 and beginning with the appointment of a bishop. Thus rather than reflecting the juncture of two distinct church-orders it is possible that K22 is an interpolation from another

---

[79] Harnack, *Lehre*, 213-214.

[80] Harnack, *Lehre*, 212.

[81] Harnack, *Lehre*, 214.

[82] The justification for this redactional intervention is discussed at 3.6.3 below. As it is, it seems artificial and superficial as noted by A. Faivre, "Apostolicité et pseudo-apostolicité dans la 'Constitution ecclésiastique des apôtres'. L'art de faire parler les origines", *RevScRel* 66 (1992) 19-67, at 42.

source or a redactional composition, which, rather than signifying the juncture of a second source, simply disrupts the flow. The subject immediately preceding is the charitable work of widows and what follows in K23 is a suggestion that the deacons should be engaged in this charitable work. Is it possible that a redactor who knew not of the work of widows, or who wished to downgrade this order, has supplemented what he found with a statement regarding the work of deacons as being that which, in essence, had been ascribed to widows? To an extent this decision is based on a decision about the redactional levels in the conclusion of the document, where the ministry of women is restricted to caring for indigent women. If this is part of a source then the source is surely different from that dictating the appointment of widows, whereas if this is a redactional composition then it too may be intended to downgrade the ministry of women in the church. It is clearly not from the same source as K16, as here it is assumed that deacons may aspire to the episcopate whereas, as will be shown below, the *episkopos* of *κκ* is elected from the number of the presbyters. The manner in which the social work of deacons mirrors that ascribed to widows is striking, and is likewise noticed by Funk, who suggests, however, that this is a single source dealing generally with diaconal works of charity.[83] He thus denies Harnack's two-source theory on the grounds that K22 is speaking of a different aspect of a deacon's duties than K20. It remains odd nonetheless that the description of the duties should be split, and so although we may agree that the connection between K21 and K22 is the issue of social work, K22 does not continue K21 but contradicts it, a reading which gains strength from the discussion of women's ministry that follows.

It is this latter option, namely that this is a redactional composition, which we intend to support. Although we have yet to reach this stage in the argument, we may for the moment set aside Harnack's two sources in favour of a hypothesis of the redactional interpolation of K22 into K's source, and the assignment of K23 to the same source as K16-21. We may, nonetheless, recognise that a source lay behind much of K16-K21 and K23.

3.2: Bartlet's hypothesis of a double revision

Harnack was not alone in discerning ancient sources behind the latter part of K. A series of interpolations in an ancient source is suggested by Bartlet. He suggests an original work from early in the third century, a revision at the end of the third century and a further revision in the fourth century. The

[83] Funk, *Doctrina*, liv-lv.

original and the first revision he places in Cilicia or Cappadocia, and the final revision in Egypt. This second revision is presumably the work of the redactor who put the document into its final shape, and corresponds to our K.[84]

Bartlet's detailed argument, alas, can not be found. His publication on the subject was posthumously edited from among his notes by Cadoux, who reports the existence of 21 sheets of unrevised work dealing with the sources that were not publishable.[85] What survives are some examples illustrating this analysis; we can only guess at the arguments that he employed to support the analysis he offered. We cite each of these examples in full using Bartlet's English version rather than that published here. The punctuation, however, is slightly altered and, rather than using Bartlet's system of brackets, his first revision is shown in boldface and his second revision is italicised and boldfaced.

> Peter said, "If there exist a paucity of men, and there be not yet to hand a full complement of those able to vote about a bishop – less (that is) than twelve men, let them write to the neighbouring church(es), where it chances to be planted, in order that thence may come three chosen men and test carefully him that is worthy - if any one has a fair repute with the heathen, **if he is free from sin, a friend of the poor, self-controlled, not a drunkard, not a fornicator, not over-reaching or abusive, or a respecter of persons, and such-like.** ***It is a fair thing indeed that he be without wife: but otherwise, having had (but) one wife, cultured, able to interpret the scriptures; but if unlettered, let him be of a meek disposition, and let him abound in love towards all***; lest perchance a bishop becomes convicted by popular opinion of any fault."

Whereas we can see why Bartlet chose to connect the final clause to the statement about good repute among the heathen, therefore attributing the intervening matter to secondary redaction, there is no reason why the final clause should not follow on from the qualification list. In that case the point is made that the qualifications should exist, and that for this reason the bishop might not be blamed in popular opinion. It is indeed possible that this last section has regard solely to the bishop's meekness, which is being seen as a consolation should he be unable to read the Scriptures, and is therefore an interpolation. With regard to the possibility that the qualification list itself has been subject to interpolation, we must immediately be suspicious of the

---

[84] J.V. Bartlet, *Church-Life and Church-Order during the First Four Centuries* (Oxford 1943) 99-105.

[85] So C.J. Cadoux at Bartlet, *Church-Life*, 103. The papers appear to have perished, as they are not among Cadoux's archive.

statement that the bishop is better unmarried, and that otherwise he should be once-married. That a bishop should be once-married is a qualification found in the pastoral epistles, and may be an ancient direction, but in its current context qualifies the statement that the bishop should be unmarried. It is unusual, though not unthinkable, that an early source should opt for an unmarried bishop,[86] but the manner in which the demonstrably more primitive qualification in this instance is the second option, gives grounds for suspicion. Likewise odd is the conjunction of the requirement that he should be educated with the recognition that he might be illiterate. We turn to this point further at 3.6.2 below, but for the moment suggest that as the role of the bishop became more of an intellectual role as the second century progressed, and as the expectation grew that the bishop should not simply be a patron but should also have competence in teaching and preaching, the requirement that he should have some education is more likely to be later than earlier, and that a latter point in the redactional history of the passage is likely to be the point at which such a requirement was inserted, whereas the provision for an unlettered bishop is more probably original.

Taking these points into consideration the following possible redactional interpolations are shown in bold.

> *ἐὰν ὀλιγανδρία ἐπάρχη καὶ μήπου πλῆθος τυγχάνῃ τῶν δυναμένων ψηφίσασθαι περὶ ἐπισκόπου ἐντὸς δεκαδύο ἀνδρῶν, εἰς τὰς πλησίον ἐκκλησίας, ὅπου τυγχάνει πεπηγυῖα, γραφέτωσαν, ὅπως ἐκεῖθεν ἐκλεκτοὶ τρεῖς ἄνδρες παραγενόμενοι δοκιμῇ δοκιμάσαντες τὸν ἄξιον ὄντα, εἴ τις φήμην καλὴν ἔχει ἀπὸ τῶν ἐθνῶν, εἰ ἀναμάρτητος ὑπάρχει, εἰ φιλόπτωχος, εἰ σώφρων, μὴ μέθυσος, μὴ πόρνος, μὴ πλεονέκτης ἢ λοίδορος ἢ προσωπολήπτης καὶ τὰ τούτοις ὅμοια.* **Καλὸν μὲν εἶναι ἀγύναιος, εἰ δὲ μή,** *ἀπὸ μιᾶς γυναικός·* ***παιδείας μέτοχος,*** *δυνάμενος τὰς γραφὰς ἑρμηνεύειν· εἰ δὲ ἀγράμματος, πραΰς ὑπάρχων, καὶ τῇ ἀγάπῃ εἰς πάντας περισσευέτω,* ***μήποτε περὶ τινος ἐλεγχθεὶς ἐπίσκοπος ἀπὸ τῶν πολλῶν γενηθείη****.*

Next Bartlet dealt with the saying ascribed to John regarding the appointment of presbyters:

[86] For R.H. Connolly, "The use of the *Didache* in the *Didascalia*", *JTS* 24 (1923) 147-157, at 155, the very provision indicates a date later than *Didasc*. See, however, 5.2 below.

John said, "The appointed bishop **knowing the devotion and love for God of those about him** shall appoint whomsoever he shall have tested, as presbyters, two in number." ***All replied to this and said, "Not two but three."*** "The presbyters, then, must be men already of long time in the world, ***in some fashion abstaining from sexual intercourse,*** generous towards the brotherhood, not respecting a man's person, ***fellow-initiates of the bishop and supporters of his, assembling the congregation together, zealous for the pastor.***"

What is obscured by Bartlet's treatment here is that all around this text there is the discussion of the manner in which the presbyters, around the bishop, represent the twenty-four elders of the apocalypse. The discussion of the elders at the right and the left is interrupted by the statement of qualifications. There are thus grounds for seeing not only the statements that are here italicised as secondary (as they certainly are), but the whole as secondary. Harnack, moreover, notes that such a treatment of the qualifications of presbyters who are not also in some sense bishops, is unique before the fourth century, though he leaves it intact in his original source.[87] Finally, we may note that the demand for celibacy is imposed more strictly upon presbyters than upon the bishop, which again indicates that this is not part of the original, but may be the work of the redactor who inserted the words *καλὸν μὲν εἶναι ἀγύναιος* in the section concerning the bishop. Thus, on the grounds of the manner in which the flow of the passage is interrupted, on the grounds that this is unique as a treatment of the qualifications of presbyters, and on the grounds of the contradiction with the earlier statement concerning the bishop, we may consider the entire passage suspect. It is true that those parts that Bartlet attributes to the original are qualifications found in more ancient contexts than the fourth century, to which he wishes to assign K, but there is no reason why a later redactor might not imitate earlier statements of qualification. Certainly, we may agree with Bartlet, as with Harnack, that the statement "All replied to this and said, 'Not two but three'" is the work of K. The way is prepared for this in K3.[88] Not only this, but the whole of the list of qualifications for a presbyter, must be assigned to K, on the basis that the discussion is interrupted, and on the basis that K is imagining presbyters who have a more distinct status than that intended in the original. *κκ* is profoundly influenced by the pastoral epistles in listing qualifications for other offices, but a sign that there is nothing here of *κκ* is the absence of any parallel.

---

[87] Harnack, *Sources*, 11 n. 9.

[88] See 3.6.3 below for a rationale for this intervention.

> James said, "Let a reader be appointed, after first having been carefully tested, **not a tongue-wagger, not a drunkard nor yet a jester, seemly in bearing, persuasive, of good sense, first to hasten to the gatherings on the Lord's Day**, easy to hear, good at exposition **knowing that he is performing the office of an Evangelist, *for he who fills the ears of one who does not understand shall be accounted as written down before God*.**"

Whereas we have suggested that Bartlet was not radical enough in his excisions in the discussion of the presbyters, in the absence of his argument it is hard to see why anything here should not be assigned to the original source. Harnack is content to attribute the whole to the source, suggesting only that K may have struck εἷς at the beginning.[89] Since the office of reader is first otherwise found at the beginning of the third century this raises the question of the date and origin of this office and the source which enshrines the appointment, but we shall turn to this at 3.6.2 below.

> Kephas said, "Let widows be appointed, three in number – two of them persevering in prayer for all those in trial and with a view to revelations touching whatsoever is needful, and one attending upon those tried by sicknesses. **Let her be fit for ministering, sober, reporting to the presbyters what things are requisite, not a lover of filthy lucre, not addicted to much wine, so that she may be able to be soberly fit for night-services and for any other sort of good deeds she may desire to do. For these things are the Lord's chief good treasures.**"

Here the point that gives rise to suspicion is that the list of qualifications for the one widow who is to care for the sick and needy is rather extensive, whereas no qualification is given for the other two, and the obvious qualifications that one might expect, namely age and length of widowhood, are not mentioned. It will be noted below that K wishes to restrict the ministry of women to service of this nature, and it may well be that it is the hand of K, rather than an intervening redactor, as Bartlet suggests, who has extended the qualifications for social care. Nonetheless, we may agree with him that the source has been extended somewhat at this point.

Thus, although as living literature it is quite likely that the church-order source which came to K had grown, there is no obvious reason why the fundamental inconsistencies that may be observed are not the result of K's own work. As we go on to examine the remainder of the document, this must be our working hypothesis. This does not exclude the possibility that *κκ* was itself the product of redactional expansion, but this expansion had taken place before coming into the hand of K, from whose work derive the

[89] Harnack, *Sources*, 15.

particular contradictions and tensions that we have noted. Bartlet does not discuss the first paragraph dealing with deacons, and we will suggest below that the whole is later than the first layer of *κκ*, but in general there is not the evidence that would enable us to trace the multiple strata in a document whose very existence is hypothetical.

3.3: Interim conclusion

Whereas Harnack suggested that there were two sources to the church-order found in K, and Bartlet suggested extensive interpolation by two redactors, we have found one ancient source only, which has been interpolated extensively by a single redactor. There is no reason to think that this redactor is other than the K redactor who joined *κκ* to *κ*. We have yet, however, to deal with the conclusion of the document.

3.4: K24-28

In seeking to determine the sources lying behind these chapters and their redactional history we may begin with three observations that give some clue to the background of the discussion.

3.4.1: Jesus as teacher

Firstly, we may concur with the observation of Harnack that at K22 and 26 Jesus is termed "the teacher".[90] This implies that both are from the same hand. Since, in contradistinction to Harnack, we have determined that K22 is the production of K, it follows that the introduction of K26 at least is also K`s construction.

3.4.2: The presence of Mary and Martha

Secondly, we may agree with Harnack that Mary and Martha are not actually present in the fictive scene, and that their statements are not part of the dialogue for, as he notes, the apostles alone are gathered;[91] rather the names as they appear are in reported speech. The prose is thus not particularly elegant, but if the two were taken as present this would stand in tension to

[90] Harnack, *Lehre*, 215.

[91] Harnack, *Sources*, 25 n. Cf. Faivre, "Apostolicité", passim, who assumes that Mary and Martha are present, make up the number 12, and are included in the opening address to sons and daughters (which is not at all to the apostles, but is epistolary).

the list of apostles at K1. This exchange is thus taken from a source, and it is entirely possible that in the source John, Martha and Mary were all present and that the passage as presently found in K stood as dialogue, and has been lifted with no editing, but that the two women are not present in the envisaged dialogue of K.

The particular source of this dialogical exchange, however, is lost to us. Harnack suggests that it is *Gospel of the Egyptians* on the grounds that there seems to have been much here about the interrelationship between male and female,[92] though he notes that in *Gospel of the Egyptians* the talk is of the negation of maleness and femaleness rather than, as would appear to be the case in the saying that the weak is saved through the strong, the subjugation of the female to the male. Harnack also noted the appearance of Mary in *Pistis Sophia* and *Acts of Philip*, in the latter of which Martha also appears. Since Harnack wrote, *Gospel of Thomas*, which states that the female must become male, has been discovered, as have other works that afford a prominence to Magdalene among the disciples, namely *Gospel of Philip*, *Epistula apostolorum*, *Gospel of Mary* and *Dialogue of the Saviour*. Although the agrapha reported in K26 do not appear in these, the scope of the possible origin of this exchange is broadened considerably (though it is not certain that the Mary here is indeed Mary Magdalene);[93] interestingly, however, all of these are products of the second century.

Also significant in terms of an investigation for the provenance of this position is the pairing of Mary with Martha. The two are paired in *Epistula apostolorum* as going to the tomb, as also in the *Book of the Resurrection of Bartholomew the Apostle*,[94] in the Hippolytean *Commentary on the Song of Songs*, and, as already observed, in *Acts of Philip*. We may also note that the gnostic *Apocalypsis Jacobi* links Martha and Mary together. This text, like other gnostic texts, is concerned to reveal the negation of femininity though absorption into the male; by contrast, *Epistula apostolorum* may be seen as an anti-gnostic text (though the section concerning Mary and Martha at the tomb is not particularly concerned with gnosticism), and the Hippolytean commentary is particularly concerned to deny the gnostic tenet of the absorption of the female by suggesting instead that women are restored to

---

[92] Harnack, *Sources*, 26.

[93] Her appearance alongside Martha would indicate that Mary of Bethany is intended. F. Bovon, "Mary Magdalene in the *Acts of Philip*", in F.S. Jones (ed.), *Which Mary: The Marys of Early Christian Tradition* (Atlanta 2002) 75-89, at 82 n. 33 however, suggests that the two are conflated by the redactor of the *Acta*.

[94] An observation first made by Baumstark, "Alte und neue Spuren eines ausserkanonischen Evangeliums"; Baumstark also observes the link with K, but is thereby led to give an Egyptian provenance to the tradition.

their original state in Eve.[95] Not only, therefore, does the presence of Mary indicate that the source employed at K26 derives from the second-century debate with gnosticism but the pairing with Martha likewise indicates a second-century and Asian provenance which engages with the gnostics. For as Harnack had noted, the emphasis here is on the subordination of the female rather than, as in gnostic literature, the transcending of gender, but nonetheless it is possible to see this source as part of the same discussion, as a response to gnostic speculation about the disappearance of gender. We may also note the particular significance of the material that is held in common with *Epistula apostolorum* since, as has already been established,[96] the apostle lists in K(κ) and *Epistula apostolorum* are linked. Given that this latter section is the work of K, we may thus observe that K is not so far removed from the context which engendered his sources.

We have already noted that κ, like *Epistula apostolorum*, was simultaneously a *Sendschreibe* and a dialogue. Whereas this section is the work of K, who continued the dialogical form adopted by κ, nonetheless we have noted that this section has likewise been excerpted from a dialogue, thus leading to a dialogue within a dialogue. The dialogue here would appear to be a revelation dialogue. This was a form much employed by gnostic groups, in particular to publish revelation given by the Lord;[97] it is the same form which *Epistula apostolorum* employs, and indeed Hermas` revelations are often reported as dialogues, which leads one to suggest that this was the recognised form of publishing new revelation, as the dialogue reflected at a literary level the discussion which might take place when early Christian prophets delivered their material.[98] Thus although the revelation dialogue is not necessarily or originally gnostic, indeed Rudolph notes that Christian dialogues preceded the gnostic dialogues and that the extant dialogues reflect a specifically Christian gnostic milieu,[99] it is in gnostic circles that the form continues to live and flourish; of the possible sources mentioned above, several are revelation dialogues with gnostic tendencies. Once again a

---

[95] Note the discussion of J.A. Cerrato, *Hippolytus between East and West* (Oxford 2002) 194-198.

[96] At 2.1 above.

[97] For a discussion, and form-critical analysis, of the gnostic revelation dialogue, see K. Rudolph, "Der gnostische Dialog als literarisches Genus", in P. Nagel (ed.), *Probleme der koptischen Literatur* (Halle 1968) 85-107.

[98] Cf. Rudolph, "Gnostische Dialog", 104, who suggests an origin in the schools, and H. Koester, "Überlieferung und Geschichte der frühchristlichen Evangelienliteratur" in W. Haase (ed.) *Aufstieg und Niedergang der Römischen Welt* II.25.2 (Berlin 1984) 1463-1542, at 1475.

[99] Rudolph, "Gnostische Dialog", 104-105.

context engendered by debate and involvement with gnosticism would seem to be the context of this exchange, since the literary tool employed to further the debate is typically gnostic. This, however, is the work of K; *κ*, although attributed to apostles, has few dialogic elements and, more significantly, is not a revelation dialogue as such, as there is no supernatural revealer. Finally significant for locating the traditions employed by K is the tension between Mary and Peter; a similar tension is to be found in *Gospel of Thomas*, *Gospel of Mary* and *Pistis Sophia.*[100] As noted below,[101] the names of apostles might be used as ciphers in polemical writings marking differences between early Christian groups, and Peter is found as the particular representative of "orthodox" thinking. Although Mary is ultimately claimed here as a similarly orthodox voice, the source would imply that originally a certain tension lay between them, which is again indicative that the use and engagement with this source indicates an engagement with heterodox groups who exalted the position of Mary above that of Peter. In time the name of Mary is substituted with that of Peter, or that of the mother of the Lord, in order precisely to remove focus from Mary Magdalene; as Brock suggests, this derives from the implicit threat posed because of her prominence in certain gnostic groups. K is faced by the same threat, but employs a different strategy to counter it.[102]

3.4.3: The offering of the body and blood

Thirdly we must observe the odd description of the eucharist as the offering of the body and blood. As Connolly puts it: "Can any parallel be brought from an ante-Nicene document to this absolute use of the 'oblation of the body and the blood?'"[103] Such is difficult, though ante-Nicene uses of the language of offering and descriptions of the eucharist as the body (or blood) of the Lord are not hard to find. However, Cyprian comes close to a doctrine as expressed here[104] and, more relevantly for K, the Syrian *Didascalia* comes close in charging that the likeness of the royal body of Christ is to be

[100] See, with full references, A.G. Brock, "Peter, Paul and Mary: canonical vs non-canonical portrayals of apostolic witnesses", in *SBL 1999 Seminar papers* (Atlanta 1999), 173-202, at 180.

[101] See 4.2.

[102] A.G. Brock, "What's in a name: the competition for authority in early Christian texts", *SBL 1998 Seminar Papers I* (Atlanta 1998) 106-124, at 112.

[103] Connolly, "Use of the Didache", 156.

[104] See the discussion in R.P.C. Hanson, *Eucharistic Offering in the Early Church* (Bramcote 1979) 17-19.

offered.[105] An absolute statement like that here is more typical of the medieval West than of any patristic author, but if it should be considered a shorthand then the shorthand is as likely to come from early in the third century as from the fourth. Thus we may note the use of Firmilian[106] who refers to the eucharist quite simply as the offering of a sacrifice. This final usage is of particular interest as it derives from Cappadocia, which is the locale to which Bartlet sought to ascribe K, and because the context is that of a woman who celebrated the eucharist. It is indeed possible that this passage lay behind Bartlet's suggestion of Cappacodia.

3.4.4: The redaction of K 24-28

We may conclude that, whereas K employs sources in this section, and in particular alludes to a dialogic gospel involving Mary and Martha, as well as deriving the agraphon concerning women sitting from a source,[107] K24-28 as a whole is his own construction. The sources are all from the second century and there is nothing in his language that prevents a similar date being ascribed to his redactional activity here. We must ask, therefore, whether it is possible to construct a *Sitz im Leben* for the discussion within that period.

These chapters are concerned with one issue, namely the impropriety that women should have any liturgical role in the eucharistic celebration, since their ministry should be restricted to care for women in need. The fact that the subject of the eucharist is introduced by Peter as soon as Andrew mentions ministry for the women is indicative that this is what really is at issue. The whole point of the discussion is to subordinate women's ministry, and in particular to legislate against women's participation in the celebration of the eucharist. We have already suggested that K introduced K22 as a qualification of what is said about the ministry of widows, and may suggest that this is part of an overall strategy to minimise the significance of women's ministry; it is the manner in which this description of deacons' duties mirrors that of the earlier description of the work of one of the widows that leads to the suggestion that the chapter is a redactional composition, and indeed leads to the suspicion that the entire exchange of K24-28 is K's production in pursuit of the same objective. At a literary level it is hard to see how K24-28 can exist as a coherent piece once the dialogic elements and the introduction to K26 is removed, and we may note that the majority of the material is a citation of diverse *testimonia* all intended to refute any claim of

[105] *Didascalia* 6.22.2.

[106] At [Cyp.] *Ep.* 75.10.5.

[107] See the notes to the translation ad loc. for further discussion of this agraphon.

women to a liturgical ministry. Whereas K was not the originator of these sayings, as he is apparently quoting from some source or sources in these chapters, it would appear to have been K who strung them together in their current form, and derived them from a source which was likewise hostile to the liturgical ministry of women.

Rather than exercising a liturgical ministry, these women are to be concerned with social care. As such they are comparable to the deaconesses of the Syrian *Didascalia*. This proximity of role has led to the suggestion that the passage here is a polemic against deaconesses, but as Gryson rightly points out, the term is not employed here.[108] Either deaconesses were never known in the K community or, given that Syria is a likely place of redaction, they had yet to emerge. The polemic, however, is not against deaconesses but against a liturgical ministry by women, and the answer that the women`s role is that of social care is one that might in turn lead to the emergence of the deaconess order. Here the functions are to be exercised by widows but in the Syrian *Didascalia* the widows are reduced to being recipients of charity rather than those who exercise good works. We may suggest that even in a charitable role widows had become too powerful for the community of *Didascalia*; Methuen thus suggests that the deaconess order is a creation of the didascalist circle as a means of bringing female ministers under episcopal control and as a means of emasculating a powerful order of widows.[109] The stage of development of K is that of widows functioning in the role which in time would be filled by deaconesses, and so K either precedes *Didascalia* or derives from an entirely different circle (though one in which similar developments are occurring.) We may, however, note that widows in *Didascalia* are to pray for the sinner undergoing repentance,[110] as for others. Is this what is meant when it said that the visionary widows are to pray for those in trouble? An additional puzzle is posed by *Testamentum Domini*, which envisages a role for widows and deaconesses alike. The order of deaconess, however, may have been a later importation into the community which produced *Testamentum Domini*, for which reason the deaconess is clearly subordinate to the widow.[111] Thus, *Testamentum Domini* knows of powerful widows who have a liturgical role, standing behind the presbyters

---

[108] R. Gryson, *The Ministry of Women in the Early Church* (Collegeville, MN 1976) 48 in response to a suggestion by J. Daniélou, *The Ministry of Women in the Early Church* (London 1961).

[109] C. Methuen, "Widows, bishops and the struggle for authority in the *Didascalia apostolorum*", *JEH* 46 (1995) 197-213, at 201-202, and building on earlier suggestions.

[110] *Didasc.* 6.6.9.

[111] *T. Dom.* 1.19; 1.23.

on one side of the bishop; is this the tradition which has come to K, and which K is opposing?

If the concern is with the liturgical role of women then this implies that some women at least had claimed a liturgical role. We have already mentioned the female prophet who caused such alarm to Firmilian; this incident may be dated to 235. But beyond noting the event we may suggest that this was no innovation, but rather an anachronism; the *Didache* recognises that prophets might celebrate the eucharist,[112] and although nothing is said of their gender, the existence of female prophets is well attested in early Christianity.[113] Firmilian may be surprised at the normative nature of the rites that she employs[114] but we should not be so. A female prophet baptising and celebrating the eucharist is simply an example of liturgical archaism.[115]

Just as prophets might give thanks at the eucharist in the community of the *Didache*, and just as at Melito's functionally eucharistic paschal rite the Lord comes to be present through prophetic utterance as much as through sacramental media,[116] so prophecy is bound up to eucharist in the ritual of the Marcosians. The presence of women at the altar in Marcosian rites that, whatever their divergence from the emerging normative eucharist, continued nonetheless to have many similarities, may likewise be seen not as an innovation but as an archaism.[117]

Having noted the prominence of women prophets in early Christianity we may suggest that the continuance of female prophecy in heterodox sects in a later period is a further example of the preservation of practices obsolete in the *Grosskirche* among heterodox and separated communities. It is to be noted that two of the widows of *κκ* are to have revelations; indeed the very qualification of widowhood as the basis for prophecy may be significant,

---

[112] *Didache* 10.7. See also the discussion of C. Trevett, *Montanism. Gender, Authority and the New Prophecy* (Cambridge 1996) 188-189.

[113] Thus note, for instance, Ammia (Eus., *H.E.* 5.17.3-4), the daughters of Philip (Eus., *H.E.* 5.17.3; 5.24.2), and the female prophetic activity described in *Acta Pauli*.

[114] Firmilian in [Cyp.] *Ep.* 75.10.5.

[115] For a further discussion of liturgical archaism in separated Christian groups see my discussion of Marcionite liturgy in "Bread, fish, water and wine: The Marcionite menu and the maintenance of purity", in G. May and K. Greschat (eds), *Marcion und seine kirchengeschichtliche Wirkung* (TU 150; Berlin 2002) 207-220.

[116] So A. Stewart-Sykes, *The Lamb's High Feast: Melito,* Peri Pascha *and the Quartodeciman Paschal Liturgy at Sardis* (Leiden 1998), 13-14 and 201 with reference to *Peri Pascha* 103.

[117] See the discussion of A. and C. Faivre, "La place des femmes dans le rituel eucharistique des marcosiens. déviance ou archaïsme?", *RevScRel* 71 (1997) 310-328.

since the original Montanist female prophets separated from their husbands at the time of prophesying.[118] Although it is possible that women continued to prophesy in orthodox circles even into the fourth century,[119] the expectation that a church that may not muster twelve males capable of offering patronage would nonetheless be able to support two (female) prophets indicates that this is indeed an ancient source. Thus, it is entirely reasonable to suggest that women had exercised a liturgical role in the K community, and possible that they continued to do so.

However, it is fair to say that female presidency at the eucharistic celebration was not known by the third century except among sectarian groups. Although Jensen argues that the anonymous woman prophet of Cappadocia was a catholic Christian, suggesting that there is no strong indication that she was a Montanist,[120] Trevett cites a number of indications that she is indeed of the new prophecy,[121] such as her ecstatic mode of delivery, the geographical setting, and her statement that she had come from "Jerusalem", which may be read as a reference to the characterisation of certain Phrygian villages as Jerusalem.[122] In Firmilian's perception, at least, she was Montanist. We may reckon with the possibility that the gap between the time of the prophet and that of Firmilian meant that the liturgical role of women had diminished and this event therefore was all the more shocking to a bishop in the middle of the third century, but even if this is the case it indicates that by the middle of the third century women did not celebrate the eucharist in catholic communities. Along similar lines Jensen suggests that the ban on female presbyters in the eleventh canon of the canons of Laodicea indicates that the presbyteral activity of women was known into that period,[123] but there is no necessity that these presbyters were liturgical presbyters.[124] It is as likely that this title is honorific or indicates a patronal

---

118 So Apollonius at Eus., *H.E.* 5.18.3.

119 So C. Trevett, "'Angelic visitations and speech she had': Nanas of Kotiaeion", in P. Allen et al. (eds), *Prayer and Spirituality in the Early Church* 2 (Brisbane 1999) 259-277.

120 A. Jensen, *God's Self-Confident Daughters* (Kampen 1996) 185-186.

121 C. Trevett, "Spiritual authority and the 'heretical' woman: Firmilian's word to the church in Carthage", in J.W. Drijvers and J.W. Watt (eds), *Portraits of Spiritual Authority: Religious Power in Early Christianity, Byzantium and the Christian Orient* (Leiden 1999) 45-62, at 48-50 in particular but also passim.

122 So Apollonius at Eus., *H.E.* 5.18. For discussion see D. Powell, "Tertullianists and Cataphrygians", *VigChr* 29 (1975) 33-54, at 44, and W. Tabbernee, "Revelation 21 and the Montanist New Jerusalem", *Australian Biblical Review* 37 (1989) 52-60.

123 Jensen, *God's Self-Confident Daughters*, 185.

124 The same objection may be levelled at the discussion of K.J. Torjeson, *When Women were Priests* (San Francisco 1993) 14-38, who, in citing evidence for women's liturgical leadership, cites evidence for women having presbyteral titles in catholic communities.

role; the assumption that the social leader of a community is also the liturgical leader needs to be examined.[125] We may re-iterate, therefore, the statement that female eucharistic presidency was unknown in Asian and Cappadocian catholic communities in the third century.

Nonetheless, widows have a place in the sanctuary at the celebration of the eucharist in *Testamentum Domini,*[126] which may imply a memory of a more prominent role in proceedings, and indicates that in this community at least women continued to have a role alongside the male *klēros*. A similar situation may be envisaged by the redactor of *Acts of Philip* 8.2, who describes Mary as preparing the bread and salt for the breaking of bread, and Martha as administering (eucharistic gifts?) to the people. The pairing of Martha and Mary here is surely significant, as this seems directly to speak to the situation envisaged by K, to the extent that we may suggest that K is a direct response to the liturgical role of women presupposed by *Acts of Philip*.[127] Thus the subjugation of women, justified by the agraphon concerning the salvation of the weak through the strong, is here particularly liturgical. The context of the dialogue may originally have related to speculation regarding maleness and femaleness, but K is solely concerned with women's ministry.

It is thus a similar context to that described by *Acts of Philip* and *Testamentum Domini* which is addressed by K, though how precisely K's context relates to these settings is less clear, in that we have to ask why female ministry, which is rooted in tradition and which occurs elsewhere, should cause such alarm to K. Possibly there was a memory of more ancient practice in the community, possibly women had demanded a role, or possibly the struggle is a literary struggle aimed either against Montanists, who had female officers, or against the gnostic groups who produced the Magdalene literature and who perhaps continued to involve women in the eucharistic celebration alongside men, (though possibly innovating in the manner in which their participation was interpreted). Or is K alarmed by a practice similar to that described in *Testamentum Domini* on the grounds that it is suspiciously close to gnostic practice?

A literary struggle is possible; given the tools employed the struggle is more probably with gnostic groups than with Montanists, though the latter

[125] I have begun such an examination of the prevailing assumption in my essay "Prophecy and patronage: the relationship between charismatic functionaries and household officers in early Christianity", in C.M. Tuckett and A.F. Gregory (eds), *Trajectories through the New Testament and the Apostolic Fathers* (Oxford 2005) 165-189.

[126] *T. Dom.* 1.19; 1.23.

[127] Such is indeed suggested by Bovon, "Mary Magdalene in the *Acts of Philip*", 83.

possibility cannot be ruled out altogether as the new prophets seem to have read a variety of material including, it has recently been argued, literature from Nag Hammadi.[128] As to internal pressures, which involvement with Christian gnostic or Montanist groups might have brought about, we can know nothing certain; however, *Testamentum Domini* would seem to describe the very situation K is seeking to prohibit, and *Acts of Philip* similarly seems to presuppose such an arrangement, which in turn implies either that there was pressure from the widows to maintain a role within the celebrations of the community or else that K is alarmed by the situation that obtains and, rather than recognising that this is ancient tradition, believes this to be a gnostic innovation, so using gnostic tools (the dialogue) and anti-gnostic tools (apostolicity) to oppose it. The K community is one distinct from that of *Didascalia*, and so knows no deaconess order, but seeks to exercise control over women through a similar strategy, namely by demoting their role to a social role and by denying them any liturgical function.

Because the whole focus of K in the end is a vision of church-order that relegates the role of women to social care, nothing is said of the widows who are to pray and prophesy whereas extensive qualifications are added to the discussion of the widow who is to engage in good works. In time even this would become controversial, but for the time being K is sufficiently motivated to redact an ancient church-order in order to clarify that women have no part in it.

3.5: The conclusion to K

As has been noted, K was produced through the adjuncture of church-order material with a document of TWT; the two openings were combined in order to produce that which is now extant. The church-order material clearly extends to K28. What, however, of the conclusion?

3.5.1: K30

Since the injunction that nothing should be added or subtracted from the content of teaching is part of TWT in D, E and K and thus, we may surmise, in δ and κ likewise, it seems most probable that the source of this statement at K30 is κ. Although K has already redacted this material at K14, the conclusion to κ provides a conclusion for his entire work.

---

128 So N. Denzey, "What did the Montanists read?", *HThR* 94 (2001) 427-448. Hippolytus, *Haer*. 8.19, refers to the large number of writings valued by the new prophecy.

The prior part of the chapter, however, goes beyond staking an apostolic claim and states that the content is commanded by the Lord. There is a superficial similarity with B4.9, and thus it is possible that the material may be attributed to *β*, but the similarity is superficial only, for whereas the point of B4.9 is to deny authority of the rabbinic type as part of the appeal to the listener, here an even higher authority is claimed.[129] Since K has used a number of agrapha attributed to Jesus earlier in his redactional construction, and is concerned to root his apostolic order in the teachings of Jesus, we may surmise that this is his redactional conclusion.

3.5.2: K29

K29 is an agraphon concerning sharing. Although not attributed to Jesus, in the light of the earlier use of non-canonical sayings, and the similarity between it and such canonical statements as Matt 6:19-21 and parallel, it may well be seen as a continuation of the catalogue of sayings and related to K's redactional argument in favour of limiting women to social work, thus being seen as the conclusion of the argument that began at K24. The possibility that it is a free-floating element of TWT material, which was attached to the end of *κ* (and omitted by E), included by K at this point due to the similarity of the material immediately preceding it cannot altogether be ruled out, but given that a similar point has already been made in K21 (in the context of the reward for the social work undertaken by widows, itself assigned to the K redaction) it seems more probable that this is K's addition to the discussion, intended to point up the charitable role of widows as opposed to any liturgical role. In either event, however, and whatever K's source, its present position relies upon K and in the final redactional creation of K belongs with the material gathered by K and suffixed to *κκ*.

3.6: The ancient church-order lying behind K

We thus conclude that K's major source was a church-order consisting of part of K1, K16-21 (less interpolations) and K23; this we have termed *κκ*. Quite possibly there was more, but even though, as we suggest below, *Didascalia* employed this church-order as one of its own sources, and may therefore preserve more of this source, it cannot readily be recognised in the context of *Didascalia* except where there is a parallel also extant in K.

[129] Schermann, *Elfapostelmoral*, 88, likewise denies a connection.

At this stage we may examine this source, insofar as it may be reconstructed, in an attempt to determine its age, provenance, and significance.

3.6.1: The bishop and presbyters in κκ

The first thing which may be deduced about the episcopate is that, given that only twelve are required to elect a bishop, the bishop is head of a single congregation. Although this may indicate a rural position, if the order is ancient we may yet be in a context in which the monepiscopate as later understood had not yet emerged, namely that a bishop may head a single congregation rather than a group of congregations, and thus it is entirely possible that the congregation in question is urban. It is also possible that the number twelve may make the congregation appear smaller than it was, in that the order not only excludes women but moreover does not state what qualified a man as an elector; we cannot simply assume that all men had a vote, for it is possible that householders or persons of property only were so competent; this position will be argued at greater length below, but for the moment we may observe that the *episkopos* is not a *monepiscopus* in the sense that he had charge of more than one congregation, but that he is what is often described as a presbyter-bishop. This argument, may, however, be overstated. Lemoine suggests that Peter's discussion of *oligandria* concerns the election of *a* bishop, as opposed to *the* bishop, and suggests that the bishop here is hardly distinguished from a presbyter,[130] and Faivre alike suggests that presbyters might not be closely distinguished from the *episkopos*, as it is to the presbyters that a fundamentally disciplinary role is assigned, and on the grounds that K17 refers to presbyters assisting the bishops (plural) at the altar.[131] To take these arguments in turn, we may first point out that the bishop is elected as a single bishop, and a definite article is unnecessary since it is clear that a single community is meant. The situation is thus probably as that envisaged by Ignatius, namely that the *episkopos* is not *episkopos* set over several communities but is *episkopos* within one church. Secondly, although it is true that the presbyters and the bishop are *summachomenoi* and *summūstai*, and even assuming that these qualifications are not, as suggested above, interpolated into κκ by K, this does not mean that they are at every level indistinguishable. Faivre points to a certain ambivalence within *Didascalia* about who has disciplinary functions, but this

---

[130] Lemoine, "Étude", 10.

[131] A. Faivre, "Le texte grec de la Constitution ecclésiastique des apôtres 16-20 et ses sources", *RevScRel* 55 (1981) 31-42 at 36.

does not impact on K. Finally the textual support for Faivre's argument has disappeared in view of the emendation to the text proposed below.[132] This said, there is a close relationship between *episkopos* and *presbūteroi* and a certain overlap of function, which may indicate that the *episkopos* had grown out of the presbyterate in this community, rather than being a graft of two systems.

The idea that the threefold order was a graft of two systems, the presbyteral and the episcopal-diaconal, was widespread in the late nineteenth century, and was held particularly by Harnack, who found support for this hypothesis in K, and particularly in the differing qualifications for presbyter and bishop; he thus suggested that this illuminates the distinct origins of the two offices.[133] However the inconsistencies he points out, such as the demand for celibacy and age of presbyters, neither of which is demanded of bishops, may be attributed to the K redaction, and so we cannot uphold the independent origin of these offices in the community of *κκ* on that basis. We may, however, deduce that by the time of K the presbyterate had been clericalised, since particular demands are made of the presbyters, whereas earlier the presbyters were simply senior male members of the community.[134]

This in turn leads us to question whether the twelve electors are not members of the congregation, but actually those who, in this community, were presbyters, that is to say property-owning patrons of the church, akin to the *presbūteroi proistamenoi* of Rome.[135] One cannot avoid being reminded of the persistence of the twelve who form a sanhedrin in Acts, of the system

---

[132] See the text and textual commentary ad loc.

[133] Harnack, *Sources*, 28-35. It is clear from Nautin's papers that he too considered that the most ancient stratum of K revealed a twofold order of bishop and deacons, and on these grounds suspected the word *πρεσβυτέρους* in K17, assigning the second part of this chapter, and the following chapter, to a distinct source, and suggesting that the appointment of deacons here described is picked up at K20 (hence his suggestion noted below that the three means the bishop and two deacons). Whereas we have seen that there is much that is suspect in K18, this does not extend to the entire chapter, but solely to the statement of qualifications. Quite apart from the fact that *κκ*'s order would appear to be fundamentally presbyteral, as argued in this section, K20 does not easily follow on from K17a, even if *πρεσβυτέρους* is replaced by *διακόνους*.

[134] That the office of *episkopos* had emerged from the presbyters in the K community does not absolutely invalidate the hypothesis that the threefold order was a graft of two systems but simply indicates that this is not what occurred in this particular community. The threefold order may have come about in different communities at different times and in different ways.

[135] The term is that of Hermas at *Vis.* 2.4.3. Duchesne, untitled review of Harnack, *Quellen*, 364, is the first to suggest that these twelve are presbyters; he would not, however, see them as patrons.

by which twelve presbyters would elect the Alexandrian patriarch from their number, and of the ordination of twelve presbyters alongside a bishop in the pseudo-Clementines.[136] Is it possible that the original situation envisaged by *κκ* was that all males who were in a position to offer patronage were considered presbyters, and that the number of twelve is set as the minimum number who might form an electoral college? We may thus note that the *oligandria* is not absolute but specifically a shortage of men who are competent to elect.

Beyond the parallels noted above, two points speak in favour of this interpretation. Firstly the election is said to take place ἐντὸς δεκαδύο ἀνδρῶν; although Harnack takes this phrase as qualifying the *oligandria* and meaning "less than twelve", the phrase is a long way from the mention of the shortage of men. It may perhaps, therefore, be taken with ψηφίσασθαι, and to be translated as "from among twelve". The twelve are thus candidates as well as electors. Secondly this avoids the oddity of having a community of twelve that nonetheless has a minimum of eight clerics![137] Although Funk notes that there would be an apparent contradiction between the existence of twelve presbyters here and the appointment of two (or three) below,[138] we may suggest that the two presbyters then appointed by the bishop make up the number of the college, given that a seat has been vacated by the departed bishop and that a further seat would be vacated the next time that an election is required. This in turn indicates that the episcopate was indeed an outgrowth from the presbyterate in this community, but that only subsequently, at the time of K, did the presbyterate become recognized as clerics, thus leading to K's expansion of the qualifications for the presbyterate.

On the basis that the twelve are actually presbyters, and because the situation envisaged is that, perhaps in a foundational community, there are not twelve, then Duchesne,[139] followed by Vilela,[140] suggests that the three men who are to come from a neighbouring church are three bishops. However, the three selected are not said to be bishops, indeed they cannot all be bishops if they come from a single congregation. Nonetheless Harnack

---

[136] Ps-Clem., *Rec.* 3.66 (Zacchaeus is ordained bishop alongside twelve presbyters and four deacons) and Ps-Clem., *Rec.* 6.15 (also *Hom.* 11.36 – Maro is ordained bishop alongside twelve presbyters, with deacons and the order of widows established).

[137] So also A. Vilela, *La condition collegiale des prêtres au IIIe siècle* (Paris 1971) 165-167.

[138] Funk, *Doctrina*, 60.

[139] Duchesne, untitled review of Harnack, *Quellen*, 364-365.

[140] Vilela, *Condition collégiale*, 166.

and Duchesne alike are certainly right in connecting this regulation to the standing rule that bishops should be consecrated by three external bishops.[141] In particular both point to the report of Cornelius' letter to Fabian of Antioch in Eusebius,[142] where Cornelius states that Novatian had obtained consecration. What is significant here is not simply that three are required for the consecration of a bishop, but that the three come to Rome in order to deal with issues that are disturbing the church. Thus we may note, again with Harnack, that *1 Clem.* 63 and 65 refer to the Roman church sending three persons to Corinth.[143]

Harnack, like Faivre points out that the duties of the presbyters are, in accordance with those of the bishop, disciplinary and economic. Some presbyters are to distribute the gifts at the altar, whereas others are to see good order. Of course this is bound up to the liturgy, but the distinction between liturgical action and economic action is a fine one. Two examples may suffice: Justin states that the offerings of the congregation made at the eucharist are received by deacons and then distributed among widows and orphans,[144] and the Syrian *Didascalia* closely connects offering for the support of the bishop and the poor to the eucharistic offering.[145] Harnack finds support in this for his hypothesis, derived from Hatch,[146] that the origins of the episcopate lay in an economic office. This view is not much found now; I will admit that it is a view that I support, but this subject is beyond the scope of this introduction. Nonetheless, the fact remains that these are the duties of the *episkopos* and of the presbyters in this community. By the time of K the eucharist is distinguished as an offering of the body and blood, but for κκ the issue is indeed that of good order at the distribution of gifts. However, the proximity of functions between presbyter and bishop is a further indication that the *episkopos*, whilst distinct from the presbyters, is a growth from the presbyterate in this community. Thus, the widows are to disclose information about women in need to the presbyters, and not, as might otherwise be expected, to the bishop.

As already noted, Faivre likewise observes the disciplinary role of the presbyters. He also notes that the provision for dealing with an insolent

[141] Duchesne, untitled review of Harnack, *Quellen*, 364-365; Harnack, *Sources*, 36-38. The rule that three bishops should ordain is subsequently confirmed by the fourth canon of Nicaea.

[142] Eus., *H.E.* 6.43.8-9.

[143] Harnack, *Sources*, 36-38.

[144] Justin, *1 Apol.* 67.6.

[145] Note especially *Didasc.* 2.36.4.

[146] E. Hatch, *The Organization of the Early Christian Churches* (London 1881).

member is closely proximate to the Essene provisions of *Community Rule* dealing with insolence.[147] Although this may perhaps point, once again, to an originally disciplinary aspect to the offices of the community of *κκ*, Faivre suggests a more direct connection to Essene practice, noting the similarity of the three chosen men and the twelve electors in the notice regarding the election of a bishop with the provision for twelve men and three priests in *Community Rule*.[148] This section of *Community Rule* is legislating for a minimal and foundational community; in this instance there is a definite linkage with the twelve of K, as in both instances we are concerned with a minimally competent group. K does not, however, concern itself with three priests; the three of *Community rule* are, moreover, additional to the twelve whereas in K they are a substitute.

On the basis of the parallels with Essene documents, Faivre characterises the community of *κκ* as Judaeo-Christian, as forming a community similar to the Essenes, and as located in Syria early in the second century. Even if the parallels are not quite so pressing as they appear to be at first sight, nonetheless the importance placed on the community of goods, which is overseen by the bishop and presbyters as well as the disciplinary functions assigned to the bishop in this context may be seen as proximate indeed to Essene practice, and so it is likewise possible that there is an organic link to the twelve who form the electoral college for the bishop and the twelve who are the minimal foundational community in Community rule.

3.6.2: The reader

Our understanding of the role of the reader depends on the statement about the unlettered bishop. As the text stands, the illiteracy of the bishop does not readily fit with the requirement that he be generous, and therefore looks like an interpolation. An emendation to the text may therefore be proposed: where the extant Greek manuscript reads *δυνάμενος τὰς γραφὰς ἑρμηνεύειν· εἰ δὲ ἀγράμματος, πραῢς ὑπάρχων* I suggest that *κκ* read: *δυνάμενος τὰς γραφὰς ἑρμηνεύειν, εἰ δ᾽ ᾖ ἀγράμματος· πραῢς ὑπάρχων.*

The reason for the emendation is that, although there is no reason why an early source might not legislate for an illiterate bishop, the connection to generosity is odd. The qualification for generosity is ancient, it is found in D, for instance, and relates to the ability of the bishop to supply financial support to the congregation but it in no way connects to literacy. Rather the

[147] Faivre, "Texte grec", 36-37, with reference to 1QS 8.16-19.

[148] Faivre, "Texte grec", 37-39, with reference to 1QS 3.1-4.

comment about literacy connects to what went before, namely the requirement that the bishop should be able to interpret the scriptures, and not what follows; thus the emendation to the text and repunctuation puts the matter of illiteracy alongside the requirement that the bishop be able to interpret the Scriptures. The point is that the bishop should be capable of interpretation, and that illiteracy is not a bar to that competence. Harnack cites several examples of illiterate bishops from the third century, and Funk two examples from the fifth![149] If the emendation is not accepted, then as an interpolation the statement "if he is unlettered" is unlikely to be the work of K, but must be assigned to some intermediate level in the growth and development of *κκ*, before it came to K, whereas the statement that he should have some education, provisionally ascribed to K above, must be original. If this is the case it is at this time likewise that the discussion of the reader, whose role in the reading and interpretation of Scripture appears to complement that of the bishop, came about. But the original probably belongs in *κκ*; the readership is complementary to the episcopate, however, because if the bishop cannot read then somebody has to read the Scripture for him in order that he may then interpret it. At this point, however, we should note again that the final comment of the chapter seems to fit the text as given in the manuscript. We have already suggested that this is K's interpolation, and may therefore suggest that K read the text as it stands in the manuscript. Either the corruption had already taken place, or possibly K simply misread what was in front of him. A deliberate alteration is unlikely.

The position of reader thus comes about as somebody has to read the text so that a bishop who is unable to read can interpret it. Such a position could simply be a local arrangement on the basis of an illiterate bishop in the *κκ* community, but it is likely that an illiterate bishop was far from being an isolated phenomenon, and thus that readers may have been widespread. Given the uncertainty of the date of *κκ*, the first clear evidence of a reader is found in Tertullian's *De praescriptione haereticorum* 41, where he states that in heretical communities a person may one day be a reader, another a deacon. Since, however, he is referring to Marcionite communities, and Marcionites were liturgically conservative,[150] the office may already have been ancient in eastern communities. We are thus reminded of the blessing upon the reader of the Apocalypse[151] as indicating that readers held some kind of position from a relatively early period.

149 Harnack, *Sources*, 10; Funk, *Doctrina*, 61.

150 On Marcionite liturgical conservatism see my "Bread, fish, water and wine".

151 Rev 1:3.

For Faivre the provision for an unlettered bishop is close in spirit to the simple priest of *Damascus document*.[152] To follow through this analogy we may see the position of the reader as close in spirit to the learned levite, who is to advise the *mebaqqer* on matters of ritual law. However, it is more probable that the similar phenomena have come about not because of a direct historical connection but because the bishop, like the *mebaqqer*, is chosen on the fundamentally social grounds that he is a person in a position to offer patronage to the community, and on these grounds need not be literate.[153] Thus the provision for a lettered reader assisting an unlettered bishop may represent the social setting in which an unlettered master may be reliant upon literate slaves for aspects of management; the context for the operation of a reader in the eucharistic setting may derive from the employment of slaves to read to a company in domestic settings.

It is said that the reader is to be *diēgētikos*. The meaning of this word is not entirely clear. Obviously, the reader is to read, and is to have a voice that is easy to hear, but it appears that something more is demanded.[154] If the term refers to something beyond reading, we may note that according to Dionysius Thrax's *Ars grammatica* 1 reading is to be followed by *exēgesis*. But this is the procedure of clarifying difficulties, and is to be distinguished from *diēgēsis*, which is the construction of a narrative. If we were to suggest that the practice here is derived from the rhetorical, rather than the grammatical, curriculum, then the role of *diēgēsis* in a speech may give a clue to the significance of the term *diēgētikos* here. The progymnasmatic authors give directions on the construction of *diēgēmata*, and Quintilian recommends that instruction in narrative should be first of that given by a rhetor as it links in with direction already given under a *grammatikos*.[155] The *narratio*, or *diēgēsis*, is part of any speech, according firstly to Aristotle, who is followed by all subsequent writers, and consists of the statement of facts preliminary to any proof to be gathered from it.[156] Thus we may suggest that the reader was to construct a narrative on the basis of the reading. The bishop, who was unable himself to read, might then *interpret* the scripture, drawing out the lesson for the hearers, thus fulfilling the rhetorical function

---

[152] Faivre, "Texte grec", 39-40, with reference to CD 13.2-6.

[153] W.V. Harris, *Ancient Literacy* (Cambridge, MA 1989) 251-252, whilst suggesting that wealthy persons are more likely to be literate, nonetheless notes cases both fictional and historical of persons of wealth who were unlettered.

[154] Cf. Funk, *Doctrina*, 65, who, rightly disagreeing with Harnack's suggestion that the term refers to an ability to interpret, takes it as indicating facility in reading, alongside εὐήκοος.

[155] Quint., *Inst.* 2.4.1.

[156] Ar., *Rh.* 3.13.1-3.

of proof which, Aristotle suggests, might consist of amplification and of the provision of examples.[157] Thus *diēgēsis* is not interpretation[158] but rather a narrative preliminary to interpretation: the pattern which seems to be implied is rather like the "word of exhortation" identified in early Christian and Jewish literature by Wills, by which ethical lessons are drawn from an *exemplum* or *exempla*.[159] The *exempla* are scriptural, and the pattern may well follow on from a reading. We may thus suggest that the reader, apart from reading the Scripture, is to narrate the *exempla*, and that the bishop is then required to draw out the ethical lesson. As such we may compare the report of Justin at *1 Apol.* 1.67, where it is said that the *προεστώς* draws out the lessons of Scripture in a word of *νουθεσία* and *πρόκλησις*, *παυσαμένου τοῦ ἀναγινώσκοντος*.

The origins for such an arrangement may be catechetical. *Canones Hippolyti* 37, in common with *κκ*, seems to suppose that the reader should be first in the assembly. If, as I have argued elsewhere, the liturgy of the word was created by the adjuncture of catechumenal instruction in the morning with a morning eucharist (with associated psalmody) transferred from the evening,[160] the direction that the reader should be first in the assembly may be a reminiscence of this earlier practice. Thus we may note that Cyprian enrolls Optatus specifically among those readers who read on behalf of those presbyters who are teaching catechumens.[161] The close association in eastern canonical material between readers and psalm-singers[162] may likewise result from this juncture of practices, due to the close association of psalmody and reading in the earliest liturgy of the word. The close association between readers and exorcists in western material[163] may likewise indicate that the origin of the readership lay in catechesis, since the preparation of catechumens was the principal occupation of both.

Harnack traces the origins of the reader as distinct from other minor orders. Although we cannot altogether follow him in tracing the origins of the readership to the routinisation and downgrading of charismatic offices such as that of the teacher and prophet,[164] and even less may follow him in

---

157 Ar., *Rh.* 3.17.3-5.

158 Cf. Harnack, *Sources*, 16; H.Y. Gamble, *Books and Readers in the Early Church* (New Haven 1995) 223, for whom they are the same.

159 L. Wills, "The form of the sermon in Hellenistic Judaism and early Christianity", *HThR* 77 (1984) 277-299.

160 "The domestic origin of the liturgy of the word", *Studia Patristica* (forthcoming).

161 Cyp., *Ep.* 29.1.2.

162 On which see Harnack, *Sources*, 66.

163 See Harnack, *Sources*, 57-58, though with a different explanation.

164 An approach followed by Gamble, *Books and Readers*, 218-224.

tracing the minor orders more generally to the adoption of a pagan sacrificial system in third-century Rome, we may, however, agree generally that there is a tendency for functions to become offices, and for offices to be seen in the light of clerical orders. For this reason *Traditio apostolica* 11 is clear that a reader does not receive a laying on of hands. As such it is resisting the tendency to clericalise the reader. In time the reader became indeed a minor cleric, and the scope of the task diminished, but we may see in κκ the distinct role of the reader and gain some insight into the origins of the office.

Finally we may note with Harnack that, like κκ, the didascalist knows no other minor order but the reader.[165] For Harnack this was the most pressing parallel to the situation found in κκ. Although we argue below that κκ was a literary source employed by the didascalist, the context in which the provision for a reader is found is not paralleled in κκ, and therefore that the presence of a reader and of no other minor order in *Didascalia* is not the result of any literary relationship, but that the situation is indeed the same, and had come about through the same process of development.

3.6.3: The deacons

Two critical matters emerge in discussing the deacons of κκ; namely, how many are to be appointed, and whether they are to be counted as part of the presbytery.

The extant text reads simply that deacons are to be appointed, and then adds: "Every matter of the Lord shall be established by three." Harnack suggests that the number three stood adjacent to deacons, and was deliberately omitted by K, in the same manner that K had increased the number of presbyters to three.[166] Otherwise it is possible that γ′ had accidentally fallen out before γέγραπται. Reasons for preferring this understanding will be advanced below. However, we must also note the possibility that two deacons were intended, though the number was not written, as it was clearly implied through the following statement that each matter of the Lord is established by three. Two would be implied as the deacons are counted alongside the bishop.[167] Before dealing with the number, however, we must first discuss the radical interpretation of the entire passage concerning presbyters and deacons proposed by Duchesne, followed by Vilela.[168]

---

[165] Harnack, *Sources*, 70-72.
[166] Harnack, *Lehre*, 212 n. 36.
[167] A suggestion derived from the unpublished notes of Pierre Nautin.
[168] Duchesne, 366-367; Vilela, *Condition collégiale*, 167-171.

Rather than seeing, as Harnack did, two presbyters as symmetrical alongside the bishop at the altar, he suggests that the citation from Apocalypse regarding the twenty-four at the altar relates to the number three. The function of keeping order in the congregation, he suggests, which is that of the presbyters on the left of the bishop, is more properly that of deacons; thus there are three on either side, forming a presbytery, of whom the three on the right are presbyters, and the three on the left deacons.

There is no theoretical objection to seeing deacons as among the presbytery,[169] and K20.3 certainly indicates that one of the diaconal functions was to keep order, but it also implies that another is to obtain gifts for distribution, which seems to fit with the presbyters on the right. In other words, the function of these deacons is almost entirely parallel to those of the presbyters, and not simply those ranked on the left. This, however, does not mean that they are to be counted as among the presbytery, for if the deacons are to be counted among the presbytery then they too would be competent to elect, and the number of the college is given as twelve.

Thus there are not necessarily twenty-four persons around the bishop at the altar, but there are more than two presbyters, as two is the number who are to be elected, and not the total. Nonetheless, both Krawutzcky and Harnack saw the two presbyters as bringing about a symmetry on either side of the bishop, and reckoned that two was therefore the minimum number of presbyters.[170] Whereas we have argued that this is a misreading (as it refers to the number appointed by the bishop on his election rather than the total), it is an easy misreading to make and it is possible that K read this in the same way. If, in turn, he saw the deacons as numbered among the presbytery, this explains the substitution of three for two at K17.2. The redactor realised that symmetry was required, but counted the deacons as part of the presbytery, and thus made provision for the appointment of three presbyters at this point in order to balance the three deacons.[171] It is for this reason that an accidental omission of the number is preferred as the explanation of the extant text, namely that K must have read the number three here, as otherwise there would be no redactional interference to adjust the number of presbyters. Thus, Duchesne is correct in his reading of K, but K had misread *κκ*, and therefore made a redactional adjustment. Harnack, however, is basically

[169] D.L. Powell, "Ordo Presbyterii", *JTS* ns 26 (1975) 290-328, at 306-307, suggests that presbyters may hold office in some contexts as deacon or bishop.

[170] Krawutzcky, "Altkirchliche Unterrichtsbuch", 400; Harnack, *Sources*, 10.

[171] So Funk, *Doctrina*, 62. Harnack, *Lehre*, 212, suggests that the redactor cannot imagine that two presbyters would be sufficient, but this is insufficient rationale for the intervention.

correct in reading *κκ* as referring to presbyters, and not deacons, around the bishop. *κκ* envisaged an even number of presbyters; K likewise envisaged an even number but, because he assumed that deacons were counted, he adjusted the number of presbyters to equal the number of deacons.

As noted above, Harnack had a theory that two systems of church-order, one presbyteral and the other episcopal-diaconal, and that the two had been conjoined. However, it was suggested that this was not the case in the K community, but rather that the episcopate in this community had emerged from the presbyterate. If, however, the *episkopos* emerges from the presbytery, rather than being a graft onto a presbyteral system, the question comes about as to the origin of deacons in a community that was originally solely presbyteral. The only possible answer, given that the diaconate is not a natural growth, is that deacons were a secondary addition to the church-order of such communities, resulting from the existence of deacons elsewhere. This in turn explains the position of deacons after readers in the hierarchy of *κκ*. These deacons have functions entirely parallel to the *episkopos* and presbyters but a sign that they are an addition to the first level of *κκ* is the fact that they are not assigned angelic functions, and are not described in keeping with the angelic typology, the promotion of which is fundamental to *κκ*'s strategy.

This in turn makes it unlikely that the number implied was two, and that the two deacons were counted alongside the bishop as making up the three in the statement that "every matter of the Lord is to be determined by three". There are yet further possible explanations of the citation. Possibly it is a reference to the threefold order of the economic ministry, justifying the introduction of deacons into this community, rather than to the number of deacons, And possibly it is, as Harnack suggests,[172] the number required for witnesses when juridical matters are brought before the presbytery. However, in the K redaction it is clearly read as referring to the number of deacons appointed, and, from the correction made to the number of presbyters, the number of deacons to be appointed as three stood at this point in the version of *κκ* which came before K. It is always possible, however, that no number stood there originally and that it was introduced in transmission, either accidentally by the same process which ultimately led to its omission (namely the collocation of γ' with another γ) or deliberately on the basis of a misunderstanding of the function of the citation!

Earlier it was suggested that *κκ* was itself the result of a redactional history, but that we were essentially limited by the evidence to studying the

---

[172] Harnack, *Sources*, 39.

K redaction. K's hand has been clearly recognised in the second paragraph concerning the diaconate (K22), following on from the discussion of the caritative work of widows, and so we may be clear that the earlier discussion of deacons, concerning their appointment (K20) was added within the development of *κκ*. We cannot, however, be certain as to the time at which the addition took place.

3.6.4: The widows

We have already discussed the role of widows above, so here need note again simply that the provision for widows who, functionally, may practise visionary prophecy, indicates an early date for *κκ*. A widow might engage in caritative functions beyond, but this is not stressed by *κκ*, rather the emphasis on this aspect of a widow's duty is a primary concern of K as a means of diminishing her liturgical leadership.

3.6.5: The text of κκ

At this point we have done enough to present a possible text for *κκ* as it came into the hands of K distinct from the reconstruction offered by Harnack.[173] Inevitably this is highly conjectural, and represents not the entirety of the document but only that preserved within K. The extent of K's interpolation is likewise not altogether certain and, most particularly, it must be stressed that it is itself the product of redactional growth, probably within the second century.

> *κατὰ κέλευσιν κυρίου ἡμῶν Ἰησοῦ Χριστοῦ τοῦ σωτῆρος συναθροισθέντων ἡμῶν καθὼς διέταξεν ἡμῖν· Πρὸ τοῦ μέλλησαι κληροῦσθαι τὰς ἐπαρχίας, καταλογίσασθε τόπων ἀριθμούς, ἐπισκόπων ἀξίας, πρεσβυτέρων ἕδρας, διακόνων παρεδρείας, ἀναγνωστῶν νουνεχίας, χηρῶν ἀνεγκλησίας καὶ ὅσα δέοι πρὸς θεμελίωσιν ἐκκλησίας, ἵνα τύπον τῶν ἐπουρανίων εἰδότες φυλάσσωνται ἀπὸ παντὸς ἀστοχήματος, εἰδότες, ὅτι λόγων ὑφέξουσιν ἐν τῇ μεγάλῃ ἡμέρᾳ τῆς κρίσεως, περὶ ὧν ἀκούσαντες οὐκ ἐφύλαξαν.*

[173] Harnack, *Sources*, 5-21.

At this point there would be the statement that a bishop should be elected, presumably couched in the passive, like the statements governing the appointment of readers, deacons and widows.[174] It is also possible that some of this material is preserved in the *Didascalia*; we have already suggested at 3.6 above that the *Didascalia* may preserve elements of *κκ* which have been omitted, and this may provide a prima facie example. The text continues:

> *ἐὰν ὀλιγανδρία ὑπάρχῃ καὶ μήπου πλῆθος τυγχάνῃ τῶν δυναμένων ψηφίσασθαι περὶ ἐπισκόπου ἐντὸς δεκαδύο ἀνδρῶν, εἰς τὰς πλησίον ἐκκλησίας, ὅπου τυγχάνει πεπηγυῖα, γραφέτωσαν, ὅπως ἐκεῖθεν ἐκλεκτοὶ τρεῖς ἄνδρες παραγενόμενοι δοκιμῇ δοκιμάσαντες τὸν ἄξιον ὄντα, εἴ τις φήμην καλὴν ἔχει ἀπὸ τῶν ἐθνῶν, εἰ ἀναμάρτητος ὑπάρχει, εἰ φιλόπτωχος, εἰ σώφρων, μὴ μέθυσος, μὴ πόρνος, μὴ πλεονέκτης ἢ λοίδορος ἢ προσωπολήπτης καὶ τὰ τούτοις ὅμοια, ἀπὸ μιᾶς γυναικός, δυνάμενος τὰς γραφὰς ἑρμηνεύειν, εἰ δ' ᾖ ἀγράμματος· πραῢς ὑπάρχων, καὶ τῇ ἀγάπῃ εἰς πάντας περισσευέτω.*
>
> *ὁ κατασταθεὶς ἐπίσκοπος, εἰδὼς τὸ προσεχὲς καὶ φιλόθεον τῶν σὺν αὐτῷ, καταστήσει οὓς ἂν δοκιμάσῃ πρεσβυτέρους δύο. εἴκοσι γὰρ καὶ τέσσαρές εἰσι πρεσβύτεροι, δώδεκα ἐξ δεξιῶν καὶ δώδεκα ἐξ εὐωνύμων. οἱ μὲν γὰρ ἐκ δεξιῶν δεχόμενοι ἀπὸ τῶν ἀρχαγγέλων τὰς φιάλας προσφέρουσι τῷ δεσπότῃ, οἱ δὲ ἐξ ἀριστερῶν ἐπέχουσι τῷ πλήθει τῶν ἀγγέλων. οἱ ἐκ δεξιῶν πρεσβύτεροι προνοήσονται τῶν ἐπισκοπούντων πρὸς τὸ θυσιαστήριον, ὅπως τιμήσωσι καὶ ἐντιμηθῶσιν εἰς ὃ ἂν δέῃ. οἱ ἐξ ἀριστερῶν πρεσβύτεροι προνοήσονται τοῦ πλήθους ὅπως εὐσταθήσῃ καὶ ἀθόρυβον ᾖ, πρῶτον μεμαθηκὸς ἐν πάσῃ ὑποταγῇ. εἰ δέ τις νουθετούμενος αὐθάδως ἀποκριθῇ, τὸ ἓν ποιήσαντες οἱ ἐπὶ τῷ θυσιαστηρίῳ τὸν τοιοῦτον μετὰ ἴσης βουλῆς, ὃ ἂν ᾖ ἄξιον, δικασάτωσαν, ἵνα καὶ οἱ λοιποὶ φόβον ἔχωσι, μήποτε ἑνὸς πρόσωπον λάβωσι, καὶ ἐπὶ πλεῖον νεμηθῇ <τὸ κακὸν> ὡς γάγγραινα, καὶ αἰχμαλωτισθῶσιν οἱ πάντες.*
>
> *ἀναγνώστης καθιστανέσθω πρῶτον δοκιμῇ δεδοκιμασμένος, μὴ γλωσσοκόπος, μὴ μέθυσος μήτε γελωτολόγος, εὔτροπος, εὐπειθής, εὐγνώμων, ἐν ταῖς κυριακαῖς συνόδοις πρῶτος σύνδρομος, εὐήκοος, διηγητικός, εἰδὼς ὅτι εὐαγγελιστῶν τόπον ἐργάζεται. ὁ γὰρ ἐμπιπλῶν ὦτα μὴ νοοῦντος ἔγγραφος λογισθήσεται παρὰ τῷ θεῷ.*

[174] The statement concerning the appointment of presbyters is different because this concerns the appointment of presbyters by the bishop on his election.

διάκονοι καθιστάσθωσαν <τρεῖς>· γέγραπται· ἐπὶ τριῶν σταθήσεται πᾶν ῥῆμα κυρίου.῞Εστωσαν δεδοκιμασμένοι πάσῃ διακονίᾳ, μεμαρτυρημένοι παρὰ τοῦ πλήθους, μονόγαμοι, τεκνοτρόφοι, σώφρονες, ἐπιεικεῖς, ἥσυχοι, μὴ γόγγυσοι, μὴ δίγλωσσοι, μὴ ὀργίλοι, ὀργὴ γὰρ ἀπόλλυσι ἄνδρα φρόνιμον, μὴ πρόσωπον πλουσίου λαμβάνοντες μηδὲ πένητα καταδυναστεύοντες μηδὲ οἴνῳ πολλῷ χρώμενοι, εὔσκυλτοι· τῶν κρυφίων ἔργων καλοὶ προτρεπτικοί, ἐπαναγκάζοντες τοὺς ἔχοντας τῶν ἀδελφῶν ἁπλοῦν τὰς χεῖρας, καὶ αὐτοὶ εὐμετάδοτοι, κονωνικοί, πάσῃ τιμῇ καὶ ἐντροπῇ καὶ φόβῳ τιμώμενοι ἀπὸ τοῦ πλήθους, ἐπιμελῶς προσέχοντες τοῖς ἀτάκτως περιπατοῦσιν, οὓς μὲν νουθετοῦντες, οὓς δὲ παρακαλοῦντες, οὓς δὲ ἐπιτιμῶντες, τοὺς δὲ καταφρονοῦντας τελέως παραπεμπόμενοι, εἰδότες ὅτι οἱ ἀντίλογοι καὶ καταφρονηταὶ καὶ λοίδοροι Χριστῷ ἀντετάξαντο.

χῆραι καθιστανέσθωσαν τρεῖς· αἱ δύο προσμένουσαι τῇ προσευχῇ περὶ πάντων τῶν ἐν πείρᾳ καὶ πρὸς τὰς ἀποκαλύψεις περὶ οὗ ἂν δέῃ. μία δὲ παρεδρεύσουσα ταῖς ἐν ταῖς νόσοις πειραζομέναις.

ὁ λαϊκὸς τοῖς λαϊκοῖς προστάγμασι περιπειθέσθω ὑποτασσόμενος τοῖς παρεδρεύσι τῷ θυσιαστρηρίῳ. ἕκαστος τῷ ἰδιῷ τόπῳ ἀρεσκέτω τῷ θεῷ μὴ φιλεχθροῦντες ἀλλήλοις περὶ τῶν τεταγμένων, ἕκαστος ἐν ᾧ ἐκλήθη παρατεθεὶς ὑπὸ Χριστοῦ. ὁ ἕτερος τοῦ ἑτέρου τὸν δρόμον μὴ παρατεμνέτω· οὐδὲ γὰρ οἱ ἄγγελοι παρὰ τὸ διατεταγμένον αὐτοῖς οὐδὲν ἕτερον ἐξελίσσουσιν.

3.6.6: The date and origin of κκ

Harnack dated *κκ* to the middle of the second century. In essence his logic was that the document demonstrated a stage of development at which institutionalisation had begun but was not complete.[175] He is, however, open to the suggestion that development was not linear or uniform.

The following indications of date may be significant.

- The eucharist still retains aspects of a *Sättigungsmahl*, as the fundamental concern of the text is the distribution of goods, rather than sacred food as such.

[175] Harnack, *Sources*, 52-53. Harnack employs other arguments, few of which would now be followed.

- The episcopate is emerging from the presbyterate, which is as yet not clericalised; the diaconate exists, but is not organically connected to the episcopate and presbyterate.
- There is no embarrassment about the prophetic activity of widows.

As such Harnack`s dating is probably accurate. We thus receive a valuable insight into the development of order in one particular congregation. Although Faivre`s linkage with the practice of Essene communities was considered uncertain though not impossible; a date as suggested here does not detract from his hypothesis of an Essene foundation to the community of *κκ*. There is nothing in the text which gives a clear indication of provenance, but since we have already suggested that *κ* derived from Asia or Syria, or from a region in between such as Cilicia or Cappadocia, and since the same will be suggested of K below, this would seem the most probable location for the growth of *κκ* as well.

4: The extent of K's editorial work

On the basis of the foregoing discussions we may now turn again to the question of the extent of K's editing. According to Harnack K`s work was as follows:

- Paragraphs 1-3 complete.
- The assignment of single groups of sentences to the several apostles.
- Unimportant additions in 4-15.
- Small but important cancellings and an addition in paragraphs 16-23.
- A certain degree of editorial work in 24-30, the extent of which is hard to ascertain.[176]

We may examine each of these in turn.

4.1: K1-3

Harnack was undoubtedly led to assign the whole of K1-3 to K on the basis of his belief that the opening greeting was derived from B and on the assumption that E, containing the list of apostles, was secondary to K.

[176] Harnack, *Sources*, 2.

However, having recognised the existence of *κ*, and having cause to doubt the use of B, we may now scrutinise this critically. If the apostle list is derived from the same context as *Epistula apostolorum*, as suggested above, then the sole involvement of K is the addition of a twelfth apostle, Judas the son of James, where previously eleven had stood in κ.

It was noted above that K2 linked closely to what followed, and for this reason the greater part of K1 was bracketed. However, a close relationship between this bracketed section and K16-21, 23 was discerned, in that whereas the preface states that the earthly hierarchy is to correspond in some way with the celestial hierarchy, we find in the latter section of the document that presbyters are to represent the angels on the left and the right of the throne; thus the presence of presbyters on either side of the bishop represents on earth what was occurring in heaven. Likewise it is said that the layperson imitates the angels in not going beyond what is proper. Thus we may suggest that this part of K1 is derived from the church-order, and that K has combined the introductions of *κκ* and *κ* in just the same way that he has combined the two church-orders overall. Harnack remarks that the introduction, which he would assign to the final redactor, demonstrates a major divergence between K's interests and those of his sources.[177] But this is far from true as the two introductions fit the two sections admirably; the inconcinnity results from the clumsy juncture of the two.

In this context we must observe the employment of the word *eparchia*. Whereas in *Lehre* Harnack suggests that this enables us to fix the date of K at around 300, on the grounds that this term indicates the imperialisation of the church, the term first being used in the canons of Nicaea,[178] he recognises in *Sources* that the term does not necessarily fix the date as such.[179] Indeed, Funk points out that provincial synods seem to have been known in Asia during the third century, and that Nicaea is regularising what already occurred.[180] Beyond this Clark notes the extent to which provincial synods were a regular feature of church life in the areas around Cappadocia and Antioch.[181] Thus, although Lemoine opines that there is a weight of technical

[177] Harnack, *Lehre*, 218.

[178] Harnack, *Lehre*, 218.

[179] Harnack, *Sources*, 4-5.

[180] Funk, *Doctrina*, lv; he cites Firmilian at [Cyp.], *Ep.* 75.4.

[181] G.W. Clarke, *The Letters of St. Cyprian of Carthage* 4 (Ancient Christian Writers 47; New York 1989) 254-255, on [Cyp.], *Ep.* 74.4, pointing out numerous incidences.

vocabulary employed here, which means that the earliest date of this section must be 220, and more probably 300,[182] it is hard to see the basis for such an assertion. The reference is to the division of the mission-field of the world among the apostles; before they do this they have to determine the manner in which each church is to be organised. This is a legend known in the third century.[183]

Finally, we should note that K3 is obviously a redactional construction,[184] preparing the way for the later qualification of the number of presbyters and for the dialogue which follows on Andrew's suggestion that ministries be established for the women, the very point which K is most concerned to contradict.

4.2: The assignment to apostles

Here, again in contradistinction to Harnack, we may suggest, again due to the existence of *κ*, that the assignment of sayings to the apostles in the first part is not the work of K. The manner of the assignment is reminiscent, as Vilela points out, of the manner in which councils and synods are reported.[185] There is nothing in this, however, which militates against the early date assigned to *κ* as, although unreported in detail, councils met in Asia to discuss Montanism in the time-frame envisaged for *κ* above.[186]

The assignment of speeches in the adaptation of the church-order section is, however, the work of K, undertaken in order to make the second part of the church-order consonant with the first, but also succeeding in answering the prominence given to Mary in anti-apostolic gnostic writings through making the apostles (and Peter in particular) the arbiters of propriety, and through the use of an apocryphal work clearly deriving from the same context as, for instance, *Gospel of Philip*. Parrott similarly notes the possibility of polemic between Christians and gnostics over the names of apostles, suggesting that Peter, John and James generally represent the voice of orthodoxy, whereas the Philip circle is claimed as gnostic.[187] It would perhaps be mistaken to schematise the apostle lists overmuch, and there is no

---

182 Lemoine, "Étude", 7.

183 *Acta Thomae* 1; something of this sort is attributed to Origen by Eus., *H.E.* 3.1.

184 So Harnack, *Lehre*, 212.

185 Vilela, *Condition collégiale*, 165.

186 So the anonymous anti-Montanist cited at Eus., *H.E.* 5.16.10.

187 D.M. Parrott, "Gnostic and orthodox disciples in the second and third centuries", in C.W. Hedrick and R. Hodgson (eds), *Nag Hammadi, Gnosticism and Early Christianity* (Peabody, MA 1986) 193-219.

obvious logic in the assignment of speeches to disciples in the church-order section of K, but it is nonetheless fair to note the prominence of Peter here, and that Peter, John and James are the first three to speak, alongside the claiming of Mary (?Magdalene) in her absence as an orthodox voice. Faivre similarly notes that in *Gospel of Mary* it is Andrew who introduces the subject of women (as in K) and Peter (again, as in K) who denies Mary's input (though unsuccessfully in the event.)[188] Again, although there is not the evidence to posit a close relationship between the two there is certainly some engagement with the polemic which Parrott identifies.

4.3: K's engagement in TWT

We have observed above the extent of K's interpolation into TWT. It was hard to determine in some instances what was interpolated and what lay in *κ*, for the interests of the two are arguably close. What is most important is the substitution of an eschatological conclusion for the *Haustafel* found in *κ*. The motivation for this is not obvious; the conclusion, moreover, is not a composition of K but probably stood in the version of TWT with which he was familiar.

Thus we may note that in the first part of the work, the hand of K appears, but reveals little about himself or his interests. A Syrian or an Asian provenance is likely, and a date earlier than the fourth century is likewise probable, but there is little here to guide us.

4.4: K16-23

Far from supplying "small...cancellings" we have suggested that K has extensively reworked his source, and supplied K22 in order to minimise the social work of widows by contrast to that of deacons. We may glean something of K from the manner in which he is involved in interpolating the sources before him.

Thus in the section concerning the qualifications for bishops he is concerned that the bishop should, by preference, be unmarried, and that presbyters likewise should be abstinent. The extensive list of qualifications for presbyters, like the demand that they should be abstinent, is unique, as Harnack notes.[189] We may also suggest that K is concerned that the bishop should have competence in preaching, and be educated to a degree that

[188] Faivre, "Apostolicité", 49.

[189] Harnack, *Sources*, 11.

enables him to do this. Finally, we may gather that K is familiar with women undertaking social work in the community, and particularly among other women. What then can be deduced from this?

Whereas for Bartlet the demand for celibacy points towards a late date, it points equally well to encratite circles in the second century. However, given that presbyters have a more extensive qualification list than is usually presented, a later date is implied, in that presbyters have grown in prominence within this community as the bishop has become a *monepiscopus*. Thus, the earlier part of the second century at least cannot be considered.

4.5: K24-30

Whereas we have suggested that part of K30 derives from *κ*, and is a doublet of the conclusion to the TWT in K14, the rest of this part of K is, we have suggested, a construction of K. It is, we have suggested, a polemic against the ministry of women.

4.6: Conclusions on K's editorial work and his sources

We may thus gather together what we have learnt. K took hold of a version of the TWT in which the material was attributed to apostles, and joined it to an ancient church-order, combining the two prefaces, in order that the whole might have the appearance of a church-order of apostolic origin. It is not clear what the function of TWT is in the church-order as a whole, but the adoption of *κ* was essential to construct the apostolic fiction. It is possible that TWT functions in K as a rehearsal of the qualifications of those who are to hold office. It is interesting that in the fourth century the material that was originally directed at catechumens comes to be directed towards clergy; thus canon 46 of the Council of Laodicea directs that "they who are of the priesthood, or of the clergy, shall not be magicians, enchanters, mathematicians, or astrologers; nor shall they make what are called amulets, which are chains for their own souls. And those who wear such, we command to be cast out of the Church". It is thus possible that K had read the material in the same light as the council, for which reason, despite the promise of hearing TWT in K4.1, only the way of life is described. Similarly, Faivre notes the extent to which the qualifications laid down for the deacon in the latter part of K mirror the moral qualities besought in the TWT section,[190] and we may note that the same transference of qualities from catechumens to clergy has occurred in *Didascalia*; "Let him not be double-minded or double tongued", states the didascalist of the qualifications of the bishop, and in discussing the meekness of a young bishop seems to echo D3.7-8,[191] the point being that this TWT material is found in *Didascalia* among the qualifications for the episcopate. All this is in accordance with Bradshaw's suggestion that the earlier of the church-order materials deal with the ethical conduct of the Christian, whereas the later orders tend to concentrate more and more upon the clergy. Bradshaw picks on *Traditio apostolica* as responsible for this development.[192] We may suggest in turn that the redactor of *Traditio apostolica* had particular reasons for beginning with the appointment of clergy and joining this statement to an earlier manual,[193] and that K has done something similar by joining together two particular kinds of document, namely *κ*, concerned with moral qualities, and *κκ* which, as a document concerning the organisation of a church under clergy, might circulate quite independently of an order for Christian conduct. Nonetheless, as a result of these movements, church-orders develop as Bradshaw describes.

κ was thus joined to the ancient church-order which we have termed *κκ*, and this ancient church-order was further interpolated, in part to conform it the better to the church-order known to the author, with a more thorough discussion of the qualifications for presbyters and with the assumption that the bishop would be unmarried, but fundamentally to legislate against a liturgical role for women.

4.7: The date and provenance of K

Throughout the work we have found hints of K's date and provenance. All the sources employed are of the second century, and are either Syrian or Asian. The language points to the early part of the third century, and nothing obliges us to see this as later. We may, however, examine the basis on which Harnack established the consensus that K derives from the fourth century, or the latter part of the third, which we seek to question here.

---

[190] A. Faivre, "La documentation canonico-liturgique de l'église ancienne", *RevScRel* 54 (1980) 204-219, 273-297 at 291-292.

[191] *Didasc.* 2.6.1; 2.1.5.

[192] P.F. Bradshaw, *The Search for the Origins of Christian Worship: Sources and Methods for the Study of Early Liturgy* (New York 2002²) 95.

[193] For the rationale see my *Hippolytus: On the Apostolic Tradition* (Crestwood 2001).

4.7.1: Harnack's dating of K

Harnack dated K to the fourth century on five bases,[194] none of which, on examination, convinces. We examine each briefly in turn, in some cases simply summarising conclusions already reached in this introduction.

4.7.1.1: The division of the regulations among the apostles

Whereas Harnack considered this the work of K, this we have seen to be the work principally of *κ*, a source which we may reasonably assign to the second century.

4.7.1.2: The clerical degrees are formed according to the type of heavenly things

Again, for Harnack, the idea that the ranks of clergy were modelled on heavenly orders indicated a later date for K. However, far from necessitating a later date, this is ideationally close to Ignatius, who sees the bishop as a type of God the Father, and the presbyters around like the angels around the throne;[195] similarly Clement sees the position of those who are subservient in the church as like that of the angels gathered around the throne of God.[196] The image of the bishop with presbyters is perhaps also taken up in Apocalypse, which represents the angels around the throne, and so the comment that the presbyters represent the angels at the left and right is a commentary on Apocalypse which is close to the fount of the image.

4.7.1.3: The appointment of the presbyters

The presupposition that the bishop alone appoints the presbyters is, for Harnack, indicative that the date is late. This, along with the extensive qualifications set out for presbyters, is the most marked indication of a later, rather than an earlier date. However, we do not know what systems were in use in which places for the appointment of presbyters such that we can claim

---

194 Harnack, *Sources*, 5.

195 Ign., *Trall.* 3.1. N.B. also Clem., *Strom.* 4.8, where the earthly church is seen as an image of that in heaven.

196 *1 Clem.* 34.1-6. One may also note that Clem., *Strom.* 4.8, in Alexandria considered that the earthly church was a type of the heavenly, though not in this case with regard to clerical degrees.

that an episcopal prerogative in the appointment necessarily points to a later date. In the third century it is reported that Boukolos appointed Polycarp as presbyter, apparently without consultation;[197] the source of this report is Smyrna, a city in which it would seem that the presbytery remained powerful. Thus K's provision for the episcopal appointment of presbyters does not preclude a date in the third century.

4.7.1.4: The offering of the body and blood

We have already examined the expression concerning the offering of the body and blood, used at K25, at 3.4.3 above, where it was observed that not only Harnack, but Connolly and Bartlet likewise, considered this a mark of a late date. However, although this usage is strange, we have already noted that this could be the usage of the third century.

4.7.1.5: The nature of the use of D

For Harnack K's omission of the second half of D is indicative of date. This argument, however, even if it had weight, would hardly apply since K made no direct use of D, but, as argued above, employed a distinct version of TWT.

4.7.2: The third-century origin of K

None of the arguments for redaction in the late third or fourth century have been found valid. Positively we may note that if the major motive for the production of K was to present apostolic opposition to the ministry of women, and to contrast this "apostolic" practice to that of gnostic groups, then the gnostic groups must still be active and in contact with members of K's community. This places K much earlier in the third century. Harnack, moreover, believes that K22-29 had been derived from a distinct source. He recognises that the engagement with apocryphal literature and the very fact that the liturgical role of women was discussed indicates a degree of antiquity for this section.[198] Since we have determined that this is a construction of K, we may attribute the same antiquity to the K redaction. The sources employed by K seem all to have derived from the second century.

---

197 *Vit. Pol.* 17.

198 Harnack, *Lehre*, 215.

Thus, all the positive indications, such as the engagement with Christian gnosticism and the second-century origin of the sources employed by K, point to the latter part of the second century or the earlier part of the third. Faivre's suggestion of 135-180 may be a little early, given the development of the presbyterate into an independent office,[199] but 200-235 would be a reasonable suggestion.

4.7.3: The provenance of K

Harnack argued for an Egyptian provenance on the grounds that the four of the five sources employed, which he believed to be D, B, the apostle list, *κκ* and his *katastasis tēs ekklēsias* (which employed, he thought, the *Gospel of the Egyptians*) were derived from Egypt.[200] However, D is no longer generally believed to be Egyptian, we have shown that the apostle list is derived from an Asian source, have suggested that B was not a source for K, and noted that the use of *Gospel of the Egyptians* is at best uncertain. In our separate examination of K's sources we have found none which is Egyptian; as far as can be seen, all are Asian or Syrian. More precisely within Egypt Harnack suggests the regions of Arsinoe, where chiliasm was present. Although *κκ*, if not K itself, may derive from a rural district, where there may not be twelve competent to elect a bishop, this is not necessarily the case, as much depends on the interpretation of the twelve, and although a region in which chiliasm was prominent would certainly be anti-gnostic, we may note the absence of any bishop from Dionysius' report of his visit to this district.[201] Hennecke thus suggests that the discussion of the presbyters is relatively early, and that only subsequently did these presbyters come under episcopal control, something of which is indicated by K16.[202] However, we have seen that, on the contrary, the discussion of presbyters is late but nonetheless that the episcopate has probably emerged from among the presbyters. Thus even if arguable the connection is tenuous.

All this results from the attempt to conform K to what is known of Egyptian practice. It would be better to abandon the idea of an Egyptian origin on the grounds of the lack of conformity of the church-order with Egyptian patterns of presbyteral government and to accept, on the basis of

---

199 See 3.6.1 above. Faivre reckons that the bishop is a presbyter-bishop. This may be so of *κκ*, but is less obviously true of K.

200 Harnack, *Lehre*, 219.

201 At Eus., *H.E.* 7.24.

202 E. Hennecke, "Zur apostolischen Kirchenordnung", *ZNW* 20 (1921) 241-248, at 244-247.

the sources employed, that it is most probable that K is a product of Asia or Syria or perhaps, if the report of Firmilian is to be given weight, of Cappadocia between the two. The situation envisaged by K, however, seems less to be the actual celebration of the eucharist by women as their presence in the sanctuary alongside a male bishop and presbyters at the celebration. This is a situation envisaged by *Testamentum Domini*. Although there is little consensus about the origin of this document there are certain similarities between practices described in *Testamentum Domini* and those of Cappadocian ascetic communities, not least in the *horarium* proposed and in the prayer practices described.[203] Thus we are again pointed in the direction of Cappadocia, or possibly Asia or West Syria.

5: K among the Church-orders

As a church-order with apostolic attribution, found in all the major ancient collections of church-orders, K is clearly identifiable as one of a group. Before concluding the introduction we may ask how it relates to the other church-orders.

5.1: The apostolic attribution of K

We have already suggested that the attribution of individual elements of K to individual apostles derived from the use of this device in *κ*, which is then picked up and extended to the other church-order material. *κ* was to be dated to some time in the second century and having employed a list of apostles broadly similar to that of *Epistula apostolorum* to attribute the TWT material to individual apostles might be considered to have arisen in a similar locale.

Unlike *Constitutiones apostolorum* there is no elaborate fictionalisation of the apostolic meeting,[204] but there is more here than the general apostolic attribution of D. It is perhaps close to *Didascalia* which likewise anchors its setting in a meeting of the apostles (though not before the ascension as K, but as an extension of the later council in Jerusalem), though this setting is not revealed until towards the end of the document, with occasional speeches in the meantime being attributed either to a single apostle or explicitly to the apostles as a group.

[203] So G. Sperry-White, *The Testamentum Domini: A Text for Students* (Bramcote 1991) 6-7, 31.
[204] Faivre, "Apostolicité", 26-27.

Faivre suggest the general principle that the more explicit and rational a reference to Scripture is, the more likely it is to be part of a later apostolic fiction.[205] This may be illustrated from the K redaction when the (κκ) discussion of twenty-four elders before the thrones is attributed to John, author of Apocalypse. There are other possible indications of this, such as the attribution of the discussion of an unlettered bishop to Peter, said at Acts 4:13 to be unlettered,[206] but these are to be found in what has already been identified as K's redaction, thus indicating that some development had been undergone. The greater part of K, however, is simply the repetition of traditional material largely derived from earlier documents and given light apostolic dress through the attribution of the material to individual apostles. Pseudepigraphy may thus be defended, as Faivre and Schöllgen in different ways suggest,[207] through noting that in large part the material is ancient and derived from tradition. Schöllgen also argues that one function of apostolic pseudepigraphy was to extend the scope of scripture; insofar as κκ material employs the pastoral epistles K, through extending the apostolic attribution to this material, may be seen as employing the apostolic device in this way. But insofar as the overall purpose of K is to create something new out of this traditional material the defence eventually fails. The all-male church-organisation which K defends is not actually apostolic! K stands between the general apostolic attribution of D and the detailed pseudepigraphy of *Constitutiones apostolorum*, but in the end leans more towards *Constitutiones apostolorum* than to D.

Given the gnostic use of the *Sendschreibe* it was suggested above that this form was adopted by *Epistula apostolorum* as a direct counter, and that κ was pursuing the same strategy, that is to say the true tradition was anchored in apostolic directions which might be traced back to Christ. It must, however, again be noted that there is a distinct difference between *Epistula apostolorum* and κ, in that there is no revealer figure as such in κ. In *Epistula apostolorum* and other revelation dialogues the revealer is supernatural, either Christ or some other supernatural revealer, whereas in κ the attribution is directly to the apostles. Thus, Aland's suggestion that early pseudepigraphy might be associated with the practice of prophecy, in which

[205] Faivre, "Apostolicité", 28.

[206] Faivre, "Apostolicité", 55.

[207] Faivre, "Apostolicité"; G. Schöllgen, "Pseudapostolizität und Schriftgebrauch in den ersten Kirchenordnungen", in G. Schöllgen and C. Scholten (eds), *Stimuli: Exegese und ihre Hermeneutik in Antike und Christentum* (*Jahrbuch für Antike und Christentum* Ergänzungsband 23; Münster 1996) 96-121.

an individual might speak in the person of a revealer figure,[208] does not really apply, as there is no evidence that prophecy was given in the person of departed individuals. Part of the reason for this is that there is no new revelation claimed in κ, but simply the repetition of what is already traditional material. As such we are nearer to the explanation of pseudonymity offered by Steimer, namely the maintenance of tradition, than that of Schöllgen, who insists that the continuation of scripture has primacy.[209] Nonetheless the manner in which traditional material is repeated, as K shows us, can reveal redactional purpose quite beyond the maintenance of tradition.

In K it was argued that we find a deliberate answer to the gnostic use of individual apostle-traditions; thus, K is following the same strategy, namely the adoption of the same form as gnostic writings, as κ, and doing so for a comparable reason, namely in order to oppose catholic order to that of gnostics.

5.2: K and the Didascalia

One of the mysteries of the church-orders continues to be the sources that each employed. The relationship of K and D has already been extensively discussed. Our conclusions were reached in section 1 above that K employed a TWT type document, which we have termed κ, which was derived from the same source as the TWT in D (termed δ). Having observed the relationship between K and D, one may enquire what relationship obtains between K and other church-orders, in particular *Didascalia*, which both contains some TWT material and material corresponding at points with the second half of K and which, as observed above, is similar in its approach to pseudonymous apostolic authorship.

With regard to TWT material Connolly persuasively argues that the didascalist knew and employed D as material with D parallels is found throughout *Didascalia*, and the parallels are, moreover, found from material distributed throughout D.[210] Thus K, or κ, cannot be the source for this as the

---

[208] K. Aland, "The problem of anonymity and pseudonymity in Christian literature of the first two centuries", *JTS* 12 (1961) 39-49.

[209] See Schöllgen's response to Steimer, *Vertex traditionis*, "Der Abfassungszweck der frühchristlichen Kirchenordnungen", *Jahrbuch für Antike und Christentum* 40 (1997) 55-77, especially 70-76.

[210] Connolly, "Use of the Didache".

parallels extend to material not found in K, and, moreover, to material which was not part of δ. The didascalist thus had access to D.[211] It may be that this is the result of one of the later redactions of *Didascalia*, material from D being incorporated at a later stage, whereas one of the sources of *Didascalia* was an independent version of TWT, but nonetheless we may safely say that the TWT within the *Didascalia* is a branch of the tradition independent of κ.

However, this leaves those points in *Didascalia* that are reminiscent of K and that are not related to TWT. Firstly, in dealing with bishops, the didascalist writes:

> If, however, the congregation in which the bishop is to be ordained is small, and nobody of age is found of whom testimony to his wisdom and suitability to stand in the episcopate might be given but, however, there is a youth, of whom those with him bear witness that he is worthy of the episcopate and who, in spite of his youth, shows evidence of maturity in his meekness and good conduct, he should be tested and if he receives such testimony from all he should be made bishop in peace. For Solomon likewise was king over Israel at the age of twelve years, and Josiah reigned in righteousness at the age of eight years, and Joash likewise reigned when he was seven years old.
>
> Therefore, even if he is young, however, let him be meek, fearful and peaceable, since the Lord God says through Isaiah: "On whom shall I look, except upon one who is meek, peaceable, and always trembling at my words." Likewise, in the Gospel, he speaks thus: "Blessed are the meek, for they shall inherit the earth."[212]

On this Connolly writes: "This and other passages leave little doubt in my mind that there has been contact between the *Apost. Ch. O.* and the *Didascalia*, and I have as little doubt that the borrowing was on the part of the first-mentioned."[213] Bartlet similarly advances the opinion that K had employed *Didascalia*, though is inclined to think that the influence was at an early redactional stage.[214]

On the grounds that K prefers a celibate bishop and on the basis of the expression concerning the offering of the body and blood, both of which are discussed above, Connolly had concluded that *Didascalia* preceded K. However, we have determined in the discussion above that neither statement

---

[211] The situation is, however, confused by the redactional complexity of the *Didascalia*; it is possible, for instance, that some of the didascalist's sources were derived from δ, and that elsewhere D is the source.

[212] *Didascalia* 2.1.3-5.

[213] Connolly, *Didascalia*, 31 n.

[214] Bartlet, *Church Life*, 102. For Bartlet's redactional theory see 3.2 above.

is inconceivable in a third-century context. However, quite apart from the fact that Connolly's arguments do not necessitate the conclusion that *Didascalia* preceded K, and thus do not necessitate the conclusion that K must have borrowed from *Didascalia*, it is also conceivable that the passage cited above indicates that the didascalist was acquainted not with K but with *κκ*. Obviously it has been thoroughly rewritten here, and shows the influence of D,[215] but we have to ask whether it is more likely that K (or rather *κκ*) should take something akin to *Didascalia* and produce what is presently extant, or whether the influence is more probably the other way around. *Didascalia* is concerned with the election of a youthful bishop, and the scriptural exempla are therefore directed at that problem, whereas *κκ* is concerned with the election of any bishop, being concerned that the election should be properly carried out when there is not a quorum. In a discussion of the qualities which are to be found in a bishop the general issue of a quorum is surely more likely to be discussed than the issue of a young bishop. Moreover, since *κκ* assumes that the presbyters provide the candidates and that these candidates form an electoral college, it is therefore less likely that a young bishop would be elected whereas the situation envisaged by *Didascalia* is one in which all participate in the election. Neither system can be said to be earlier than the other, but they are different, and whichever, therefore, used the other as source would have to make the necessary alterations. If an electoral college system were being written into a source instead of a system of popular election then one would expect that it would be more explicit, whereas a popular election need not be described. Finally, when the passage turns to the qualifications of a bishop, the statement in *κκ* simply states that the bishop should be generous, even though he be unlettered. *Didascalia*, however, expands the statement with further TWT material, as noted above, but does this again pursuing the question of the bishop's youth, rather than moving the subject on to the qualities expected of a bishop. Again, it seems less likely that the discussion extant in K would emerge from that of *Didascalia*, with no sign of the question of a youthful bishop, than that the didascalist, in pursuit of a particular issue in that community, should recast directions for the election and particular qualities of the bishop. Finally we may compare K's conservative treatment of TWT received through *κ* to the free treatment which TWT, whether received

[215] We may particularly note that some material from TWT has been included. This TWT material is not from K since, as Connolly, "Use of the Didache", 150, points out, the phrase translated above as "always", διὰ παντός (represented in the Latin version and in the parallel section of *Constitutiones apostolorum* though omitted from the Syriac version) is present in D but not in K.

through D or from an earlier part of the tradition, receives in *Didascalia*. Elsewhere in *Didascalia* where any source is extant, for instance in *Didascalia* 21, the source has received a free treatment and considerable expansion. Thus, it is far less likely that K reworked *Didascalia* than that the didascalist reworked *κκ*. This is the conclusion which was reached by Nautin, though the grounds of his conclusion are not clear.[216]

Faivre also notes several parallels between the judicial role of the bishop and presbyters, set out in the *Didascalia*, and that of the bishop and presbyters of K, one of which, the image of a gangrene spreading through the body, is particularly close.[217] Again, however, it is possible that this image is taken from *κκ*, since it derives from the discussion of the disciplinary role of presbyters. This is hardly the place to begin a discussion of the sources of *Didascalia*,[218] but we may suggest that *κκ* was one of the sources employed, entirely independently of its subsequent incorporation into K, and that when *Didascalia* turns to the appointment of a bishop, and subsequently to the duties of deacons and the appointment of widows, it is following the lines laid down in *κκ*.

Finally Connolly notes that a number of adjectives found as qualifications for various offices, namely *εὔσκυλτοι*, *εὐήκοος* and *εὐμετάδοτος* are presents in both in K and *Didascalia*. He concludes that whereas "the *Apost. Ch. Order* is appreciably later than the *Didascalia*...there has been borrowing on one side or the other."[219] We may, however, suggest that the appearance of these adjectives in passages concerning the qualifications for ministries indicates not borrowing on the part of either finished church-order, but a use by the didascalist, or one of his sources, of *κκ*.

Quite apart from these literary parallels, however, we have already found certain similarities between K and *Didascalia*; it was argued above that a common catechetical tradition underlay certain statements in K and

---

[216] P. Nautin announced in *Annuaire de l'École pratique des hautes Études, V^e section: sciences religieuses* 90 (1981-1982) 335-339, that he had uncovered a common source to K and *Didascalia*, corresponding roughly to what here has been termed *κκ*. No work on this was, however, published. I have examined Nautin's notes, and as noted above Nautin believed that K employed a source consisting of K16-17a, 20-21. However, there are no notes connecting this to *Didascalia*. He does note that both *Didascalia* and K open with a gathering of apostles, but this scene within the *Didascalia* is the result of a secondary and late recension.

[217] Faivre, "Texte grec", 35, citing *Didasc.* 2.42.1, and 2.46.6, 2.47.1.

[218] I hope, however, to essay such a discussion in my forthcoming translation of *Didascalia* to be published by St Vladimir's Seminary Press.

[219] Connolly, *Didascalia*, lxxxv.

Didascalia concerning the bishop, and both confront the issue of women's ministry (though in different ways.) Both, moreover, are concerned with the role of the bishop in the distribution of the community's goods as well as in discipline. We need not, however, seek a common literary stratum to explain all of this; the one point concerning discipline where there is the possibility of a literary relationship does not concern the bishop but the role of deacons, who at this point in *Didascalia* are performing a role analogous to that performed by presbyters in K.[220] What is pertinent is not the possibility of a literary source but our argument that K derives from a Syrian or Cappadocian context from the earlier part of the third century. It is hardly co-incidental that a similar date, and a Syrian locale, is ascribed to *Didascalia* by the consensus, for, quite apart from any literary relationship the two share a common thought-world. In constructing their apostolic fictions, therefore, the two readily draw upon the same traditional material.

6: Conclusion

In this introduction we set out to revisit Harnack's conclusions on the date and provenance of K, and as part of this to determine the sources employed both for their own sake and in order to uncover K's redactional purpose through understanding the manner in which the sources were used.

We have argued, broadly in line with Harnack, that two main sources were employed, a document of the TWT type (*κ*) and a church-order (*κκ*). Both appear to be documents of the second century, both of an Asian or Syrian provenance. *κ* had employed a tradition concerning the names of the apostles deriving from this context and of this date, which is brought into K. In distinction to Harnack, however, we have suggested that there was no other church-order source, though it is possible that some of the material employed towards the end of the document was gathered from other written sources.

In terms of redactional history I have sought to show that there is no evidence for intervening levels of redaction, but that it is entirely reasonable to see the sources being put into their current shape by a single redactor. The final chapters would seem to indicate that fundamental to the redactor's purpose was the exclusion of women from a liturgical role, and the promotion in lieu thereof of a caritative role, particularly among women. The nature of ministry and qualifications for ministry are established, using

[220] *Didasc.* 2.57.5-7; cf. to this K18.3. The passage is cited in the notes to the translation ad loc.

traditional material, prior to the clarification that women are excluded from any liturgical role or any form of leadership.

The nature of the redactional purpose and the date of the sources employed would tend to point to an earlier date than that assigned to K by Harnack. Yet more certainly we may suggest that an Egyptian provenance is most unlikely, but that the area between West Syria and Asia is most probable.

That K has been seriously and unduly neglected is beyond doubt. The purpose of this introduction has been to suggest that the document is of the greatest interest both in the sources it employs and in the use to which it puts them.

Text
and textual commentary

The following abbreviations are employed in the textual commentary:

A	Arabic version. G. Horner (ed.), *The Statutes of the Apostles or Canones Ecclesiastici* (London 1904) 89-95. This version is not much used as it is dependent upon S.
Arendzen	J.P. Arendzen, "An entire Syriac text of the 'Apostolic Church Order'", *JTS* 3 (1901) 59-80.
D	The Didache. W. Rordorf and A. Tuilier (eds), *La doctrine des douze apôtres* (Paris 1998) 140-199.
E	Epitome of the canons of the apostles. T. Schermann (ed.), *Eine Elfapostelmoral oder die X-Rezension der "beiden Wege"* (Munich 1903) 16-18. Due to the significance of this document for the study of K, Schermann's text is reproduced in appendix A.
Eth.	Ethiopic version. G. Horner (ed.), *The Statutes of the Apostles or Canones Ecclesiastici* (London 1904) 1-10. This version is not much used as it is dependent upon S.
Funk	F.X. Funk, *Doctrina duodecim apostolorum* (Tübingen 1887) 50-73.
Harnack	A. von Harnack, *Die Lehre der zwölf Apostel nebst Untersuchungen zur ältesten Geschichte der Kirchenverfassung und des Kirchenrechts* (TU 2.1; Leipzig 1886)
Harnack, *Sources*	A. von Harnack, *The Sources of the Apostolic Canons* (Eng. trans.; London 1895).
Hauler	First edition of the Latin version. Hauler's apparatus is reproduced by Tidner (see Lat. below)
Hennecke	E. Hennecke, "Zur apostolischen Kirchenordnung", *ZNW* 20 (1921) 241-248.
Hilgenfeld	A. Hilgenfeld, *Novum Testamentum extra canonem receptum* 4 (Leipzig 1864) 95-106.
L	*Doctrina apostolorum.* W. Rordorf and A. Tuilier (eds), *La doctrine des douze apôtres* (Paris 1998) 207-210.
Lagarde:	P. Lagarde, *Reliquiae iuris ecclesiastici antiquissimae* (Leipzig 1856) 74-79.
Lat.	Latin version. E. Tidner (ed.), *Didascaliae apostolorum, canonum ecclesiasticorum, traditionis apostolicae versiones Latinae* (TU 75; Berlin 1963).

Mosq.	Codex Mosquensis 125, O. Gebhardt et al. (eds), *Patrum apostolicorum opera* 1.2 (Leipzig 1878) xxix-xxxi. This is an abbreviated version of the TWT in K.
Pitra	J.B. Pitra, *Iuris ecclesiastici Graecorum historia et monumenta* I (Rome 1864) 77-88.
S	Sahidic version. P. Lagarde (ed.), *Aegyptiaca* (Göttingen 1883) 238-248.
Schermann	T. Schermann, *Die allgemeine Kirchenordnung, frühristliche Liturgien und kirchliche Überlieferung* I (Paderborn 1914) 12-34.
Syr.	Syriac version, J.P. Arendzen (ed.); q.v.
V	Codex Vindob. gr. hist. 7. This fourteenth-century MS is the basis for all editions.
WM	U. von Wilamowitz Moellendorff, "In libellum ΠΕΡΙ ΤΨΟΤΣ coniectanea", *Hermes* 10 (1876) 334-346, in note on 341-342.

Αἱ διαταγαὶ αἱ διὰ Κλήμεντος καὶ κανόνες τῶν ἁγίων ἀποστόλων[1]

Χαίρετε υἱοὶ καὶ θυγατέρες ἐν ὀνόματι κυρίου Ἰησοῦ Χριστοῦ. Ἰωάννης καὶ Ματθαῖος καὶ Πέτρος καὶ Ἀνδρέας καὶ Φίλιππος καὶ Σίμων καὶ Ἰάκωβος καὶ Ναθαναὴλ καὶ Θωμᾶς καὶ Κηφᾶς καὶ Βαρθολομαῖος καὶ Ἰούδας Ἰακώβου.

1

κατὰ κέλευσιν κυρίου ἡμῶν Ἰησοῦ Χριστοῦ τοῦ σωτῆρος συναθροισθέντων ἡμῶν καθὼς διέταξεν ἡμῖν·[2] Πρὸ τοῦ μέλλησαι κληροῦσθαι τὰς ἐπαρχίας,[3] καταλογίσασθε[4] τόπων ἀριθμούς, ἐπισκόπων ἀξίας, πρεσβυτέρων ἕδρας, διακόνων παρεδρείας, ἀναγνωστῶν νουνεχίας, χηρῶν ἀνεγκλησίας[5] καὶ ὅσα δέοι πρὸς θεμελίωσιν ἐκκλησίας, ἵνα τύπον τῶν ἐπουρανίων εἰδότες φυλάσσωνται ἀπὸ παντὸς ἀστοχήματος, εἰδότες, ὅτι λόγων ὑφέξουσιν ἐν τῇ μεγάλῃ ἡμέρᾳ τῆς κρίσεως, περὶ ὧν ἀκούσαντες οὐκ ἐφύλαξαν. καὶ ἐκέλευσεν ἡμᾶς ἐκπέμψασθαι τοὺς λόγους εἰς ὅλην τὴν οἰκουμένην.

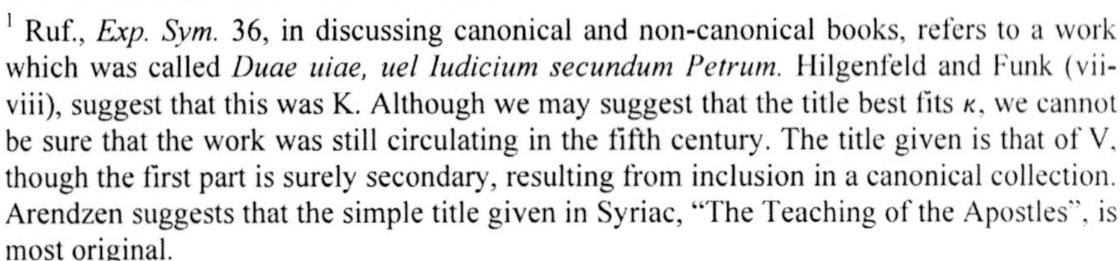

[1] Ruf., *Exp. Sym.* 36, in discussing canonical and non-canonical books, refers to a work which was called *Duae uiae, uel Iudicium secundum Petrum.* Hilgenfeld and Funk (vii-viii), suggest that this was K. Although we may suggest that the title best fits *κ*, we cannot be sure that the work was still circulating in the fifth century. The title given is that of V, though the first part is surely secondary, resulting from inclusion in a canonical collection. Arendzen suggests that the simple title given in Syriac, "The Teaching of the Apostles", is most original.

[2] ἡμῖν is added following Syr. and S (Eth.).

[3] ἐπαρχίας: ὑπαρχίας may be preferred on the basis of the Syriac transliteration, but this is unnecessary. V has ἐπ' ἀρχείας.

[4] Πρὸ τοῦ μέλλησαι κληροῦσθαι τὰς ἐπαρχίας, καταλογίσασθε... Cf. edd. who punctuate ...πρὸ τοῦ. Μέλλετε κληροῦσθαι τὰς ἐπαρχίας, καταλογίσασθαι... The punctuation and text here is adopted following the suggestion of Arendzen that the reading underlying the Syriac text is preferable. There is some support for this in S and, moreover, it should be noted that V reads μέλλεται. If πρὸ τοῦ is taken with διέταξεν the text is difficult; πρὸ τοῦ might be emended to πρότερον, but this seems somewhat radical.

[5] ἀνεγκλησίας: V has ἀνεκκλησίας. Pitra suggested παρακλήσεις, but Lagarde's conjecture printed here won editorial acceptance.

2

ἔδοξεν οὖν[6] ἡμῖν πρὸς ὑπόμνησιν τῆς ἀδελφότητος καὶ νουθεσίαν ἑκάστῳ ὡς ὁ κύριος ἐπεκάλυψε κατὰ τὸ θέλημα τοῦ θεοῦ διὰ πνεύματος ἁγίου μνησθεῖσι λόγου ἐντείλασθαι ὑμῖν.

3

Ἰωάννης εἶπεν· ἄνδρες ἀδελφοί, εἰδότες, ὅτι λόγον ὑφέξομεν περὶ τῶν διατεταγμένων ἡμῖν, εἷς[7] ἑνὸς πρόσωπον μὴ λαμβάνωμεν,[8] ἀλλ᾽ ἐάν τις δοκῇ τι ἀσύμφορον λέγειν,[9] ἀντιλεγέσθω αὐτῷ. ἔδοξε δὲ πᾶσι πρῶτον Ἰωάννην εἰπεῖν.

4

1 Ἰωάννης εἶπεν· ὁδοὶ δύο εἰσί, μία τῆς ζωῆς καὶ μία τοῦ
θανάτου, διαφορὰ δὲ πολλὴ μεταξὺ τῶν δύο ὁδῶν. 2 ἡ μὲν γὰρ
ὁδὸς τῆς ζωῆς[10] ἐστιν αὕτη· πρῶτον ἀγαπήσεις τὸν θεὸν τὸν
ποιήσαντά σε ἐξ ὅλης τῆς καρδίας σου[11] καὶ δοξάσεις τὸν
λυτρωσάμενόν σε ἐκ θανάτου, ἥτις ἐστὶν ἐντολὴ πρώτη. 3
δευτέρα δέ·[12] ἀγαπήσεις τὸν πλησίον σου ὡς ἑαυτόν, ἥτις ἐστὶν
ἐντολὴ δευτέρα, ἐν οἷς ὅλος ὁ νόμος κρέμαται καὶ προφῆται.

---

[6] *οὖν*: Lagarde suggested that this word be deleted. I believe that it was provided by K, to link to the *κκ* material previously cited. See the introduction at 2.2.

[7] *εἷς*: V, whereas a later corrector to V writes *εἰς*.

[8] *λαμβάνωμεν*: so V, followed by Lagarde, Hilgenfeld and Harnack. Schermann prints *λαμβάνομεν*; WM suggests *λάβωμεν*.

[9] *ἐάν τις δοκῇ τι ἀσύμφορον λέγειν*: so Harnack and Funk following Syr., S (Eth.); Cf. V and Schermann: *ἐάν τις δοκῇ συμφέρον ἀντιλέγειν*.

[10] *ἡ μὲν γὰρ ὁδὸς τῆς ζωῆς*: so V and Funk; since D reads *ἡ μὲν οὖν ὁδὸς τῆς ζωῆς*, and E reads *ἡ οὖν τῆς ζωῆς* Schermann is led to suggest *ἡ μὲν οὖν τῆς ζωῆς*, and Harnack *ἡ μὲν οὖν ὁδὸς τῆς ζωῆς*. Mosq. reads simply: *ἡ μὲν τῆς ζωῆς*. Decisive is Syr., which reads: ܐܘܪܚܐ ܕܝܢ ܗܝ ܕܚܝܐ, whereas S (A, Eth.) supports the inclusion of *μέν* and *ὁδός*. It seems to me that Harnack and Schermann are unduly influenced in their inclusion of *οὖν* by D and E; this may have been the reading of *κ*, but K is clearly an independent witness. See also the introduction at 1.1.

[11] So V; cf. Schermann, who conforms to E: *ἐξ ὅλης σου καρδίας*.

[12] *δευτέρα*: V, supported by Syr., reads *δευτέρα* and Mosq., supported by S, reads *δευτέρα δὲ ἐντολή*. Although Lagarde, Pitra and Hilgenfeld prefer *δεύτερον*, on the basis of E, and Harnack, Funk and Schermann follow them, with further support from the reading of D, the better textual support for K seems to lie with *δευτέρα*. *δέ* is probably necessary on stylistic grounds.

5

Ματθαῖος εἶπεν· πάντα ὅσα μὴ θέλῃς σοι γενέσθαι, σὺ μηδὲ ἄλλῳ ποιήσῃς·[13] τούτων δὲ τῶν λόγων τὴν διδαχὴν εἰπέ, ἀδελφὲ Πέτρε.

6

1 Πέτρος εἶπεν· οὐ φονεύσεις, οὐ μοιχεύσεις, οὐ πορνεύσεις, οὐ
παιδοφθορήσεις, οὐ κλέψεις, οὐ μαγεύσεις,[14] οὐ φαρμακεύσεις,
οὐ φονεύσεις τέκνον ἐν φθορᾷ οὐδὲ γεννηθὲν ἀποκτενεῖς, οὐκ
ἐπιθυμήσεις τὰ τοῦ πλησίον. οὐκ ἐπιορκήσεις,[15] 2 οὐ
ψευδομαρτυρήσεις, οὐ κακολογήσεις, οὐδὲ μνησικακήσεις, οὐκ
ἔσῃ δίγνωμος οὐδὲ δίγλωσσος· παγὶς γὰρ θανάτου ἐστιν ἡ
διγλωσσία· οὐκ ἔσται ὁ λόγος σου κενὸς οὐδὲ ψευδής. 3 οὐκ ἔσῃ
πλεονέκτης οὐδὲ ἅρπαξ οὐδὲ ὑποκριτὴς οὐδὲ κακοήθης, οὐδὲ
ὑπερήφανος· οὐ λήψῃ βουλὴν πονηρὰν κατὰ τοῦ πλησίον σου·
οὐ μισήσεις πάντα ἄνθρωπον, ἀλλ᾽ οὓς μὲν ἐλέγξεις, οὓς δὲ
ἐλεήσεις, περὶ ὧν δὲ προσεύξῃ, οὓς δὲ ἀγαπήσεις ὑπὲρ τὴν
ψυχήν σου.

7

᾿Ανδρέας εἶπεν· τέκνον μου, φεῦγε ἀπὸ παντὸς πονηροῦ καὶ ἀπὸ παντὸς ὁμοίου αὐτοῦ· μὴ γίνου ὀργίλος· ὁδηγεῖ γὰρ ἡ ὀργὴ πρὸς τὸν φόνον. ἔστι γὰρ δαιμόνιον ἀρρενικὸν ὁ θυμός.

---

[13] E here adds: *τουτέστιν ὃ σὺ μισεῖς ἄλλῳ μὴ ποιήσῃς*, and the addition of these words to K would appear to be supported by Syr. and by S. However, it is possibly a gloss deriving from Tob 4:16 that entered early into some texts. The phrase appears neither in V nor in Mosq.

[14] *οὐ πορνεύσεις, οὐ παιδοφθορήσεις, οὐ κλέψεις, οὐ μαγεύσεις* do not appear in V; Mosq. has *οὐ παιδοφθορήσεις, οὐ κλέψεις, οὐ μαντεύσῃ*. Harnack, followed by Schermann, supplied *οὐ παιδοφθορήσεις, οὐ κλέψεις, οὐ μαγεύσεις* from D, with some justification, since Syr. and S both contain these commandments. Syr. and S., moreover, add the commandment not to fornicate after the commandment not to commit adultery; this commandment is also in D (though in a different position), and the paraphrase in E might lead one to expect such a commandment here and so it is added by Funk in this position, in addition to those supplied by Harnack. The text presented here is thus a retroversion based on the versions. The *μαντεύσεις* which Mosq. suggests is possible instead of *μαγεύσεις*, but could equally be a scribal error in that MS.

[15] *οὐκ ἐπιθυμήσεις τὰ τοῦ πλησίον. οὐκ ἐπιορκήσεις*: not in V, but is present in Mosq. and the versions as well as E.

μὴ γίνου ζηλωτὴς μηδὲ ἐριστικὸς μηδὲ θυμαντικός·[16] *ἐκ γὰρ τούτων φόνος γεννᾶται.*

8

1 *Φίλιππος εἶπεν· τέκνον μου, μὴ γίνου ἐπιθυμητής. ὁδηγεῖ*
γὰρ ἡ ἐπιθυμία πρὸς τὴν πορνείαν και ἕλκει τοὺς ἀνθρώπους
πρὸς ἑαυτήν.[17] *Ἔστι γὰρ θηλυκὸν δαιμόνιον ἡ ἐπιθυμία, καὶ ὃ*
μὲν μετ᾿ ὀργῆς, ὃ δὲ μεθ᾿ ἡδονῆς[18] *ἀπόλλυσι τοὺς*
εἰσερχομένους αὐτά.[19]
2 *Ὁδὸς δὲ πονηροῦ πνεύματος ἁμαρτία ψυχῆς, καὶ ὅταν*
βραχεῖαν εἴσδυσιν σχῇ ἐν αὐτῷ,[20] *πλατύνει αὐτὴν καὶ ἄγει ἐπὶ*
πάντα τὰ κακὰ τὴν ψυχὴν ἐκείνην καὶ οὐκ ἐᾷ διαβλέψαι τὸν
ἄνθρωπον καὶ ἰδεῖν τὴν ἀλήθειαν.[21] 3 *Ὁ θυμὸς ὑμῶν μέτρον*
ἐχέτω καὶ ἐν βραχεῖ διαστήματι αὐτὸν ἡνιοχεῖτε καὶ
ἀνακρούετε, ἵνα μὴ ἐμβάλλῃ ὑμᾶς εἰς ἔργον πονηρόν. 4 *Θυμὸς*
γὰρ καὶ ἡδονὴ πονηρὰ ἐπὶ πολὺ παραμένουσα κατὰ ἐπίτασιν
δαιμόνια γίνεται, καὶ ὅταν ἐπιτρέψῃ αὐτοῖς ὁ ἄνθρωπος,
οἰδαίνουσιν ἐν τῇ ψυχῇ αὐτοῦ καὶ γίνονται μείζονες καὶ
ἐπάγουσιν αὐτὸν εἰς ἔργα ἄδικα καὶ ἐπιγελῶσιν αὐτῷ καὶ
ἥδονται ἐπὶ τῇ ἀπωλείᾳ τοῦ ἀνθρώπου.

---

[16] *θυμαντικός*: so V. Although not the most common word in Greek literature, I agree with Funk that this is the right reading. Harnack and Schermann print *θυμώδης*, which is the reading of Mosq., but this may be an alteration in the interests of comprehension. Most significantly, E has *μανικός*, taken as the reading of K by Lagarde and Hilgenfeld. If *θυμαντικός* stood in *κ* then the reading of E is more readily understandable than it would be should we seek to see a derivation from *θυμώδης*. We may also understand that *θυμαντικός* might derive from the *θυμικός* of D (and *δ*?).

[17] *ἑαυτήν*: Funk suggests *αὐτήν*.

[18] *καὶ ὃ μὲν μετ᾿ ὀργῆς, ὃ δὲ μεθ᾿ ἡδονῆς*: WM suggests *καὶ ὁ μὲν θυμὸς μετ᾿ ὀργῆς, ἡ δὲ μεθ᾿ ἡδονῆς*; although there is a degree of support in S, the text in S is probably a clarification and there is no need for such extensive emendation.

[19] *τοὺς εἰσερχομένους αὐτά*: V, followed by edd. apart from Harnack, reads: *τοὺς εἰσδεχομένους αὐτά*. WM suggests *ἀποδεχομένους*. Harnack prefers Mosq.: *τοὺς εἰσερχομένους εἰς αυτήν*, and this has some support from Syr., which has ܡܬܩܪܒܝܢ ܠܘܬܗܘܢ ܕܐܝܠܝܢ ܒܗܘܢ. Here, however, there is ambiguity about whether the spirits or the person affected is making the approach. Certainly on the basis of Mosq. and Syr., the word *εἰσερχομένους* was present in K, and the text given is an attempt at restoration.

[20] P. Nautin, in unpublished notes, suggests *αὐτῇ*. This may well be an improvement.

[21] Mosq. adds: *ἐπιγελᾷ δὲ τὸ πονηρὸν πνεῦμα τῷ ἀνθρώπῳ ἐκείνῳ καὶ εὐφραίνεται ἐπὶ τῇ ἀπωλείᾳ αὐτοῦ*. This seems misplaced from further below.

9

Σίμων εἶπεν· τέκνον, μὴ γίνου αἰσχρολόγος μηδὲ ὑψηλόφθαλμος. ἐκ γὰρ τούτων μοιχεῖαι γίνονται.[22]

10

Ἰάκωβος εἶπεν· τέκνον μου,[23] μὴ γίνου οἰωνοσκόπος, ἐπειδὴ ὁδηγεῖ εἰς τὴν εἰδωλολατρίαν, μηδὲ ἐπαοιδός, μηδὲ μαθηματικὸς μηδὲ περικαθαίρων, μηδὲ θέλε αὐτὰ ἰδεῖν[24] μηδὲ ἀκούειν· Ἐκ γὰρ τούτων ἁπάντων εἰδωλολατρεῖαι γεννῶνται.

11

1 Ναθαναὴλ εἶπεν· τέκνον μου,[25] μὴ γίνου ψεύστης, ἐπειδὴ
ὁδηγεῖ τὸ ψεῦσμα ἐπὶ τὴν κλοπήν, μηδὲ φιλάργυρος, μηδὲ
κενόδοξος· ἐκ τούτων ἁπάντων κλοπαὶ γεννῶνται. 2 Τέκνον
μου,[26] μὴ γίνου γόγγυσος, ἐπειδὴ ἄγει πρὸς τὴν βλασφημίαν,
μηδὲ αὐθάδης, μηδὲ πονηρόφρων· ἐκ γὰρ τούτων ἁπάντων
βλασφημίαι γεννῶνται. 3 Ἴσθι δὲ πραΰς, ἐπειδὴ πραεῖς
κληρονομήσουσι τὴν βασιλείαν τῶν οὐρανῶν.[27] 4 Γίνου
μακρόθυμος, ἐλεήμων, εἰρηνοποιός, καθαρὸς τῇ καρδίᾳ ἀπὸ
παντὸς κακοῦ, ἄκακος καὶ ἡσύχιος, ἀγαθός καὶ φυλάσσων καὶ
τρέμων τοὺς λόγους οὓς ἤκουσας. 5 Οὐχ ὑψώσεις σεαυτόν, οὐδὲ
δώσεις τὴν ψυχήν σου μετὰ ὑψηλῶν ἀλλὰ μετὰ δικαίων καὶ

---

[22] *μοιχεῖαι γίνονται*: so V, Lagarde, Hilgenfeld, Funk, Syr., E. Schermann emends to *γεννῶνται* in order to conform the text to D. There is no reason, however, to conform the text to D. Mosq. reads *γεννᾶται μοιχεία*, which leads Harnack to suggest *μοιχεία γεννᾶται*; but the reading of Mosq. might come about through a misreading of *γίνονται*, and thus tends to support the text as given here.

[23] *μου* is not in V, but is supplied from Mosq., supported by Syr. and S, as well as D. The entire phrase is dropped from E. So also Harnack, Funk and Schermann.

[24] *ἰδεῖν*: so WM, followed by Funk, Harnack and Schermann. Codd. and other eds read *εἰδέναι*.

[25] *μου* is again inserted on the basis of Syr. and S, as well as D, though with less certainty than at the beginning of K10, as there is not the support of Mosq. (which lacks this chapter altogether).

[26] *μου* is once again inserted on the basis of the versions and D. The entire phrase is omitted from E and the entire chapter from Mosq., thus leaving the text uncertain.

[27] *τὴν βασιλείαν τῶν οὐρανῶν*: S (though unsupported by A, Eth.) and D read *τὴν γῆν*. However Syr. concurs with V in the reading given. *τὴν γῆν* in S is perhaps an attempt to bring the text into line with Scripture.

ταπεινῶν ἀναστραφήσῃ. 6 Τὰ δὲ συμβαίνοντά σοι ἐνεργήματα ὡς ἀγαθὰ προσδέξῃ, εἰδὼς ὅτι ἄτερ θεοῦ οὐδὲν γίνεται.

12

1 Θωμᾶς εἶπεν· τέκνον,[28] τὸν λαλοῦντά σοι τὸν λόγον τοῦ θεοῦ καὶ παραίτιόν σοι γινόμενον τῆς ζωῆς καὶ δόντα σοι τὴν ἐν κυρίῳ σφραγῖδα ἀγαπήσεις ὡς κόρην ὀφθαλμοῦ σου, μνησθήσῃ[29] αὐτοῦ νύκτα καὶ ἡμέραν, τιμήσεις αὐτὸν ὡς τὸν κύριον. ὅθεν γὰρ ἡ κυριότης λαλεῖται, ἐκεῖ κύριός ἐστιν. 2
Ἐκζητήσεις δὲ τὸ πρόσωπον αὐτοῦ καθ᾽ ἡμέραν καὶ τοὺς λοιποὺς ἁγίους, ἵνα ἐπαναπαύσῃ τοῖς λόγοις αὐτῶν· κολλώμενος γὰρ ἁγίους ἅγιος ἁγιασθήσῃ.[30] 3 Τιμήσεις δὲ αὐτὸν καθ᾽ ὃ δυνατὸς εἶ ἐκ τοῦ ἱδρῶτός σου καὶ ἐκ τοῦ πόνου τῶν χειρῶν σου. Εἰ γὰρ ὁ κύριος δι᾽ αὐτοῦ ἠξίωσέν σοι δοθῆναι πνευματικὴν τροφὴν καὶ ποτὸν καὶ ζωὴν αἰώνιον, σὺ ὀφείλεις πολὺ μᾶλλον τὴν φθαρτὴν καὶ πρόσκαιρον προσφέρειν τροφήν. ἄξιος γὰρ ὁ ἐργάτης τοῦ μισθοῦ αὐτοῦ, καὶ βοῦν ἀλοῶντα οὐ φιμώσεις καὶ οὐδεὶς φυτεύει ἀμπελῶνα καὶ ἐκ τοῦ καρποῦ αὐτοῦ οὐκ ἐσθίει.

13

1 Κηφᾶς εἶπεν· οὐ ποιήσεις σχίσματα,[31] εἰρηνεύσεις δὲ μαχομένους, κρινεῖς δικαίως, οὐ λήψῃ πρόσωπον ἐλέγξαι τινὰ[32] ἐπὶ παραπτώματι, οὐ γὰρ ἰσχύει πλοῦτος παρὰ κυρίῳ· οὐ γὰρ ἀξία[33] προσκρίνει οὐδὲ κάλλος ὠφελεῖ, ἀλλ᾽ ἰσότης ἐστι

---

[28] On this occasion *τέκνον* is allowed to stand without *μου* as at this point. Although the versions and D have *μου* this chapter is contained in Mosq., which reads simply *τέκνον*.

[29] *μνησθήσῃ*: V and eds except Funk. Cf. Mosq., Funk, *μνήσθητι*. *μνησθήσῃ* has support from Syriac.

[30] *ἁγιασθήσῃ*: although E and S read *ἁγιασθήσεται*, the saying is virtually proverbial, and may therefore have been written from memory.

[31] *σχίσματα*: Mosq. reads *συνάψαι τινὰ μάχην πρὸς ἕτερον*. D and E have *σχίσμα*.

[32] *τινά*: V and Mosq. S, however, has "the sinner", and Arendzen, 76, suggests that this is the true reading, as Syr. here has a redundant *ὄντα*, which may in turn be explained by a misreading of *ἁμαρτόντα*. In addition the *τινά* here is somewhat harsh. Therefore, although the text of V is left intact here, the possibility of emendation should receive serious consideration.

[33] *ἀξία*: Such is the emendation offered by WM, accepted by Harnack, by Funk and by Schermann. V however reads *ἀξίας*, and this was likewise clearly read by the Syriac

πάντων παρ᾽ αὐτῷ. 2 ἐν προσευχῇ σου μὴ διψυχήσεις πότερον ἔσται ἢ οὔ. 3 Μὴ γίνου πρὸς μὲν τὸ λαβεῖν ἐκτείνων τὰς χεῖρας, πρὸς δὲ τὸ δοῦναι συσπῶν. Ἐὰν ἔχῃς διὰ τῶν χειρῶν σου, δώσεις[34] λύτρωσιν τῶν ἁμαρτιῶν σου. οὐ διστάσεις διδόναι[35] οὐδὲ διδοὺς γογγύσεις· γνώσῃ γάρ, τίς ἐστιν ὁ τοῦ μισθοῦ καλὸς ἀνταποδότης.[36] 4 Οὐκ ἀποστραφήσῃ ἐνδεούμενον, κοινωνήσεις δὲ ἁπάντων[37] τῷ ἀδελφῷ σου καὶ οὐκ ἐρεῖς ἴδια εἶναι· εἰ γὰρ ἐν τῷ ἀθανάτῳ[38] κοινωνοί ἐστε, πόσῳ μᾶλλον ἐν τοῖς φθαρτοῖς;[39]

14

1 Βαρθολομαῖος εἶπεν· Ἐρωτῶμεν ὑμᾶς, ἀδελφοί, ὡς ἔτι καιρός ἐστι καὶ ἔχετε[40] εἰς οὓς ἐργάζεσθε μεθ᾽ ἑαυτῶν μὴ ἐκλίπητε ἐν μηδενί ἐξ οὗ ἂν ἔχητε.[41] 2 Ἐγγυς γὰρ ἡ ἡμέρα κυρίου, ἐν ᾗ συναπολεῖται πάντα σὺν τῷ πονηρῷ· ἥξει γὰρ ὁ

---

translator; I am thus not entirely confident in the text I have printed here. I would be more confident if *οὐ γὰρ* read *οὐδὲ*, as WM proposed to emend the text.

[34] *δώσεις*: Pitra suggested *δὸς* on the basis of *Constitutiones apostolorum*, a reading which is supported by E and Mosq., but this is insufficient reason to essay an emendation here.

[35] *διδόναι*: so V; cf. Harnack, followed by Schermann, who, on the basis of D and Mosq., amends to *δοῦναι*.

[36] Mosq. concludes here with a doxology. Chapter 14, however, is misplaced and thus Mosq. provides a witness to the chapter.

[37] *κοινωνήσεις δὲ ἁπάντων*: so V and Funk. Cf. Harnack (followed by Schermann) who, on the basis of D and E, emends to *συγκοινωνήσεις δὲ πάντα*.

[38] E reads *θάνατῳ*, a reading supported by L, though not D. This is probably the reading of *κ*, since it seems improbable that E would make the error; the originality of the reading is supported by L, which has the same reading. We cannot therefore be sure whether K made the "correction", or whether this results from the scribal tradition, though Syr. clearly implies *ἀθανάτοις*. D reads *ἀθάνατῳ*. See Giet, "Didache", 232-233.

[39] *φθαρτοῖς*: V, Pitra, Lagarde, Hilgenfeld, Syr., Funk. Cf. again Harnack and Schermann who, on the basis of D and E, read *θνητοῖς*. Although the reading here imbalances the clauses, this is explained in the introduction at 1.2.4.1.3.3 as the result of a recollection by K of a different version of the saying.

[40] Schermann inserts *οὐκ* here.

[41] *ἐξ οὗ ἂν ἔχητε·* Such is the conjecture of Lagarde, based on his reading of V as *ἐξοῦ ἐὰν ἔχητε*. Mosq., however, reads *ἐξουσίαν ἔχητε*, which is the manner in which Bickell read V! Thus, with the exception of Lagarde, eds have given the text as *ἐξουσίαν ἐὰν ἔχητε*. Apart from being closer to V, Lagarde's conjecture is confirmed by the versions, whereas the version of Mosq. can be understood as a misreading.

κύριος καὶ ὁ μισθὸς αὐτοῦ μετ' αὐτοῦ.[42] 3 Ἑαυτῶν γίνεσθε νομοθέται,[43] ἑαυτῶν γίνεσθε σύμβουλοι ἀγαθοί, θεοδίδακτοι·[44] φυλάξεις ἃ παρέλαβες μήτε προσθεὶς μήτε ὑφαιρῶν.

15

Πέτρος εἶπεν· ἀδελφοί, τὰ περὶ τῶν λοιπῶν νουθεσιῶν αἱ γραφαὶ διδάξουσιν,[45] ἡμεῖς δὲ ἃ ἐκελεύσθημεν διατάξωμεν. πάντες εἶπαν· Πέτρος λεγέτω.

16

1 Πέτρος εἶπεν· ἐὰν ὀλιγανδρία ὑπάρχῃ καὶ μήπου πλῆθος τυγχάνῃ τῶν δυναμένων ψηφίσασθαι περὶ ἐπισκόπου ἐντὸς δεκαδύο ἀνδρῶν, εἰς τὰς πλησίον ἐκκλησίας, ὅπου τυγχάνει πεπηγυῖα, γραφέτωσαν, ὅπως ἐκεῖθεν ἐκλεκτοὶ τρεῖς ἄνδρες παραγενόμενοι δοκιμῇ δοκιμάσαντες[46] τὸν ἄξιον ὄντα,[47] εἴ τις φήμην καλὴν ἔχει ἀπὸ τῶν ἐθνῶν, εἰ ἀναμάρτητος ὑπάρχει,[48] εἰ φιλόπτωχος, εἰ σώφρων, μὴ μέθυσος, μὴ πόρνος, μὴ πλεονέκτης ἢ λοίδορος ἢ προσωπολήπτης καὶ τὰ τούτοις
ὅμοια. 2 Καλὸν μὲν εἶναι ἀγύναιος, εἰ δὲ μή, ἀπὸ μιᾶς γυναικός· παιδείας μέτοχος, δυνάμενος τὰς γραφὰς ἑρμηνεύειν· εἰ δὲ ἀγράμματος, πραῢς ὑπάρχων,[49] καὶ τῇ ἀγάπῃ

---

[42] *ὁ μισθὸς αὐτοῦ μετ' αὐτοῦ*: so V, Syr., S (with A, Eth.), Funk. Cf. however, Mosq., followed by Harnack and Schermann, *ὁ μισθὸς αὐτοῦ*. This is the reading of B, but there is no reason to suppose that this was the reading of K, unless under the prior conviction that K is following B. The reading of Mosq. is simply a manifestation of the tendency of this MS to abbreviate.

[43] *Ἑαυτῶν γίνεσθε νομοθέται*: these words appear in neither V nor Mosq., but are added by Harnack, Funk and Schermann on the basis of Syr. and S (A, Eth.) as well as B. Although B should not figure in any calculation of the text here, the universal witness of the versions is significant.

[44] *θεοδίδακτοι*: so Mosq., Syr. S (A, Eth.), Harnack, Funk, Schermann. V has *διδακτοί*.

[45] It is possible that, following Syr. and S, *ὑμᾶς* should be added to *διδάξουσιν*.

[46] *δοκιμάσαντες*: Funk, with support from Syr. and S, suggests *δοκιμάσωσι*. Arendzen, 77, suggests that this might be a correction on the part of the translators, providing a verb after *ὅπως*, especially as *δοκιμῇ* is not rendered in either version.

[47] S, with some support from A and Eth., adds *τοῦ βαθμοῦ τούτου*.

[48] Syr. and S (with A, Eth.) add "and not prone to anger." The sole reason not to insert *εἰ μὴ ὀργίλος* in the text is that this is a negative quality, whereas the other qualities at this point are positive. Hennecke, 242, supports this reading.

[49] *δυνάμενος τὰς γραφὰς ἑρμηνεύειν· εἰ δὲ ἀγράμματος, πραῢς ὑπάρχων*. So V, versions and edd. However, as noted in the introduction at 3.6.2, this is awkward for a

εἰς πάντας περισσευέτω, μήποτε περὶ τινος ἐλεγχθεὶς
ἐπίσκοπος ἀπὸ τῶν πολλῶν γενηθείη.

17

1 Ἰωάννης εἶπεν· ὁ κατασταθεὶς ἐπίσκοπος, εἰδὼς τὸ προσεχὲς
καὶ φιλόθεον τῶν σὺν αὐτῷ, καταστήσει οὓς ἂν δοκιμάσῃ
πρεσβυτέρους δύο. 2 πάντες ἀντεῖπον· ὅτι οὐ δύο ἀλλὰ τρεῖς.[50]
εἴκοσι γὰρ καὶ τέσσαρές εἰσι πρεσβύτεροι, δώδεκα ἐξ δεξιῶν
καὶ δώδεκα ἐξ εὐωνύμων.

18

1 Ἰωάννης εἶπεν· καλῶς ὑπεμνήσατε, ἀδελφοί. οἱ μὲν γὰρ ἐκ
δεξιῶν δεχόμενοι ἀπὸ τῶν ἀρχαγγέλων τὰς φιάλας
προσφέρουσι τῷ δεσπότῃ, οἱ δὲ ἐξ ἀριστερῶν ἐπέχουσι τῷ
πλήθει τῶν ἀγγέλων. 2 δεῖ οὖν εἶναι τοὺς πρεσβυτέρους ἤδη
κεχρονικότας ἐπὶ τῷ κόσμῳ, τρόπῳ τινὶ ἀπεχομένους τῆς πρὸς
γυναῖκας συνελεύσεως, εὐμεταδότους εἰς τὴν ἀδελφότητα,
πρόσωπον ἀνθρώπου μὴ λαμβάνοντας, συμμύστας τοῦ
ἐπισκόπου καὶ συνεπιμάχους, συναθροίζοντας τὸ πλῆθος,
προσθυμουμένους τὸν[51] ποιμένα. 3 οἱ[52] ἐκ δεξιῶν πρεσβύτεροι
προνοήσονται τῶν ἐπισκοπούντων[53] πρὸς τὸ θυσιαστήριον, ὅπως

---

number of reasons. Thus I have conjectured that the text of κκ read: δυνάμενος τὰς γραφὰς ἑρμηνεύειν, εἰ δ᾿ ᾖ ἀγράμματος· πραῢς ὑπάρχων. However, in view of the following interpolation I eventually conclude that the text of K read as printed here. We cannot tell whether the text had already suffered mutilation, or was misread or even deliberately recast by K.

[50] πρεσβυτέρους δύο. πάντες ἀντεῖπον· ὅτι οὐ δύο ἀλλὰ τρεῖς. Cf. Pitra and Hilgenfeld, who would emend to πρεσβυτέρους δεκαδύο. πάντες ἀντεῖπον· ὅτι οὐ δεκαδύο ἀλλὰ εἴκοσι καὶ τέσσαρες (κδ´). This passage is discussed in the introduction at 3.6.3; here we may simply note that Hilgenfeld`s emendation, whilst intended to simplify matters, does not actually succeed in making sense of the passage, and is hard to explain on orthographical grounds.

[51] προσθυμουμένους τὸν: so V. Syr., however, inserts ܠܘܬ here and, as Arendzen, 77, remarks, it seems that some preposition is needed in the Greek. The obvious preposition would be πρὸς, but this is stylistically awkward after προσθυμουμένους.

[52] Funk suggests οἱ δὲ.

[53] ἐπισκοπούντων: V has τῶν ἐπισκόπων whereas the oriental versions indicate that the word present was κοπιόντων, a reading supported by Hennecke, 242-243. ἐπισκοπούντων is thus a conjecture intended to account for both possible readings. If the conjecture is not accepted, then I must suggest that of the two existing readings, that of the Greek text is

τιμήσωσι καὶ ἐντιμηθῶσιν[54] εἰς ὃ ἂν δέῃ. οἱ ἐξ ἀριστερῶν πρεσβύτεροι προνοήσονται τοῦ πλήθους ὅπως εὐσταθήσῃ καὶ ἀθόρυβον ᾖ,[55] πρῶτον μεμαθηκὸς ἐν πάσῃ ὑποταγῇ.[56] 4 εἰ δέ τις νουθετούμενος αὐθάδως ἀποκριθῇ, τὸ[57] ἓν ποιήσαντες[58] οἱ ἐπὶ τῷ θυσιαστηρίῳ τὸν τοιοῦτον μετὰ ἴσης βουλῆς, ὃ ἂν ᾖ ἄξιον, δικασάτωσαν, ἵνα καὶ οἱ λοιποὶ φόβον ἔχωσι, μήποτε ἑνὸς πρόσωπον λάβωσι, καὶ ἐπὶ πλεῖον νεμηθῇ <τὸ κακὸν> ὡς γάγγραινα, καὶ αἰχμαλωτισθῶσιν οἱ πάντες.[59]

19

Ἰάκωβος εἶπεν· ἀναγνώστης καθιστανέσθω πρῶτον δοκιμῇ δεδοκιμασμένος,[60] μὴ γλωσσοκόπος, μὴ μέθυσος μήτε γελωτολόγος, εὔτροπος, εὐπειθής, εὐγνώμων, ἐν ταῖς κυριακαῖς συνόδοις πρῶτος σύνδρομος, εὐήκοος, διηγητικός, εἰδὼς ὅτι

---

the less probable, as K really seems not to take account of the possibility of more than one bishop.

[54] *ἐντιμηθῶσιν*: Syr. and S (A Eth.) all read *ἐπιτιμήσωσιν*. The acceptance of the reading depends to a great extent on the interpretation of the passage. It seems to me that Harnack is right in seeing the focus on the distribution of gifts, and thus it is possible that the versions had misunderstood the passage, leading to the reading which they present. *ἐπιτιμήσωσιν* is supported by Hennecke, 243-244.

[55] *εὐσταθήσῃ καὶ ἀθόρυβον ᾖ*: so Lagarde, and all subsequent eds V has *εὐσταθὴς ᾖ καὶ ἀθόρυβον εἴη*.

[56] Arendzen, 77, suggests on the basis of Syr. and S that an infinitive, probably *ὑπάρχειν*, has fallen out here. Although this would be an improvement in the text, it may be that the versions are making such an improvement, whereas the somewhat awkward Greek is original.

[57] *ἀποκριθῇ, τὸ*: so V and edd. except Pitra, who conjectures *ἀποκριθήτω*.

[58] *ἓν ποιήσαντες*: so V, followed by eds, Syr. and S imply *ἓν νοήσαντες*, a reading supported by Arendzen. However, this is to an extent made redundant by *μετὰ ἴσης βουλῆς*. Pitra conjectured *ἐμποιήσαντες*.

[59] *μήποτε ἑνὸς πρόσωπον λάβωσι, καὶ ἐπὶ πλεῖον νεμηθῇ <τὸ κακὸν> ὡς γάγγραινα, καὶ αἰχμαλωτισθῶσιν οἱ πάντες*: I have supplied *τὸ κακὸν* as something is clearly missing here, but I have been as conservative as possible in supplying a noun as Lat. commences here, and supports the text of V. For this reason I reject the far more extensive restoration proposed by Arendzen, largely on the basis of Syr., as an attempt by the Syriac translator to make sense of a text which he did not understand. Arendzen's proposed restoration is: *μήποτε ἐὰν πρόσωπον λάβωσιν τολμήσωσιν οἱ ἀδικοῦντες καὶ ἐπὶ πλεῖον νεμηθῇ τὸ κακὸν καὶ νομὴν σχῇ ὡς γάγγραινα*.

[60] *δοκιμῇ δεδοκιμασμένος*: both Lat. (*probatione omni probatus*) and Syr. ܒܒܘܩܝܐ ܡܠܝܐ ܒܗܐ imply that some word intervened between the two, but there is no agreement as to which.

εὐαγγελιστῶν τόπον ἐργάζεται. ὁ γὰρ ἐμπιπλῶν ὦτα μὴ νοοῦντος ἔγγραφος λογισθήσεται παρὰ τῷ θεῷ.

20

1 Ματθαῖος εἶπεν· διάκονοι καθιστάσθωσαν <τρεῖς>.[61]
γέγραπται· ἐπὶ τριῶν σταθήσεται πᾶν ῥῆμα κυρίου. 2 Ἔστωσαν
δεδοκιμασμένοι πάσῃ διακονίᾳ, μεμαρτυρημένοι παρὰ τοῦ πλήθους, μονόγαμοι, τεκνοτρόφοι, σώφρονες, ἐπιεικεῖς, ἥσυχοι, μὴ γόγγυσοι, μὴ δίγλωσσοι, μὴ ὀργίλοι, ὀργὴ γὰρ ἀπόλλυσι ἄνδρα φρόνιμον, μὴ πρόσωπον πλουσίου[62] λαμβάνοντες μηδὲ πένητα καταδυναστεύοντες μηδὲ οἴνῳ
πολλῷ χρώμενοι, εὔσκυλτοι· 3 τῶν κρυφίων ἔργων καλοὶ
προτρεπτικοί, ἐπαναγκάζοντες τοὺς ἔχοντας τῶν ἀδελφῶν ἁπλοῦν τὰς χεῖρας, καὶ αὐτοὶ εὐμετάδοτοι, κονωνικοί, πάσῃ τιμῇ καὶ ἐντροπῇ καὶ φόβῳ τιμώμενοι ἀπὸ τοῦ πλήθους, ἐπιμελῶς προσέχοντες τοῖς ἀτάκτως περιπατοῦσιν, οὓς μὲν νουθετοῦντες, οὓς δὲ παρακαλοῦντες, οὓς δὲ ἐπιτιμῶντες, τοὺς δὲ καταφρονοῦντας τελέως παραπεμπόμενοι, εἰδότες ὅτι οἱ ἀντίλογοι καὶ καταφρονηταὶ καὶ λοίδοροι Χριστῷ ἀντετάξαντο.

21

1 Κηφᾶς εἶπεν· χῆραι καθιστανέσθωσαν τρεῖς· αἱ δύο
προσμένουσαι τῇ προσευχῇ περὶ πάντων τῶν[63] ἐν πείρᾳ καὶ
πρὸς τὰς ἀποκαλύψεις περὶ οὗ ἂν δέῃ. 2 μία δὲ παρεδρεύσουσα
ταῖς ἐν ταῖς νόσοις πειραζομέναις· εὐδιάκονος ᾖ, νηπτική, τὰ δέοντα ἀπαγέλλουσα τοῖς πρεσβυτέροις, μὴ αἰσχροκερδής, μὴ οἴνῳ πολλῷ προσέχουσα, ἵνα δύνηται νήφειν πρὸς τὰς

---

[61] Bickell and Funk supply the number *τρεῖς*, following whom it is supplied here; whereas Harnack suggests that the number has been deliberately omitted by K, Hauler (apparatus reproduced in Tidner in Lat., 106) suggests that the omission is accidental, and that *γ´* fell out before *γέγραπται*. The issue is discussed in the introduction at 3.6.3, where an accidental explanation of the absence of the number in V is preferred, on the basis that K read the number here. The number is present in Syriac but not in the other versions.

[62] *Πλουσίου*: Schermann prints *πλησίου*.

[63] *τῶν*: not in V and supplied by Lagarde.

νυκτερινὰς ὑπηρεσίας καὶ εἴ τις ἕτερα[64] *βούλοιτο ἐργαγαθεῖν. καὶ γὰρ ταῦτα πρῶτα κυρίου*[65] *θησαυρίσματά εἰσιν ἀγαθά.*

22

1 Ἀνδρέας *εἶπεν· διάκονοι ἐργάται τῶν καλῶν ἔργων. νυχθήμερον ἐπελεύσονται*[66] *πανταχοῦ, μήτε πένητα ὑπεροπτεύοντες μήτε πλούσιον προσωποληπτοῦντες, ἐπιγνώσονται τὸν θλιβόμενον καὶ ἐκ τῆς λογίας οὐ παραπέμψονται,* 2 *ἐπαναγκάσουσι δὲ τοὺς δυναμένους ἀποθησαυρίζειν εἰς ἔργα ἀγαθά, προορῶντας τοὺς λόγους τοῦ διδασκάλου ἡμῶν· εἴδετέ με πεινῶντα καὶ οὐκ ἐθρεψατέ με. Οἱ γὰρ καλῶς διακονήσαντες καὶ ἀμέμπτως τόπον ἑαυτοῖς περιποιοῦνται*[67] *τὸν ποιμενικόν.*

---

[64] *ἕτερα*: The accentuation here (reading a neuter plural) is that implied by the Syriac translation and as given by Hilgenfeld (who attributes the reading to E. Bochmer) and Harnack. Serious consideration, however should be given to accenting the word with Lagarde, followed by Funk and Schermann, and also in accordance with the reading of Lat. and S (with A, Eth.), as *ἑτέρα* (feminine singular). In this event the translation would read: "If another wished to perform good words, and indeed these are the good treasures of the Lord." This could well be an expansion by K, as part of his response to the proper ministries of women, and coheres, moreover, with the statement at K29. It is, however, difficult to make sense of the clause, as it seems incomplete. S (with A, Eth.) expands the clause, adding, "let her act in accordance with her heart". It is quite possible, however, that this expansion is a rationalising addition by the translator. Thus the accentuation as given is, after due consideration, preferred on the grounds of sense, and rendered in the opposite translation, but the suspicion remains that the text read otherwise. For discussion see Gryson, *Ministry of Women*, 46 (who prefers the accentuation as given here).

[65] *πρῶτα κυρίου*: so V, Lagarde, Hilgenfeld, Harnack, Funk. Schermann omits *πρῶτα*. Pitra's conjecture of *παρὰ τῷ κυρίῳ* should, however, be given serious consideration, though unsupported by the versions.

[66] *ἐπελεύσονται*: V reads *ἐπελεύσοντε*, and Bickell gave *ἐπελεύσοντες* which, as Harnack, *Sources*, 21, remarks, "is no word at all." M. Schmidt (apud Hilgenfeld) proposed *ἐπιλεύσοντες*, but I can make no sense of this suggestion, though it is accepted by Schermann. Harnack, *Sources*, 21, suggested instead *ἐπιλεύσσοντες*, though he was not sure of the emendation, as the word is purely Homeric (though *λεύσσω* without a prefix is more widespread). The emendation proposed is that of Funk. It represents only a minor change in the text of V and, most importantly, is entirely coherent with the versions, all of which agree in having "going around."

[67] *περιποιοῦνται*: Funk reads *προσποιοῦνται*, but there seems no good reason to make the emendation.

23

1 Φίλιππος εἶπεν· ὁ λαϊκὸς τοῖς λαϊκοῖς προστάγμασι[68]
περιπειθέσθω[69] ὑποτασσόμενος τοῖς παρεδρεύσι τῷ
θυσιαστηρίῳ. 2 ἕκαστος τῷ ἰδιῷ τόπῳ ἀρεσκέτω τῷ θεῷ[70] μὴ
φιλεχθροῦντες ἀλλήλοις περὶ τῶν τεταγμένων, ἕκαστος ἐν ᾧ
ἐκλήθη παρατεθεὶς ὑπὸ Χριστοῦ.[71] 3 ὁ ἕτερος τοῦ ἑτέρου τὸν
δρόμον μὴ παρατεμνέτω·[72] οὐδὲ γὰρ οἱ ἄγγελοι παρὰ τὸ
διατεταγμένον αὐτοῖς οὐδὲν ἕτερον ἐξελίσσουσιν.

24

Ἀνδρέας εἶπεν· εὔχρηστόν ἐστιν, ἀδελφοί, ταῖς γυναιξὶ διακονίαν καταστῆσαι.

25

Πέτρος εἶπεν· ἐφθάσαμεν τάξαντες· περὶ δὲ τῆς προσφορᾶς τοῦ σώματος καὶ τοῦ αἵματος ἀκριβῶς μηνύσωμεν.

---

[68] *προστάγμασι*: so Lat., Syr., S (with A, Eth.), Hennecke, 242, Schermann. V, followed by other eds, has *πράγμασι*.

[69] *περιπειθέσθω*: so Lagarde and subsequent eds except Hilgenfeld, who suggests *περιτιθέσθω* or *περιπλεκέσθω*. V has *περιποιθέσθω*. M. Schmidt, apud Hilgenfeld, suggests *ἐπιτερπέσθω*.

[70] *θεῷ*: so V, S. Lat. and Syr., however, agree in having *κυρίῳ*.

[71] *ἕκαστος ἐν ᾧ ἐκλήθη παρατεθεὶς ὑπὸ Χριστοῦ*: The last three words are conjectural. Cf. V: *ἕκαστος ἐν ᾧ ἐκλήθη παρὰ τῷ θεῷ*. Harnack, *Sources*, 24, suggests that *ἐν τούτῳ μενέτω θεέτω* has fallen out before *παρὰ τῷ θεῷ*. The addition of *ἐν τούτῳ μενέτω* would conform the text to 1 Cor 7:24, but there is no reason to suspect such a conformity. The further addition of *θεέτω* is suggested in the light of S (A, Eth.) and in the light of the *δρόμος* which appears below, and may indeed fall out in proximity to *θεῷ*, but there is no support in Syr., though Arendzen, 78, supports the thrust of Harnack's argument (nonetheless noting that Harnack's additional words would appear to be in the wrong place). However the passage is difficult, and, even with Harnack's emendation, the dative after *παρά* is difficult. Latin reads: "quae singulis decreta sunt loca, unusquisque in quo vocatus est a Christo". There are thus two deviations from V, namely the explicit mention of an allotted place and the term "Christo" rather than *θεῷ*. The conjectural emendation is thus made in order to account for these two points, as well as the dative after *παρά* and the mention of a *δρόμος* (the term *παρατίθημι* being understood as placement in a lane or course, which would lead the Latin translator to infer the idea of an allotted place), and suggests that *παρὰ τοῦ θεῷ* is a misreading of *παρατεθείς*, leading to the loss of the final words as redundant. The corruption had already occurred by the time that the text came before the Syriac translator, whereas the Sahidic translator freely adapts in order to make sense of the passage.

[72] *παρατεμνέτω*: V has *παρατεμνεῖτο*. Funk reads *παρατεμνέσθω*.

26

Ἰωάννης εἶπεν· ἐπελάθεσθε, ἀδελφοί, ὅτε ᾔτησεν ὁ διδάσκαλος τὸν ἄρτον καὶ τὸ ποτήριον καὶ ηὐλογήσεν αὐτὰ λέγων· τοῦτο ἐστι τὸ σῶμα μου· καὶ τὸ αἶμα, ὅτι οὐκ ἐπέτρεψε ταύταις συστῆναι ἡμῖν.

Μάρθα εἶπεν· διὰ Μαριάμ, ὅτι εἶδεν αὐτὴν μειδιῶσαν· Μαρία εἶπεν· οὐχ ὅτι[73] ἐγέλασα· προέλεγε γὰρ ἡμῖν, ὅτε ἐδίδασκεν, ὅτι τὸ ἀσθενὲς διὰ τοῦ ἰσχυροῦ σωθήσεται.

27

Κηφᾶς εἶπεν· ἐνίων μεμνῆσθαι δεῖ ὅτι ταῖς γυναιξὶ μὴ ὀρθαῖς προσεύχεσθαι,[74] ἀλλὰ ἐπὶ[75] τῆς γῆς καθεζομέναις.[76]

28

Ἰάκωβος εἶπεν· πῶς οὖν δυνάμεθα περὶ γυναικῶν διακονίαν[77] ὁρίσαι, εἰ μή τι διακονίαν ἵνα ἐπισχύσωσι[78] ταῖς ἐνδεομέναις;

---

[73] *οὐχ ὅτι* is read with Lat., following Hauler. The emendation was suggested by WM without reference to the Latin text. Cf. V and eds *οὐκέτι*.

[74] *ἐνίων μεμνῆσθαι δεῖ ὅτι ταῖς γυναιξὶ μὴ ὀρθαῖς προσεύχεσθαι*: Cf. V *ἐνίων μέμνησθε δὲ ὅτι*... The emendation is made following a suggestion of Arendzen, derived from Syr. In order to make better sense of the unemended text, and to conform it in some way to Lat., which reads: "aliquantorum memores estis, quoniam hoc iubebat mulieribus..." Hauler and Schermann supplied *προσέταξεν* after *ὅτι*, and Pitra, Lagarde, Hilgenfeld, Harnack and Funk similarly supplied *πρέπει* after *ὀρθαῖς*; this is unnecessary once the *δὲ* is emended, as the force of "iubebat" may be contained within *δεῖ*, and as *δεῖ* explains the infinitive.

[75] *ἐπί* is given following the suggestions of WM, Funk and Harnack. V, however has *ἀπὸ*, accepted by Schermann, and Latin has "de", whereas the other versions offer no guidance.

[76] The entire phrase is questioned by A.J. Maclean, *The Ancient Church Orders* (Cambridge 1910) 28, who prefers the rendering of the Syriac that women should approach the sacrifice with heads covered. He suggests a misreading of *προσέρχεσθαι* as *προσεύχεσθαι*. Whereas it is possible that there was some misreading here, it would surely be a misreading by the Syriac translator. As noted in the comments to the translation, Maclean in part prefers the reading because it is paralleled elsewhere in the church-orders.

[77] *διακονίαν*: so V, Lat., Lagarde, Hilgenfeld, Schermann; cf. Harnack and Funk, who read *διακονίας*.

[78] *ἐπισχύσωσι*: WM suggests *ἐπισχήσωσι*, Lagarde *ἐπισχῶσι*. I cannot see that any emendation is necessary. Hilgenfeld, Harnack, Funk and Schermann leave the text so.

29

Φίλιππος εἶπεν· τοῦτο, ἀδελφοί, περὶ τῆς μεταδόσεως· ὁ ποιῶν ἔργον ἑαυτῷ θησαυρὸν καλὸν[79] περιποιεῖται· ὁ γὰρ θησαυρίζων ἐν τῇ βασιλείᾳ ἔγγραφος ἐργάτης λογισθήσεται παρὰ τῷ θεῷ.

30

Πέτρος εἶπεν· ταῦτα, ἀδελφοί, οὐχ ὡς ἐξουσίαν τινὸς ἔχοντες πρὸς ἀνάγκην, ἀλλ᾽ ἐπιταγὴν ἔχοντες παρὰ κυρίου. ἐρωτῶμεν ὑμᾶς, φυλάξαι τὰς ἐντολὰς μηδὲν ἀφαιροῦντας ἢ προστιθέντας ἐν τῷ ὀνόματι τοῦ κυρίου ἡμῶν,[80] ᾧ ἡ δόξα εἰς τοὺς αἰῶνας. ἀμήν.

---

[79] *ἔργον ἑαυτῷ θησαυρὸν καλὸν*: so V and all versions and edd. except Lagarde, who ventures *ἔργον καλὸν ἑαυτῷ θησαυρὸν*.

[80] *κυρίου ἡμῶν*: Lat., Syr, S add Ἰησοῦ Χριστοῦ. Although loath to leave the text as it is against the unanimous versional witness, doxologies are so prone to alteration that I have left the text as it stands.

The directions through Clement and the canons of the holy apostles

Greetings, sons and daughters, in the name of the Lord Jesus Christ. John and Matthew and Peter and Andrew and Philip and Simon and James and Nathanael and Thomas and Kephas and Bartholomew and Jude the son of James.

1

In accordance with the command of Our Lord Jesus Christ the Saviour we gathered ourselves together, as he laid down for us: Before you determine the eparchies,[1] you are to calculate the numbers of the places,[2] the dignities of bishops, the seats of presbyters, the assistance offered by deacons, the understanding of readers, the blamelessness of widows and whatever is necessary for the foundation of the church so that, knowing the type of those things which are heavenly,[3] they should guard themselves against every fault, seeing that, in the great day of judgement, they should give an account of those who heard and did not keep. And he ordered us to send these words out to the whole inhabited world.

2

It seemed to us, therefore, that we should command you as an admonition of brotherhood and an exhortation, so that you might be mindful through the account of what the Lord revealed to each of us in accordance with the will of God through the Holy Spirit.

3

John said: Brethren, since we know that we shall have to give an account of what was commanded us, let us not have regard for any person, but if someone should seem to say something which is improper, he should be contradicted. It seemed to all that John should speak first.

---

[1] Or, if the emendation proposed is not accepted: ... as he laid down before. "You are to determine the eparchies..."

[2] This is to be taken as the number of episcopal seats, which are to be established before any provincial arrangements are made.

[3] See the introduction, 4.7.1.2, on the idea that the earthly church should typify that in heaven.

4

1 John said: There are two ways, the one of life and the one of death, and the
difference between the two ways is great. 2 For the way of life is this. First you
shall love the God who created you with all your heart and you shall glorify him
who ransomed you from death. Such is the first commandment. 3 The second:
you shall love your neighbour as yourself. Such is the second commandment,
on which the whole of the law and the prophets is dependent.

5

Matthew said: Whatever you would not wish done to you, do to nobody else. State the teaching of these maxims, brother Peter.

6

1 Peter said: You shall not murder, you shall not commit adultery, you shall
not fornicate, you shall not despoil a child, you shall not steal, you shall not
employ charms, you shall not be a sorcerer, you shall not destroy a child
through abortion nor kill it once born, you shall not covet what is your
neighbour's, 2 you shall not swear falsely, you shall not bear false witness,
you shall not speak evil, you shall not store up wrongs, you shall not be
double-minded or double-tongued. For being double-tongued is a snare of
death. Your word shall not be empty, nor false. 3 You shall not be grasping,
nor rapacious, nor hypocritical, nor malicious, nor arrogant. You shall not
plot evil against your neighbour. You shall not hate any person, but some
you shall rebuke, some you shall pity, for some you shall pray, and some you
shall love more than your own life.

7

Andrew said: My child, shun every evil person and all who are like to him. Do not be quick-tempered, for anger leads to murder. For rage is a male demon. Do not be jealous or quarrelsome or ragingly aggressive. For murder is begotten from these.

8

1 Philip said: My child, do not be given over to passion. For lust leads to
fornication and drags people towards itself. For lust is a female demon, and
one with anger, the other with pleasure, destroys those who go close to them.
2 The way of an evil spirit is a soul's sin, and when it has a narrow place of
entry in somebody it expands itself and leads that soul on to all evil things,
and does not allow the person to look out and see the truth. 3 Let your rage be

measured and rein it in and bring it to a halt in a short distance, so that it
cannot lead you to an evil deed. 4 For rage and evil pleasure, when they
remain a long time, gain strength to become demons, and when a person
yields to them they swell up in his soul and become greater and lead him on
to unjust deeds and they mock him and take pleasure in the person's
destruction.

9

Simon said: Child, do not be a speaker of base words, nor immodestly curious.[4] For from these adulteries come about.

10

James said: My child, do not be an examiner of omens, since this leads to idolatry, nor an enchanter nor an astrologer nor a lustrator, nor desire to see or hear these things. For from all of these are idolatries begotten.

11

1 Nathanael said: My child, do not be a liar, since falsehood leads to theft,[5]
nor a lover of money nor vain glory. For from all of these are thefts begotten.
2 My child, do not be a grumbler, since it leads to blasphemy, nor self-willed
nor evil-minded. For from all of these are blasphemies begotten. 3 Be
generous, for the generous will inherit the kingdom of the heavens. 4 Be
patient, merciful, a peacemaker, pure in heart from every evil, guileless and
peaceable, good and guarding and fearing the words which you heard. 5 Do
not make yourself haughty, nor commit your life to the exalted, but associate
with the righteous and lowly. 6 Whatever befalls you, accept these
experiences as good, knowing that nothing happens without God.

12

1 Thomas said: Child, you shall love as the apple of your eye the one who
speaks to you the word of God and is the cause of life to you and gives you
the seal of the Lord. You shall remember him night and day, you shall
honour him as the Lord. For inasmuch as the dominion is discussed, the Lord
is there. 2 You shall daily seek out his face, as well as the rest of the saints, so
that you may find refreshment in their words. For in being cemented with the
saints you shall be sanctified as a saint.[6] 3 You shall honour him as much as

[4] Literally, "a lifter up of the eyes." The rendition is that of the *Patristic Greek Lexicon*, drawn to my attention by Allen Brent.

[5] Cited by Clem., *Strom.* 1.20.

[6] This phrase is cited as scriptural by *1 Clem.* 46.2.

you are able from your sweat and from the labour of your hands. If the Lord through him has made you worthy to be given spiritual food and drink and eternal life, much the more should you bring him corruptible and temporary food. "For the workman is worthy of his hire" and "You shall not muzzle a threshing ox" and "Nobody plants a vine and does not eat the fruit of it."

13

1 Kephas said: "You shall not make schisms, you shall make peace between those who are disputing, you shall judge justly, you shall not show partiality in rebuking any transgression, for wealth does not count before the Lord. Status does not impress nor does beauty give advantage, for before him all are equal. 2 In your prayer you shall not be divided in your mind, whether it will be or not. 3 Do not be one who stretches out hands to take, whilst retracting them to avoid giving. If you have gained through your hands, you shall give a ransom for your sins. Do not hesitate to give, nor grumble in your giving, for you know who is the good dispenser of rewards. 4 You shall not turn away a beggar. You shall have all things in common with your brother, and you shall not claim anything as your own. For if you are companions in immortality, are you not much more so in what is corruptible?

14

1 Bartholomew said: We ask you, brethren, for as long as there is time, while you have amongst yourselves those for whom to labour, do not withhold anything that you possess. 2 For the day of the Lord is near, on which all things will perish alongside the evil one. For the Lord will come and his reward with him. 3 Be legislators for yourselves, be good counsellors one to another, taught of God. You shall guard what you have received, neither adding nor subtracting.

15

Peter said: Brothers, the scriptures will teach of the remaining exhortations. But let us draw up in order what we have commanded. All said: Let Peter speak.

16

1 Peter said: If there should occur a shortage of men, and there are insufficient competent to elect to the episcopate from among twelve,[7] they should write to the neighbouring churches, where one is established, so that

[7] Cf. Harnack, *Sources*, 7: "and there are not twelve who are competent to vote at the election of a bishop". See the introduction at 3.6.1 for some discussion of the phrase.

three selected men might come from there carefully to determine[8] which is worthy,[9] whether any has a good reputation among the heathen,[10] being without fault,[11] whether a friend of the poor, whether temperate,[12] not a drunkard,[13] not a fornicator, not grasping or abusive,[14] or a respecter of persons[15] or anything of that nature. 2 It is good should he be unmarried, otherwise he should be of one wife, having some education, and able to interpret the scriptures, even if he is unlettered. He should be generous,[16] and overflowing with love for all,[17] so that a bishop should not come under accusation on any account by the many.

17

1 John said: The bishop who has been installed, knowing the care and the love of God of those who are with him, should install two presbyters of whom he approves. 2 All said in reply: Not two but three. For there are twenty-four presbyters, twelve on the right and twelve on the left.

18

1 John said: You have recalled this well, brothers. For those on the right receive the phials from the archangels and bear them to the master, and those on the left have authority over the company of angels.[18] 2 Therefore the presbyters should have been a long time in the world, having kept themselves from congress with women in their lives, generous towards the brotherhood,

---

[8] *δοκιμῇ δοκιμάσαντες*. Cf. 2 Cor 8:22; 1 Tim. 3:10; *1 Clem.* 42.4, 44.2, 47.4; *Did.* 15.1.
[9] *ἄξιον*. The word enters ordination rites. See P.F. Bradshaw, *Ordination Rites of the Ancient Churches of East and West* (New York 1990) 23-24.
[10] 1 Tim 3:7.
[11] Cf. 1 Tim 3:2.
[12] Cf. 1 Tim 3:2.
[13] Cf. Tit 1:8; 1 Tim 3:2.
[14] For this list cf. 1 Cor 5:11. The debt to the pastoral epistles overall in the list of qualities is noteworthy; the sole qualification not so derived is that the bishop should be *φιλόπτωχος*, which is that which, given the economic office of the bishop in *κκ*, is most authentic and primitive.
[15] Cf. Polycarp, *Ad Phil.* 61 (of presbyters). This is demanded frequently of the bishop in the Syrian *Didasc.*, so that he should not be partial in exercising judgement.
[16] Note that the text has been emended here. The unemended text reads: "... able to interpret the scriptures. If he is unlettered, it is sufficient that he should be generous." For further discussion see the introduction. The influence of the pastoral epistles has perhaps brought about the requirement that the bishop should have some ability in teaching, which is at odds with the duties described.
[17] Cf. 1 Thess 3:12.
[18] Cf. Rev 4:4, 8.

not respecters of persons, struggling alongside the bishop and participating in the mysteries together with him,[19] gathering the people and devoted to the pastor.[20] 3 The presbyters on the right are to assist those who oversee[21] the altar, so that they may distribute the gifts of honour and receive them as necessary.[22] The presbyters on the left are to assist the congregation, so that it may be peaceful and without disturbance, once it has been instructed in all submission.[23] 4 But if anyone who has been warned should respond rashly,

---

[19] This may be a reference to Wis 8:4, stating in effect that the presbyter is to share with the bishop in having knowledge of God; Ign., *Eph.* 12.2, uses the term of the Ephesians, as fellow-initiates with Paul. However, I am persuaded by A. Brent of the rightness of Arendzen's suggestion that the term simply means that the presbyters concelebrate the eucharist with the bishop, as it is hard to see ordination as meaning initiation.

[20] As A.J. Maclean, *The Ancient Church Orders* (Cambridge 1910) 68 n., observes, the use of the term "shepherd" absolutely to refer to the bishop is not common in church order literature, but is found most prominently in *T. Dom.*, as well as occasionally in the *Didasc.* and *Constitutiones Apostolorum*. This is to be considered alongside other indications of a common interest between *T. Dom.* and K/κκ.

[21] Following the conjecture made opposite. This, as does the reading of the oriental versions, solves the difficulty regarding the sudden plurality of bishops, and balances the functions of the presbyters on the left and the right.

[22] The interpretation of Harnack, *Sources*, 13-14, who sees the verbs as referring to the distribution and receipt of gifts, is followed. According to this reading the meaning of the passage is that the gifts are received at the altar, and that they are distributed according to need to the congregation. This task is that of the bishop and deacons, who are assisted (and perhaps overseen) in this task by the presbyters on the right (if the term presbyters does not indeed refer to deacons as well). There is one difference with the interpretation of Harnack, who felt that the subject was the bishops. However, as the result of an emendation, these bishops have disappeared, and so the task is that of "those who oversee the altar". Funk, *Doctrina*, 64, however, suggested that the subject was the πλῆθος, and that the verbs referred to the giving of gifts, rather than the distribution thereof; the πλῆθος, however, does not appear in this sentence. See also Hennecke, "Apostolischen Kirchenordnung", 243-244.

[23] To this whole passage cf. *Didasc.* 2.57.5-7. "The presbyters are to be seated in the eastern part of the house with the bishops, and then the laymen, and then the women, so that when you stand up to pray the leaders should stand first, and then the laymen and subsequently the women. For it is required that your prayers should be directed towards the East, as you know what is written: 'Give glory to God who rides upon the heavens of heaven, towards the East.' One of the deacons should continue to stand by the offerings of the eucharist; another should stand outside the door observing those who come in. And afterwards, when you are offering, they should minister together in the church. And if anyone is found sitting in a place which is not his the deacon within should warn him and make him stand up and seat him in the place which is his own, as is right."

Not only is this indicative of a literary relationship, as suggested in the introduction, but it may be observed that here deacons are performing duties comparable to those of presbyters in K. It would seem that *Didasc.* knew an episcopal-diaconal church-order.

those at the altar, acting in concert, should pronounce a like decision, as is deserved, so that the rest might be in fear, and so that they do not accept any person, and so that the evil might not spread further like a cancer and all be infected.[24]

19

James said: A reader should be appointed after careful testing. He should not be a babbler, or a drunkard, or a jester. He should be of upstanding life, submissive, well-intentioned, taking the lead in the assemblies on the Lord`s days,[25] who is good to listen to and is able to construct a narrative, aware that he labours in the place of an evangelist.[26] For whoever fills the ears of the ignorant shall be reckoned as written before God.

20

1 Matthew said: Three[27] deacons should be appointed. It is written: "Every matter of the Lord shall be established by three."[28] 2 They should be proved in every ministry, with witness borne by the congregation,[29] married once,[30] educating their children,[31] temperate,[32] fair,[33] peaceable, not grumblers, not double-tongued, not irascible,[34] for anger distracts a reasonable man,[35] who

---

Most significantly this disciplinary activity is placed explicitly at the eucharist. Although K does not make this explicit, that would seem to be the context of the activity here. However it is to be noted that the arguments would seem to be less about the distribution of sacred food but of food in general. We may imagine *sportulae* being prepared and distributed at the altar on the same occasion and in the same context that sacred food is distributed. Hence there is a need for jealousy and dispute to be policed (as any parish priest who has presided over the distribution of harvest offerings will know well). By the time of the construction of the *Didasc.* the distribution of offerings has been separated from the distribution of eucharistic food and so the disciplinary provisions are brought to apply to the matter of honour in seating, rather than honour in the receipt of foodstuffs.

[24] The word "evil" here is not in the text but is supplied to make sense.

[25] Cf. *Canones Hippolyti* 37.

[26] Cf. 2 Tim 4:5.

[27] The appearance of this number is not absolutely certain. See the discussion in the introduction at 3.6.3.

[28] Deut 19:15; Matt 18:16; 2 Cor 8:1. Since none of these passages exactly cited, it is not clear which is intended. Faivre, "Apostolicité", *ReScRel* 43-44, interestingly suggests that, in view of the disciplinary context, Deut 17 lies behind this provision.

[29] Cf. *1 Clem.* 44.3.

[30] Cf. 1 Tim 3:12.

[31] Cf. 1 Tim 3:12.

[32] Cf. 1 Tim 3:2.

[33] Cf. 1 Tim 3:3.

[34] Cf. Tit 1:7.

neither accept the persons of the rich nor oppress the poor, not given to much use of wine,[36] intelligent, 3 good at exhorting to secret works, as they oblige the brothers who have possessions to open their hands, and themselves generous, communicative, honoured by the congregation with all honour, esteem and fear, carefully mindful of those who are conducting themselves in a disorderly manner, warning some, encouraging others, threatening others, but leaving the scoffers entirely alone, mindful that those opposed to reason, the scoffers and the abusive have resisted Christ.

21

1 Kephas said: Three widows should be appointed. Two are to continue in prayer[37] for all who are in temptation and for revelations concerning whatever is necessary. 2 One is to assist women who are being troubled by sickness.[38] She is to be a good minister, discreet in communicating what is necessary to the presbyters,[39] not avaricious, not fond of much wine, so that she may be sober in her service during the night, and in whatever other acts of charity[40] she desires to perform. These foremost treasures of the Lord are good.

22

1 Andrew said: Deacons perform noble deeds; they go around everywhere, night and day, neither looking down upon the poor or paying undue attention to the wealthy, recognising any who is oppressed and not excluding him from the collections, 2 obliging those who are able to put something aside for good works, having in mind the words of our teacher: "You saw me hungry, and fed me not." Those who serve nobly and blamelessly set aside for themselves the position of the pastorate.

23

1 Philip said: The layman should be content to concern himself with the ordinances of the laity,[41] submitting to whose who attend to the altar. 2 Each

---

[35] Prov 15:1. Whereas this may look like a later gloss, the same text is quoted, in the same context (though with regard to the appointment of bishops rather than deacons) by *Didasc.* 2.3.

[36] Cf. 1 Tim 3:8.

[37] Cf. 1 Tim 5:5.

[38] Cf. *Canones Hippolyti* 9: widows are to pray, to care for the sick and to fast.

[39] Cf. *Didasc.* 2.44.3 (of the deacon and the bishop).

[40] Cf. 1 Tim 5:10.

[41] Cf. *1 Clem.* 40.5.

should please God in his own position,[42] not striving with each other in the matter of rank, each in that to which he was called and is placed by Christ.[43] 3 None should obstruct the path of another, for neither do the angels anything contrary to their station,[44] or take another`s route.

24

Andrew said: It would be useful, brothers, to establish ministry for the women.

25

Peter said: We have previously legislated. Let us carefully explain regarding the offering of the Body and the Blood.

26

John said: You are forgetting, brothers, that when the teacher requested the bread and the cup and blessed them saying: This is my Body and Blood,[45] he did not permit the women to stand alongside us. Martha said it was on account of Mary because he saw her smiling. Mary said: I did not laugh at this. Previously he said to us, when he was teaching, that the weak would be saved through the strong.

27

Kephas said: Some things should be remembered: that women should not pray upright but seated on the ground.[46]

---

[42] Cf. *1 Clem.* 41.1.

[43] Or, if the emendation is not accepted: "in that in which he was called beside God."

[44] Cf. *1 Clem.* 34.5.

[45] This is clearly a loose paraphrase. This in turn indicates, however, that there is no established use of the words of institution in the liturgy.

[46] As Harnack, *Sources*, 27 n. 13 notes, this is a strange statement, as there is ample evidence of women praying in a standing position. I can make one suggestion only which might cast some light.

In the *Quaestiones Bartholomaei* Mary is gathered with the disciples. When they come to pray, she says: "Let us stand up in prayer." However, when the apostles stand behind Mary she suggests that Peter should not stand behind her but before, and quotes 1 Cor 11:3 as from the Lord: "The head of the man is Christ, but the head of the woman is the man." Eventually they prevail upon her and she stands, spreads out her hands and prays. Thus a standing position is established, but there is debate concerning the propriety of women leading prayer. It seems that Mary is only permitted to lead prayer on this occasion on the basis of her particular significance as the one who bore Jesus, which is the subject which the apostles wish to discuss.

After they pray she says:

28

James said: How then can we establish ministry[47] for the women, except the ministry of supporting women in need?[48]

"Let us sit down on the ground. Come, Peter, chief of the apostles, sit on my right hand and put your left hand under my shoulder. And you, Andrew, do the same on my left hand. And you, chaste John, hold my breast. And you, Bartholomew, place your knees on my shoulders and press close my back so that, when I begin to speak, my limbs are not loosed." Thus she sits, as Peter in K states that women should. It seems that this is related to prophecy; are the apostles perhaps holding her down lest the mantic manifestations of a prophet under ecstasy become too extreme? Is it possible that the agraphon cited by K originally related not to the prayer of women but to their prophesying, insisting that women should prophesy seated? The holding of the arms is interesting, as the same is found in Hermas, *Vis.* 1.3.4, where the old lady (who, incidentally, is likewise seated, a posture arguably derived from the circles of magic and ritual; on which see E. Petersen, "Beiträge zur Interpretation der Visionen im 'Pastor Hermae'", *Frühkirche Judentum und Gnosis* [Rome 1959] 254-270) is carried away being held by the arms when she has finished her revelation.

The fact that this illuminating parallel is to be found in *Quaestiones Bartholomaei* is significant since, as A.G. Brock, "What's in a name: the competition for authority in early Christian texts", *SBL 1998 seminar papers I* (Atlanta 1998) 106-124, at 121-123, observes, this text is intended to exalt Peter's authority as a cipher for "apostolic" orthodoxy over female disciples in much the way that K does.

The versions are clearly puzzled by the statement. Syriac completely alters the direction, stating instead that women should approach the sacrifice with heads covered. Sahidic makes the statement the opposite of that here. In both cases there seems to be some attempt to correct and update the statement, though Maclean, *Ancient Church Orders*, 27-28, partly on the basis that a similar direction to that found in the Syriac is found in *Apostolic Constitutions* 2.47 and elsewhere in the church-order literature, reckons the Syriac reading original. However, the very existence of these parallels indicates an attempt to correct the text and Maclean's suggestion of an erroneous reading, as noted in the textual commentary, does not explain the extensive departure from V and Latin.

[47] An indication of the development of the deaconess order is indicated in that Lat. reads "It would be useful to appoint the deaconess order for women" and S reads "to designate women to be deaconesses." As argued in the introduction, K knows no such order, but such knowledge is assumed on the part of the versions.

[48] This may also be translated as "Support those who are in chains." If this translation is followed, then this must refer to some form of exorcistic ministry, as no kind of persecution is apparently envisaged. But a ministry of healing and evangelism, rather than social support, hardly seems to be what K is envisaging for women. See, for discussion, though with a different conclusion, Faivre, "Apostolicité", 60-61.

29

Philip said: This, brothers, concerning sharing: whoever does a deed gathers for himself a good treasury. Whoever gathers treasure in the kingdom is reckoned an enrolled labourer by God.

30

Peter said: Brothers, we do not command these things as those who have the power to compel, but as having a command from the Lord. We ask you to keep the commandments, neither detracting from them or adding, in the name of Our Lord, to whom be glory for ever. Amen.

Appendix A: The text of E as given by Schermann

Ἐπιτομὴ ὅρων τῶν ἁγίων ἀποστόλων καθολικῆς παραδόσεως.

Ἰωάννης εἶπεν· ὁδοὶ δύο εἰσί, μία τῆς ζωῆς καὶ μία τοῦ θανάτου, καὶ διαφορὰ πολλὴ τῶν δύο. ἡ οὖν τῆς ζωῆς ἐστιν αὕτη· πρῶτον ἀγαπήσεις τὸν θεὸν τὸν ποιήσαντά σε ἐξ ὅλης σου καρδίας· δεύτερον ἀγαπήσεις τὸν πλησίον σου ὡς ἑαυτόν.

Ματθαῖος εἶπεν· πᾶν ὃ μὴ θέλῃς γενέσθαι σοι, μηδὲ σὺ ἄλλῳ ποιήσῃς, τουτέστιν ὃ σὺ μισεῖς ἄλλῳ μὴ ποιήσῃς.

Πέτρος εἶπεν· οὐ φονεύσεις, οὐ ποιήσεις ἁμαρτίαν τινὰ τῇ σαρκί σου, οὐ κλέψεις, οὐ μαγεύσεις, οὐ φαρμακεύσεις, οὐκ ἐπιθυμήσεις τὰ τοῦ πλησίον σου. οὐκ ἐπιορκήσεις, οὐ ψευδομαρτυρήσεις, οὐ κακολογήσεις, οὐδὲ μνησικακήσεις, οὐκ ἔσῃ δίγνωμος οὐδὲ δίγλωσσος· οὐκ ἔσται σοι λόγος κενός, οὐκ ἔσῃ πλεονέκτης, οὐχ ἅρπαξ οὐδὲ ὑποκριτής, οὐκ ἔσῃ κακοήθης, οὐχ ὑπερήφανος· οὐ λήψῃ βουλὴν πονηρὰν κατὰ τὸν πλησίον σου· οὐ μισήσεις πάντα ἄνθρωπον, ἀλλ᾽ οὓς μὲν ἐλέγξεις, περὶ ὧν δὲ καὶ προσεύξῃ, οὓς δὲ ἀγαπήσεις ὑπὲρ τὴν ψυχήν σου.

Ἀνδρέας εἶπε· φεῦγε ἀπὸ παντὸς κακοῦ καὶ ἀπὸ παντὸς ὁμοίου αὐτοῦ· μὴ γίνου ὀργίλος μήτε ζηλωτής, μὴ ἐριστικὸς μηδὲ μανικός· ὁδηγεῖ γὰρ ταῦτα πρὸς τὸν φόνον.

Φίλιππος εἶπε· μὴ γίνου ἐπιθυμητής, ὁδηγεῖ γὰρ πρὸς τὴν πορνείαν.

Σίμων εἶπεν· μὴ γίνου αἰσχρολόγος μηδὲ ὑψηλόφθαλμος. ἐκ γὰρ τούτων μοιχεῖαι γίνονται.

Ἰάκωβος εἶπεν· μὴ γίνου οἰωνοσκόπος, μὴ ἐπαοιδός, μὴ μαθητικὸς μήτε ἃ ἐρεῖ περικαθαίρων, μήτε θέλε αὐτὰ εἰδέναι μηδὲ ἀκούειν· ἐκ γὰρ τούτων ἁπάντων εἰδωλολατρίαι γίνονται.

Ναθαναὴλ εἶπεν· μὴ γίνου ψεύστης, μηδὲ φιλάργυρος, μηδὲ κενόδοξος· ἐκ τούτων ἁπάντων κλοπαὶ γίνονται· μὴ γίνου γόγγυσος, μὴ θυμώδης, μὴ αὐθάδης, μήτε πονηρόφρων· ἐκ γὰρ τούτων ἁπάντων βλασφημίαι γίνονται. Ἴσθι δὲ πραΰς, ἐπειδὴ πραεῖς κληρονομήσουσι τὴν βασιλείαν τοῦ θεοῦ. Γίνου μακρόθυμος, ἐλεήμων, εἰρηνοποιός, καθαρὸς τὴν καρδίαν, ἄκακος, ἥσυχος, ἀγαθός, φυλάσσων καὶ τρέμων τοὺς λόγους τοῦ θεοῦ. Οὐχ ὑψώσεις σεαυτόν, οὐ δώσεις τῇ ψυχῇ σου θράσος, οὐδὲ κολληθήσῃ τῇ ψυχῇ σου μετὰ ὑψηλῶν· ἀλλὰ μετὰ δικαίων καὶ ταπεινῶν. Τὰ συμβαίνοντά σοι ἐνεργήματα ὡς ἀγαθὰ προσδέξαι, εἰδὼς ὅτι ἄτερ τοῦ θεοῦ οὐδὲν γίνεται.

Θωμᾶς εἶπεν· τὸν λαλοῦντά σοι τὸν λόγον τοῦ θεοῦ καὶ παραίτιόν σοι γινόμενον τῆς ζωῆς καὶ δόντα σοι τὴν ἐν κυρίῳ σφραγῖδα ἀγαπήσεις αὐτὸν ὡς κόρην ὀφθαλμοῦ σου, μνησθήσῃ αὐτοῦ νυκτὸς καὶ ἡμέρας, τιμήσεις δὲ αὐτὸν ὡς κύριον, ὅθεν γὰρ Ἰησοῦς Χριστὸς λαλεῖται, ἐκεῖ κύριος ἐστιν. Ἐκζητήσεις δὲ αὐτὸν καὶ τοὺς λοιποὺς ἁγίους, ἵνα ἐπαναπαυσθῇς τοῖς λόγοις αὐτῶν· κολλώμενος γὰρ ἁγίους ἅγιος ἁγιασθήσεται. Ὁ γὰρ κύριος ἠξίωσέ σε δι᾽ αὐτοῦ δοθῆναι πνευματικὴν τροφὴν καὶ ζωὴν αἰώνιον.

Κηφᾶς εἶπεν· οὐ ποιήσεις σχίσμα, εἰρηνεύσεις δὲ μαχομένους, κρινεῖς δικαίως, οὐ λήψῃ πρόσωπον ἐλέγξαι τινὰ ἐπὶ παραπτώματι, ἰσότης γὰρ ἐστι παρὰ θεῷ· ἐν προσευχῇ σου μὴ διψυχήσῃς. Ἐὰν ἔσται ἔχειν σε ἀπὸ τῶν χειρῶν σου, δὸς εἰς ἄφεσιν ἁμαρτιῶν σου. Οὐκ ἀποστραφήσῃ ἐνδεούμενον, συγκοινωνήσεις δὲ πάντα τοῖς ἀδελφοῖς σου καὶ οὐκ ἐρεῖς ἴδια εἶναι· εἰ γὰρ ἐν τῷ θανάτῳ κοινωνοί ἐστε, πόσῳ μᾶλλον ἐν τοῖς θνητοῖς;

Βαρθολομαῖος εἶπεν· οὐκ ἄρῃς τὴν χεῖρά σου ἀπὸ τοῦ υἱοῦ οὐδὲ ἀπὸ τῆς θυγατρός σου, ἀλλ᾽ ἅμα ἀπὸ νεότητος διδάξεις αὐτοὺς τὸν φόβον τοῦ κυρίου. Ἐξομολογήσῃ τὰ παραπτώματά σου, οὐκ ἐγκαταλείψῃ ἐντολὰς κυρίου, οὐ προσελεύσῃ ἐν προσευχῇ σου ἐν συνειδήσει πονηρᾷ, μισήσεις πᾶσαν ὑπόκρισιν καὶ πᾶν ὃ μὴ ἀρέσκει κυρίῳ, φυλάξῃ δὲ ἃ παρέλαβες μήτε προστιθεὶς μήτε ὑφαιρῶν. Αὕτη ἐστὶν ἡ ὁδὸς τῆς ζωῆς.

Appendix B: A synoptic table of TWT in D, K and E

D	K	E
ὁδοὶ	Ἰωάννης εἶπεν· ὁδοὶ	Ἰωάννης εἶπεν· ὁδοὶ
δύο εἰσί, μία τῆς	δύο εἰσί, μία τῆς	δύο εἰσί, μία τῆς
ζωῆς καὶ μία τοῦ	ζωῆς καὶ μία τοῦ	ζωῆς καὶ μία τοῦ
θανάτου, διαφορὰ	θανάτου, διαφορὰ	θανάτου, καὶ
δὲ πολλὴ μεταξὺ	δὲ πολλὴ μεταξὺ	διαφορὰ πολλὴ
τῶν δύο ὁδῶν.	τῶν δύο ὁδῶν.	τῶν δύο.
ἡ μὲν οὖν ὁδὸς τῆς	ἡ μὲν γὰρ ὁδὸς τῆς	ἡ οὖν τῆς
ζωῆς ἐστιν αὕτη·	ζωῆς ἐστιν αὕτη·	ζωῆς ἐστιν αὕτη·
πρῶτον ἀγαπήσεις	πρῶτον ἀγαπήσεις	πρῶτον ἀγαπήσεις
τὸν θεὸν τὸν	τὸν θεὸν τὸν	τὸν θεὸν τὸν
ποιήσαντά σε,	ποιήσαντά σε ἐξ	ποιήσαντά σε ἐξ
	ὅλης τῆς καρδίας	ὅλης σου καρδίας·
	σου καὶ δοξάσεις	
	τὸν λυτρωσάμενόν	
	σε ἐκ θανάτου,	
	ἥτις ἐστὶν ἐντολὴ	
	πρώτη. .	
δεύτερον	δευτέρα δὲ·	δεύτερον
τὸν	ἀγαπήσεις τὸν	ἀγαπήσεις τὸν
πλησίον σου ὡς	πλησίον σου ὡς	πλησίον σου ὡς
σεαυτόν	ἑαυτόν, ἥτις ἐστὶν	ἑαυτόν.
	ἐντολὴ δευτέρα, ἐν	
	οἷς ὅλος ὁ νόμος	
	κρέμαται καὶ	
	προφῆται.	
	Ματθαῖος εἶπεν·	Ματθαῖος εἶπεν·
πάντα δὲ ὅσα ἐὰν	πάντα ὅσα	πᾶν ὃ
μὴ θελήσῃς μὴ	μὴ θέλῃς σοι	μὴ θέλῃς
γίνεσθαί σοι, καὶ	γενέσθαι, σὺ μηδὲ	γενέσθαι σοι, μηδὲ
σὺ ἄλλῳ μὴ ποίει.	ἄλλῳ ποιήσῃς·	σὺ ἄλλῳ ποιήσῃς,
τούτων δὲ τῶν	τούτων δὲ τῶν	τουτέστιν ὃ σὺ
λόγων ἡ διδαχή	λόγων τὴν διδαχὴν	μισεῖς ἄλλῳ μὴ
ἐστιν αὕτη·	εἰπε, ἀδελφὲ	ποιήσῃς.
εὐλογεῖτε τοὺς	Πέτρε.	
καταρωμένους ὑμῖν		
καὶ προσεύχεσθε		
ὑπὲρ τῶν ἐχθρῶν		
ὑμῶν, νηστεύετε δὲ		

ὑπὲρ τῶν διωκόντων
ὑμᾶς· ποία γὰρ
χάρις ἐὰν ἀγαπᾶτε
τοὺς ἀγαπῶντας
ὑμᾶς; οὐχὶ καὶ τὰ
ἔθνη τὸ αὐτὸ
ποιοῦσιν; ὑμεῖς δὲ
ἀγαπᾶτε τοὺς
μισοῦντας ὑμᾶς,
καὶ οὐχ ἕξετε
ἐχθρόν.
ἀπέχου τῶν
σαρκικῶν καὶ
σωματικῶν
ἐπιθυμιῶν· ἐάν τίς
σοι δῷς ῥάπισμα
εἰς τὴν δεξιὰν
σιαγόνα, στρέψον
αὐτῷ καὶ τὴν
ἄλλην, καὶ ἔσῃ
τέλειος· ἐὰν
ἀγγαρεύσῃ σέ τις
μίλιον ἕν, ὕπαγε
μετ᾽ αὐτοῦ δύο·
ἐὰν ἄρῃ τις τὸ
ἱμάτιόν σου, δὸς
αὐτῷ καὶ τὸν
χιτῶνα· ἐὰν λάβῃ
τις ἀπό σου τὸ σόν,
μὴ ἀπαίτει· οὐδὲ
γὰρ δύνασαι. παντὶ
τῷ αἰτοῦντί σε
δίδου καὶ μὴ
ἀπαίτει. πᾶσι γὰρ
θέλει δίδοσθαι ὁ
πατὴρ ἐκ τῶν ἰδίων
χαρισμάτων.
μακάριος ὁ διδοὺς
κατὰ τὴν ἐντολήν·
ἀθῷος γάρ ἐστιν.
οὐαὶ τῷ

λαμβάνοντι· εἰ μὲν γὰρ χρείαν ἔχων λαμβάνει τις, ἀθῷος ἔσται· ὁ δὲ μὴ χρείαν ἔχων δώσει δίκην, ἱνατί ἔλαβε καὶ εἰς τί. ἐν συνοχῇ δὲ γενόμενος ἐξετασθήσεται περὶ ὧν ἔπραξε, καὶ οὐκ ἐξελεύσεται ἐκεῖθεν, μέχρις οὗ ἀποδῷ τὸν ἔσχατον κοδράντην. ἀλλὰ καὶ περὶ τούτου δὲ εἴρηται· Ἱδρωσάτω ἐλεημοσύνη σου εἰς τὰς χεῖράς σου, μέχρις ἂν γνῷς, τίνι δῷς.

Δευτέρα δὲ ἐντολὴ τῆς διδαχῆς·	Πέτρος εἶπεν·	Πέτρος εἶπεν·
οὐ φονεύσεις, οὐ μοιχεύσεις, οὐ παιδοφθορήσεις, οὐ πορνεύσεις, οὐ κλέψεις, οὐ μαγεύσεις, οὐ φαρμακεύσεις, οὐ φονεύσεις τέκνον ἐν φθορᾷ οὐδὲ γεννηθὲν ἀποκτενεῖς,	οὐ φονεύσεις, οὐ μοιχεύσεις, οὐ πορνεύσεις, οὐ παιδοφθορήσεις, οὐ κλέψεις, οὐ μαγεύσεις, οὐ φαρμακεύσεις, οὐ φονεύσεις τέκνον ἐν φθορᾷ οὐδὲ γεννηθὲν ἀποκτενεῖς,	οὐ φονεύσεις, οὐ ποιήσεις ἁμαρτίαν τινὰ τῇ σαρκί σου, οὐ κλέψεις, οὐ μαγεύσεις, οὐ φαρμακεύσεις,
οὐκ ἐπιθυμήσεις τὰ τοῦ πλησίον.	οὐκ ἐπιθυμήσεις τὰ τοῦ πλησίον.	οὐκ ἐπιθυμήσεις τὰ τοῦ πλησίον σου.
οὐκ ἐπιορκήσεις, οὐ ψευδομαρτυρήσεις, οὐ κακολογήσεις, οὐδὲ μνησικακήσεις, οὐκ	οὐκ ἐπιορκήσεις, οὐ ψευδομαρτυρήσεις, οὐ κακολογήσεις, οὐδὲ μνησικακήσεις, οὐκ	οὐκ ἐπιορκήσεις, οὐ ψευδομαρτυρήσεις, οὐ κακολογήσεις, οὐδὲ μνησικακήσεις, οὐκ

ἔσῃ διγνώμων οὐδὲ	ἔσῃ δίγνωμος οὐδὲ	ἔσῃ δίγνωμος οὐδὲ
δίγλωσσος· παγὶς	δίγλωσσος· παγὶς	δίγλωσσος·
γὰρ θανάτου	γὰρ θανάτου ἐστιν	
ἡ διγλωσσία· οὐκ	ἡ διγλωσσία· οὐκ	οὐκ
ἔσται ὁ λόγος σου	ἔσται ὁ λόγος σου	ἔσται σοι λόγος
ψευδής, οὐ κενός,	κενὸς οὐδὲ ψευδής.	κενός,
ἀλλὰ		
μεμεστωμένος		
πράξει.		
οὐκ ἔσῃ	οὐκ ἔσῃ	οὐκ ἔσῃ
πλεονέκτης οὐδὲ	πλεονέκτης οὐδὲ	πλεονέκτης, οὐχ
ἅρπαξ οὐδὲ	ἅρπαξ οὐδὲ	ἅρπαξ οὐδὲ
ὑποκριτὴς οὐδὲ	ὑποκριτὴς οὐδὲ	ὑποκριτής, οὐκ ἔσῃ
κακοήθης, οὐδὲ	κακοήθης, οὐδὲ	κακοήθης, οὐχ
ὑπερήφανος· οὐ	ὑπερήφανος· οὐ	ὑπερήφανος· οὐ
λήψῃ βουλὴν	λήψῃ βουλὴν	λήψῃ βουλὴν
πονηρὰν κατὰ τοῦ	πονηρὰν κατὰ τοῦ	πονηρὰν κατὰ τὸν
πλησίον σου· οὐ	πλησίον σου· οὐ	πλησίον σου· οὐ
μισήσεις πάντα	μισήσεις πάντα	μισήσεις πάντα
ἄνθρωπον, ἀλλὰ	ἄνθρωπον, ἀλλ᾽	ἄνθρωπον, ἀλλ᾽
οὓς μὲν ἐλέγξεις,	οὓς μὲν ἐλέγξεις,	οὓς μὲν ἐλέγξεις,
	οὓς δὲ ἐλεήσεις,	
περὶ δὲ ὧν	περὶ ὧν δὲ	περὶ ὧν δὲ καὶ
προσεύξῃ, οὓς δὲ	προσεύξῃ, οὓς δὲ	προσεύξῃ, οὓς δὲ
ἀγαπήσεις ὑπὲρ	ἀγαπήσεις ὑπὲρ	ἀγαπήσεις ὑπὲρ
τὴν ψυχήν σου.	τὴν ψυχήν σου.	τὴν ψυχήν σου.
	Ἀνδρέας εἶπεν·	Ἀνδρέας εἶπε·
τέκνον μου, φεῦγε	τέκνον μου, φεῦγε	φεῦγε
ἀπὸ παντὸς	ἀπὸ παντὸς	ἀπὸ παντὸς
πονηροῦ καὶ ἀπὸ	πονηροῦ καὶ ἀπὸ	κακοῦ καὶ ἀπὸ
παντὸς ὁμοίου	παντὸς ὁμοίου	παντὸς ὁμοίου
αὐτοῦ· μὴ γίνου	αὐτοῦ· μὴ γίνου	αὐτοῦ· μὴ γίνου
ὀργίλος· ὁδηγεῖ	ὀργίλος· ὁδηγεῖ	ὀργίλος
γὰρ ἡ ὀργὴ πρὸς	γὰρ ἡ ὀργὴ πρὸς	
τὸν φόνον,	τὸν φόνον. ἔστι	
	γὰρ δαιμόνιον	
	ἀρρενικὸν ὁ θυμός.	
μηδὲ ζηλωτὴς	μὴ γίνου ζηλωτὴς	μήτε ζηλωτής,
μήδὲ ἐριστικὸς	μήδὲ ἐριστικὸς	μὴ ἐριστικὸς
μηδὲ θυμικός·	μηδὲ θυμαντικός·	μηδὲ μανικός·
ἐκ γὰρ τούτων	ἐκ γὰρ τούτων	ὁδηγεῖ γὰρ ταῦτα

ἁπάντων φόνοι γεννῶνται.

τέκνον μου, μὴ γίνου ἐπιθυμητής, ὁδηγεῖ γὰρ ἡ ἐπιθυμία πρὸς τὴν πορνείαν,

φόνος γεννᾶται.

Φίλιππος εἶπεν· τέκνον μου, μὴ γίνου ἐπιθυμητής. ὁδηγεῖ γὰρ ἡ ἐπιθυμία πρὸς τὴν πορνείαν και ἕλκει τοὺς ἀνθρώπους πρὸς ἑαυτήν. Ἔστι γὰρ θηλυκὸν δαιμόνιον ἡ ἐπιθυμία, καὶ ὃ μὲν μετ᾽ ὀργῆς, ὃ δὲ μεθ᾽ ἡδονῆς ἀπόλλυσι τοὺς εἰσερχομένους αὐτά. Ὁδὸς δὲ πονηροῦ πνεύματος ἁμαρτία ψυχῆς, καὶ ὅταν βραχεῖαν εἴσδυσιν σχῇ ἐν αὐτῷ, πλατύνει αὐτὴν καὶ ἄγει ἐπὶ πάντα τὰ κακὰ τὴν ψυχὴν ἐκείνην καὶ οὐκ ἐᾷ διαβλέψαι τὸν ἄνθρωπον καὶ ἰδεῖν τὴν ἀλήθειαν. Ὁ θυμὸς ὑμῶν μέτρον ἐχέτω καὶ ἐν βραχεῖ διαστήματι αὐτὸν ἡνιοχεῖτε καὶ ἀνακρούετε, ἵνα μὴ ἐμβάλλῃ ὑμᾶς εἰς ἔργον πονηρόν. Θυμὸς γὰρ καὶ ἡδονὴ πονηρὰ ἐπὶ πολὺ παραμένουσα κατὰ

πρὸς τὸν φόνον.

Φίλιππος εἶπε· μὴ γίνου ἐπιθυμητής, ὁδηγεῖ γὰρ πρὸς τὴν πορνείαν.

μηδὲ
αἰσχρολόγος μηδὲ
ὑψηλόφθαλμος. ἐκ
γὰρ τούτων
ἁπάντων μοιχεῖαι
γεννῶνται.

τέκνον μου, μὴ
γίνου οἰωνοσκόπος,
ἐπειδὴ ὁδηγεῖ εἰς
τὴν εἰδωλολατρίαν,
μηδὲ ἐπαοιδός,
μηδὲ μαθηματικὸς
μηδὲ
περικαθαίρων,
μηδὲ θέλε αὐτὰ
βλέπειν·
ἐκ γὰρ
τούτων ἁπάντων
εἰδωλολατρία
γεννᾶται.

τέκνον μου, μὴ
γίνου ψεύστης,
ἐπειδὴ ὁδηγεῖ τὸ
ψεῦσμα εἰς τὴν

ἐπίτασιν δαιμόνια
γίνεται, καὶ ὅταν
ἐπιτρέψῃ αὐτοῖς ὁ
ἄνθρωπος,
οἰδαίνουσιν ἐν τῇ
ψυχῇ αὐτοῦ καὶ
γίνονται μείζονες
καὶ ἐπάγουσιν
αὐτὸν εἰς ἔργα
ἄδικα καὶ
ἐπιγελῶσιν αὐτῷ
καὶ ἥδονται ἐπὶ τῇ
ἀπωλείᾳ τοῦ
ἀνθρώπου.
Σίμων εἶπεν·
τέκνον, μὴ γίνου
αἰσχρολόγος μηδὲ
ὑψηλόφθαλμος. ἐκ
γὰρ τούτων
μοιχεῖαι
γίνονται.
Ἰάκωβος εἶπεν·
τέκνον μου, μὴ
γίνου οἰωνοσκόπος,
ἐπειδὴ ὁδηγεῖ εἰς
τὴν εἰδωλολατρίαν,
μηδὲ ἐπαοιδός,
μηδὲ μαθηματικὸς
μηδὲ
περικαθαίρων,
μηδὲ θέλε αὐτὰ
ἰδεῖν μηδὲ
ἀκούειν· ἐκ γὰρ
τούτων ἁπάντων
εἰδωλολατρεῖαι
γεννῶνται.
Ναθαναὴλ εἶπεν·
τέκνον μου, μὴ
γίνου ψεύστης,
ἐπειδὴ ὁδηγεῖ τὸ
ψεῦσμα ἐπὶ τὴν

Σίμων εἶπεν·
μὴ γίνου
αἰσχρολόγος μηδὲ
ὑψηλόφθαλμος. ἐκ
γὰρ τούτων
μοιχεῖαι
γίνονται.
Ἰάκωβος εἶπεν·
μὴ
γίνου οἰωνοσκόπος,
μὴ ἐπαοιδός,
μὴ μαθητικὸς
μήτε ἃ ἐρεῖ
περικαθαίρων,
μήτε θέλε αὐτὰ
εἰδέναι μηδὲ
ἀκούειν· ἐκ γὰρ
τούτων ἁπάντων
εἰδωλολατρίαι
γίνονται.
Ναθαναὴλ εἶπεν·
μὴ
γίνου ψεύστης,

κλοπήν, μηδὲ φιλάργυρος, μηδὲ κενόδοξος· ἐκ γὰρ τούτων ἁπάντων κλοπαὶ γεννῶνται. Τέκνον μου, μὴ γίνου γόγγυσος, ἐπειδὴ ὁδηγεῖ εἰς τὴν βλασφημίαν, μηδὲ αὐθάδης, μηδὲ πονηρόφρων· ἐκ γὰρ τούτων ἁπάντων βλασφημίαι γεννῶνται. Ἴσθι δὲ πραΰς, ἐπεὶ οἱ πραεῖς κληρονομήσουσι τὴν γῆν.

Γίνου μακρόθυμος, ἐλεήμων καὶ ἄκακος καὶ ἡσύχιος καὶ ἀγαθός καὶ τρέμων τοὺς λόγους διὰ παντός οὓς ἤκουσας. Οὐχ ὑψώσεις σεαυτόν, οὐδὲ δώσεις τῇ ψυχῇ σου θράσος. οὐ κολληθήσεται ἡ ψυχή σου μετὰ ὑψηλῶν, ἀλλὰ μετὰ δικαίων καὶ ταπεινῶν ἀναστραφήσῃ. Τὰ

κλοπήν, μηδὲ φιλάργυρος, μηδὲ κενόδοξος· ἐκ τούτων ἁπάντων κλοπαὶ γεννῶνται. Τέκνον μου, μὴ γίνου γόγγυσος, ἐπειδὴ ἄγει πρὸς τὴν βλασφημίαν, μηδὲ αὐθάδης, μηδὲ πονηρόφρων· ἐκ γὰρ τούτων ἁπάντων βλασφημίαι γεννῶνται. Ἴσθι δὲ πραΰς, ἐπειδὴ πραεῖς κληρονομήσουσι τὴν βασιλείαν τῶν οὐρανῶν.

Γίνου μακρόθυμος, ἐλεήμων, εἰρηνοποιός, καθαρὸς τῇ καρδίᾳ ἀπὸ παντὸς κακοῦ, ἄκακος καὶ ἡσύχιος, ἀγαθός καὶ φυλάσσων καὶ τρέμων τοὺς λόγους οὓς ἤκουσας. Οὐχ ὑψώσεις σεαυτόν, οὐδὲ δώσεις τὴν ψυχήν σου μετὰ ὑψηλῶν ἀλλὰ μετὰ δικαίων καὶ ταπεινῶν ἀναστραφήσῃ. Τὰ

μηδὲ φιλάργυρος, μηδὲ κενόδοξος· ἐκ τούτων ἁπάντων κλοπαὶ γίνονται· μὴ γίνου γόγγυσος, μὴ θυμώδης, μὴ αὐθάδης, μήτε πονηρόφρων· ἐκ γὰρ τούτων ἁπάντων βλασφημίαι γίνονται. Ἴσθι δὲ πραΰς, ἐπειδὴ πραεῖς κληρονομήσουσι τὴν βασιλείαν τοῦ θεοῦ.

Γίνου μακρόθυμος, ἐλεήμων, εἰρηνοποιός, καθαρὸς τὴν καρδίαν, ἄκακος, ἥσυχος, ἀγαθός, φυλάσσων καὶ τρέμων τοὺς λόγους τοῦ θεοῦ. Οὐχ ὑψώσεις σεαυτόν, οὐ δώσεις τῇ ψυχῇ σου θράσος, οὐδὲ κολληθήσῃ τῇ ψυχῇ σου μετὰ ὑψηλῶν· ἀλλὰ μετὰ δικαίων καὶ ταπεινῶν. Τὰ

δὲ συμβαίνοντά σοι	δὲ συμβαίνοντά σοι	συμβαίνοντά σοι
ἐνεργήματα ὡς	ἐνεργήματα ὡς	ἐνεργήματα ὡς
ἀγαθὰ προσδέξῃ,	ἀγαθὰ προσδέξῃ,	ἀγαθὰ προσδέξαι,
εἰδὼς ὅτι ἄτερ	εἰδὼς ὅτι ἄτερ	εἰδὼς ὅτι ἄτερ τοῦ
θεοῦ οὐδὲν γίνεται.	θεοῦ οὐδὲν γίνεται.	θεοῦ οὐδὲν γίνεται.
	Θωμᾶς εἶπεν·	Θωμᾶς εἶπεν·
τέκνον μου, τοῦ	τέκνον, τὸν	τὸν
λαλοῦντός σοι τὸν	λαλοῦντά σοι τὸν	λαλοῦντά σοι τὸν
λόγον τοῦ θεοῦ	λόγον τοῦ θεοῦ καὶ	λόγον τοῦ θεοῦ καὶ
	παραίτιόν σοι	παραίτιόν σοι
	γινόμενον τῆς ζωῆς	γινόμενον τῆς ζωῆς
	καὶ δόντα σοι τὴν	καὶ δόντα σοι τὴν
	ἐν κυρίῳ σφραγῖδα	ἐν κυρίῳ σφραγῖδα
	ἀγαπήσεις	ἀγαπήσεις αὐτὸν
	ὡς κόρην ὀφθαλμοῦ	ὡς κόρην ὀφθαλμοῦ
μνησθήσῃ	σου, μνησθήσῃ	σου, μνησθήσῃ
νυκτὸς καὶ	αὐτοῦ νύκτα καὶ	αὐτοῦ νυκτὸς καὶ
ἡμέρας, τιμήσεις	ἡμέραν, τιμήσεις	ἡμέρας, τιμήσεις
δὲ αὐτὸν ὡς	αὐτὸν ὡς τὸν	δὲ αὐτὸν ὡς
κύριον. Ὅθεν γὰρ	κύριον. Ὅθεν γὰρ	κύριον, ὅθεν γὰρ
ἡ κυριότης	ἡ κυριότης	Ἰησοῦς Χριστὸς
λαλεῖται, ἐκεῖ	λαλεῖται, ἐκεῖ	λαλεῖται, ἐκεῖ
κύριός ἐστιν.	κύριός ἐστιν.	κύριός ἐστιν.
Ἐκζητήσεις δὲ καθ'	Ἐκζητήσεις δὲ	Ἐκζητήσεις δὲ
ἡμέραν τὰ	το	αὐτὸν
πρόσωπα τῶν	πρόσωπον αὐτοῦ	
ἁγίων,	καθ' ἡμέραν καὶ	καὶ
	τοὺς λοιποὺς	τοὺς λοιποὺς
ἵνα	ἁγίους, ἵνα	ἁγίους, ἵνα
ἀπαναπαῇς τοῖς	ἐπαναπαύσῃ τοῖς	ἐπαναπαυσθῇς τοῖς
λόγοις αὐτῶν.	λόγοις αὐτῶν·	λόγοις αὐτῶν·
	κολλώμενος γὰρ	κολλώμενος γὰρ
	ἁγίους ἅγιος	ἁγίους ἅγιος
	ἁγιασθήσῃ.	ἁγιασθήσεται.
	Τιμήσεις δὲ αὐτὸν	
	καθ' ὃ δυνατὸς εἶ	
	ἐκ τοῦ ἱδρῶτός σου	
	καὶ ἐκ τοῦ πόνου	
	τῶν χειρῶν σου.	
	Εἰ γὰρ ὁ κύριος δι'	Ὁ γὰρ κύριος
	αὐτοῦ ἠξίωσέν σοι	ἠξίωσέ σε δι' αὐτοῦ

	δοθῆναι πνευματικὴν τροφὴν καὶ ποτὸν καὶ ζωὴν αἰώνιον, σὺ ὀφείλεις πολὺ μᾶλλον τὴν φθαρτὴν καὶ πρόσκαιρον προσφέρειν τροφήν. ἄξιοσ γὰρ ὁ ἐργάτης τοῦ μισθοῦ αὐτοῦ, καὶ βοῦν ἀλοῶντα οὐ φιμώσεις καὶ οὐδεὶς φυτεύει ἀμπελῶνα καὶ ἐκ τοῦ καρποῦ αὐτοῦ οὐκ ἐσθίει.	δοθῆναι πνευματικὴν τροφὴν καὶ ζωὴν αἰώνιον.
οὐ ποιήσεις σχίσμα, εἰρηνεύσεις δὲ μαχομένους, κρινεῖς δικαίως, οὐ λήψῃ πρόσωπον ἐλέγξαι ἐπὶ παραπτώμασιν.	Κηφᾶς εἶπεν· οὐ ποιήσεις σχίσματα, εἰρηνεύσεις δὲ μαχομένους, κρινεῖς δικαίως, οὐ λήψῃ πρόσωπον ἐλέγξαι τινὰ ἐπὶ παραπτώματι, οὐ γὰρ ἰσχύει πλοῦτος παρὰ κυρίῳ· οὐ γὰρ ἀξία προσκρίνει οὐδὲ κάλλος ὠφελεῖ, ἀλλ' ἰσότης ἐστι πάντων παρ' αὐτῷ.	Κηφᾶς εἶπεν· οὐ ποιήσεις σχίσμα, εἰρηνεύσεις δὲ μαχομένους, κρινεῖς δικαίως, οὐ λήψῃ πρόσωπον ἐλέγξαι τινὰ ἐπὶ παραπτώματι, ἰσότης γὰρ ἐστι παρὰ θεῷ·
οὐ διψυχήσεις πότερον ἔσται ἢ οὐ. Μὴ γίνου πρὸς μὲν τὸ λαβεῖν ἐκτείνων τὰς χεῖρας, πρὸς δὲ τὸ δοῦναι συσπῶν. Ἐὰν ἔχῃς	ἐν προσευχῇ σου μὴ διψυχήσεις πότερον ἔσται ἢ οὐ. Μὴ γίνου πρὸς μὲν τὸ λαβεῖν ἐκτείνων τὰς χεῖρας, πρὸς δὲ τὸ δοῦναι συσπῶν. Ἐὰν ἔχῃς	ἐν προσευχῇ σου μὴ διψυχήσῃς. Ἐὰν ἔσται ἔχειν σε

διὰ τῶν χειρῶν σου, δώσεις λύτρωσιν ἁμαρτιῶν σου. οὐ διστάσεις δοῦναι οὐδὲ διδοὺς γογγύσεις· γνώσῃ γάρ, τίς ἐστιν ὁ τοῦ μισθοῦ καλὸς ἀνταποδότης.	διὰ τῶν χειρῶν σου, δώσεις λύτρωσιν τῶν ἁμαρτιῶν σου. οὐ διστάσεις διδόναι οὐδὲ διδοὺς γογγύσεις· γνώσῃ γάρ, τίς ἐστιν ὁ τοῦ μισθοῦ καλὸς ἀνταποδότης.	ἀπὸ τῶν χειρῶν σου, δὸς εἰς ἄφεσιν ἁμαρτιῶν σου.
Οὐκ ἀποστραφήσῃ τὸν ἐνδεούμενον, συγκοινωνήσεις δὲ πάντα τῷ ἀδελφῷ σου καὶ οὐκ ἐρεῖς ἴδια εἶναι· εἰ γὰρ ἐν τῷ ἀθανάτῳ κοινωνοί ἐστε, πόσῳ μᾶλλον ἐν τοῖς θνητοῖς;	Οὐκ ἀποστραφήσῃ ἐνδεούμενον, κοινωνήσεις δὲ ἁπάντων τῷ ἀδελφῷ σου καὶ οὐκ ἐρεῖς ἴδια εἶναι· εἰ γὰρ ἐν τῷ ἀθανάτῳ κοινωνοί ἐστε, πόσῳ μᾶλλον ἐν τοῖς φθαρτοῖς;	Οὐκ ἀποστραφήσῃ ἐνδεούμενον, συγκοινωνήσεις δὲ πάντα τοῖς ἀδελφοῖς σου καὶ οὐκ ἐρεῖς ἴδια εἶναι· εἰ γὰρ ἐν τῷ θανάτῳ κοινωνοί ἐστε, πόσῳ μᾶλλον ἐν τοῖς θνητοῖς;
οὐκ ἄρῃς τὴν χεῖρά σου ἀπὸ τοῦ υἱοῦ σου ἢ ἀπὸ τῆς θυγατρός σου, αλλὰ ἀπὸ νεότητος διδάξεις αὐτοὺς τὸν φόβον τοῦ θεοῦ. οὐκ ἐπιτάξεις δούλῳ σου ἢ παιδίσκῃ, τοῖς ἐπὶ τὸν αὐτὸν θεὸν ἐλπίζουσιν, ἐν πικρίᾳ σου, μήποτε οὐ μὴ φοβηθήσονται τὸν ἐπ᾽ ἀμφοτέροις θεόν· οὐ γὰρ ἔρχεται κατὰ πρόσωπον καλέσαι, ἀλλ᾽ ἐφ᾽ οὓς τὸ	Βαρθολομαῖος εἶπεν· Ἐρωτῶμεν ὑμᾶς, ἀδελφοί, ὡς ἔτι καιρός ἐστι καὶ ἔχετε εἰς οὓς ἐργάζεσθε μεθ᾽ ἑαυτῶν μὴ ἐκλίπητε ἐν μηδενί, ἐξ οὗ ἂν ἔχητε. Ἐγγυς γὰρ ἡ ἡμέρα κυρίου, ἐν ᾗ συναπολεῖται πάντα σὺν τῷ πονηρῷ· ἥξει γὰρ ὁ κύριος καὶ ὁ μισθὸς αὐτοῦ. Ἑαυτῶν γίνεσθε νομοθέται, ἑαυτῶν γίνεσθε σύμβουλοι ἀγαθοί, θεοδίδακτοι·	Βαρθολομαῖος εἶπεν· οὐκ ἄρῃς τὴν χεῖρά σου ἀπὸ τοῦ υἱοῦ οὐδὲ ἀπὸ τῆς θυγατρός σου, ἀλλ᾽ ἅμα ἀπὸ νεότητος διδάξεις αὐτοὺς τὸν φόβον τοῦ κυρίου. Ἐξομολογήσῃ τὰ

πνεῦμα ἡτοίμασεν, ὑμεῖς δὲ οἱ δοῦλοι ὑποταγήσεσθε τοῖς κυρίοις ὑμῶν ὡς τύπῳ θεοῦ ἐν αἰσχύνῃ καὶ φόβῳ. Μισήσεις πᾶσαν ὑπόκρισιν καὶ πᾶν ὃ μὴ ἀρεστὸν τῷ κυρίου. οὐ μὴ ἐγκαταλίπῃς ἐντολὰς κυρίου,		παραπτώματά σου, οὐκ ἐγκαταλείψῃ ἐντολὰς κυρίου, οὐ προσελεύσῃ ἐν προσευχῇ σου ἐν συνειδήσει πονηρᾷ, μισήσεις πᾶσαν ὑπόκρισιν καὶ πᾶν ὃ μὴ ἀρέσκει κυρίῳ,
φυλάξεις δὲ ἃ παρέλαβες μήτε προστιθεὶς μήτε ἀφαιρῶν.	φυλάξεις ἃ παρέλαβες μήτε προσθεὶς μήτε ὑφαιρῶν.	φυλάξῃ δὲ ἃ παρέλαβες μήτε προστιθεὶς μήτε ὑφαιρῶν.
ἐν ἐκκλησίᾳ ἐξομολογήσῃ τὰ παραπτώματά σου, καὶ οὐ προσελεύσῃ ἐπὶ προσευχήν σου ἐν συνειδήσει πονηρᾷ·		Cf. supra.
Αὕτη ἐστὶν ἡ ὁδὸς τῆς ζωῆς.		Αὕτη ἐστὶν ἡ ὁδὸς τῆς ζωῆς.

Appendix C: K14 with parallel B material

K	B
Βαρθολομαῖος εἶπεν·	καλὸν οὖν ἐστὶν μαθόντα τὰ δικαιώματα τοῦ κυρίου, ὅσα γέγραπται, ἐν τούτοις περιπατεῖν. ὁ γὰρ ταῦτα ποιῶν ἐν τῇ βασιλείᾳ τοῦ θεοῦ δοξασθήσεται· ὁ ἐκεῖνα ἐκλεγόμενος μετὰ τῶν ἔργων αὐτοῦ συναπολεῖται. διὰ τοῦτο ἀνάστασις, διὰ τοῦτο ἀνταπόδομα.
ἐρωτῶμεν ὑμᾶς, ἀδελφοί, ὡς ἔτι καιρός ἐστι καὶ ἔχετε εἰς οὓς ἐργάζεσθε μεθ᾽ ἑαυτῶν μὴ ἐκλίπητε ἐν μηδενί, ἐξ οὗ ἂν ἔχητε.	ἐρωτῶ τοὺς ὑπερέχοντας, εἴ τινά μου γνώμης ἀγαθῆς λαμβάνετε συμβουλίαν· ἔχετε μεθ᾽ ἑαυτῶν εἰς οὓς ἐργάσησθε τὸ καλόν· μὴ ἐλλείπητε.
Ἔγγυς γὰρ ἡ ἡμέρα κυρίου, ἐν ᾗ συναπολεῖται πάντα σὺν τῷ πονηρῷ· ἥξει γὰρ ὁ κύριος καὶ ὁ μισθὸς αὐτοῦ μετ᾽ αὐτοῦ.	ἐγγυς ἡ ἡμέρα ἐν ᾗ συναπολεῖται πάντα τῷ πονηρῷ. ἐγγὺς ὁ κύριος καὶ ὁ μισθὸς αὐτοῦ.
	ἔτι καὶ ἔτι ἐρωτῶ ὑμᾶς·
ἑαυτῶν γίνεσθε νομοθέται, ἑαυτῶν γίνεσθε σύμβουλοι ἀγαθοί,	ἑαυτῶν γίνεσθε νομοθέται ἀγαθοί, ἑαυτῶν μένετε σύμβουλοι πιστοί, ἄρατε ἐξ ὑμῶν πᾶσαν ὑπόκρισιν. ὁ δὲ θεός, ὁ τοῦ παντὸς κόσμου κυριεύων, δῴη ὑμῖν σοφίαν, σύνεσιν, ἐπιστήμην, γνῶσιν τῶν δικαιωμάτων αὐτοῦ, ὑπομονήν.
θεοδίδακτοι· φυλάξεις ἃ παρέλαβες μήτε προσθεὶς μήτε ὑφαιρῶν.	γίνεσθε δὲ θεοδίδακτοι, ἐκζητοῦντες τί ζητεῖ κύριος ἀφ᾽ ὑμῶν, καὶ ποιεῖτει ἵνα εὑρεθῆτε ἐν ἡμέρᾳ κρίσεως.

Appendix D: A synoptic table of TWT in D, K and B*

D	K	B
	Ἰωάννης εἶπεν·	19.1-2b:
ὁδοὶ δύο εἰσί, μία τῆς ζωῆς καὶ μία τοῦ θανάτου,	ὁδοὶ δύο εἰσί, μία τῆς ζωῆς καὶ μία τοῦ θανάτου,	ὁδοὶ δύο εἰσιν διδαχῆς καὶ ἐξουσίας, ἥ τε τοῦ φωτὸς καὶ ἡ τοῦ σκότους.
διαφορὰ δὲ πολλὴ μεταξὺ τῶν δύο ὁδῶν.	διαφορὰ δὲ πολλὴ μεταξὺ τῶν δύο ὁδῶν.	διαφορὰ δὲ πολλὴ τῶν δύο ὁδῶν. ἐφ' ἧς μὲν γὰρ εἰσιν τεταγμένοι φωταγωγοὶ ἄγγελοι τοῦ θεοῦ, ἐφ' ἧς δὲ ἄγγελοι τοῦ σατανᾶ. καὶ ὁ μέν ἐστιν κύριος ἀπὸ αἰώνων καὶ εἰς τοὺς αἰῶνας, ὁ δὲ ἄρχων καιροῦ τοῦ νῦν τῆς ἀνομίας.
ἡ μὲν οὖν ὁδὸς τῆς ζωῆς ἐστιν αὕτη·	ἡ μὲν γὰρ ὁδὸς τῆς ζωῆς ἐστιν αὕτη·	ἡ οὖν ὁδὸς τοῦ φωτός ἐστιν αὕτη· ἐάν τις θέλων ὁδὸν ὁδεύειν ἐπὶ τὸν ὡρισμένον τόπον, σπεύσῃ τοῖς ἔργοις αὐτοῦ. ἔστιν οὖν ἡ δοθεῖσα ἡμῖν γνῶσις τοῦ περιπατεῖν ἐν αὐτῇ τοιαύτη.
πρῶτον ἀγαπήσεις τὸν θεὸν τὸν ποιήσαντά σε,	πρῶτον ἀγαπήσεις τὸν θεὸν τὸν ποιήσαντά σε ἐξ ὅλης τῆς καρδίας	ἀγαπήσεις τὸν ποιήσαντά σε, φοβηθήσῃ τόν σε

* As noted in the introduction the order of topics in B is significantly different from that of D/K. This synopsis follows the order of D/K and shows verbal parallels with B by reorganizing and disordering the B material.

	σοῦ καὶ δοξάσεις τὸν λυτρωσάμενόν σε ἐκ θανάτου, ἥτις ἐστὶν ἐντολὴ πρώτη.	πλάσαντα, δοξάσεις τόν σε λυτρωσάμενον ἐκ θανάτου·
δεύτερον τὸν πλησίον σου ὡς σεαυτόν	δευτέρα δὲ· ἀγαπήσεις τὸν πλησίον σου ὡς ἑαυτόν, ἥτις ἐστὶν ἐντολὴ δευτέρα, ἐν οἷς ὅλος ὁ νόμος κρέμαται καὶ προφῆται.	Cf. 19.5c: ἀγαπήσεις τὸν πλησίον σου ὑπὲρ τὴν ψυχήν σου.
	Ματθαῖος εἶπεν·	
πάντα δὲ ὅσα ἐὰν μὴ θελήσῃς μὴ γίνεσθαί σοι, καὶ σὺ ἄλλῳ μὴ ποίει. τούτων δὲ τῶν λόγων ἡ διδαχή ἐστιν αὕτη· εὐλογεῖτε τοὺς καταρωμένους ὑμῖν καὶ προσεύχεσθε ὑπὲρ τῶν ἐχθρῶν ὑμῶν, νηστεύετε δὲ ὑπὲρ τῶν διωκόντων ὑμᾶς· ποία γὰρ χάρις ἐὰν ἀγαπᾶτε τοὺς ἀγαπῶντας ὑμᾶς; οὐχὶ καὶ τὰ ἔθνη τὸ αὐτὸ ποιοῦσιν; ὑμεῖς δὲ ἀγαπᾶτε τοὺς μισοῦντας ὑμᾶς, καὶ οὐχ ἕξετε ἐχθρόν. ἀπέχου τῶν σαρκικῶν καὶ σωματικῶν	πάντα ὅσα μὴ θέλῃς σοι γενέσθαι, σὺ μηδὲ ἄλλῳ ποιήσῃς· τούτων δὲ τῶν λόγων τὴν διδαχὴν εἰπέ. ἀδελφὲ Πέτρε.	

ἐπιθυμιῶν· ἐάν τίς σοι δῷς ῥάπισμα εἰς τὴν δεξιὰν σιαγόνα, στρέψον αὐτῷ καὶ τὴν ἄλλην, καὶ ἔσῃ τέλειος· ἐὰν ἀγγαρεύσῃ σέ τις μίλιον ἕν, ὕπαγε μετ᾽ αὐτοῦ δύο· ἐὰν ἄρῃ τις τὸ ἱμάτιόν σου, δὸς αὐτῷ καὶ τὸν χιτῶνα· ἐὰν λάβῃ τις ἀπό σου τὸ σὸν, μὴ ἀπαίτει· οὐδὲ γὰρ δύνασαι. παντὶ τῷ αἰτοῦντί σε δίδου καὶ μὴ ἀπαίτει. πᾶσι γὰρ θέλει δίδοσθαι ὁ πατὴρ ἐκ τῶν ἰδίων χαρισμάτων. μακάριος ὁ διδοὺς κατὰ τὴν ἐντολήν· ἀθῷος γάρ ἐστιν. οὐαὶ τῷ λαμβάνοντι· εἰ μὲν γὰρ χρείαν ἔχων λαμβάνει τις, ἀθῷος ἔσται· ὁ δὲ μὴ χρείαν ἔχων δώσει δίκην, ἱνατί ἔλαβε καὶ εἰς τί. ἐν συνοχῇ δὲ γενόμενος ἐξετασθήσεται περὶ ὧν ἔπραξε, καὶ οὐκ ἐξελεύσεται ἐκεῖθεν, μέχρις οὗ ἀποδῷ τὸν ἔσχατον κοδράντην. ἀλλὰ

καὶ περὶ τούτου δὲ		
εἴρηται· Ἱδρωσάτω		
ἐλεημοσύνη σου εἰς		
τὰς χεῖράς σου,		
μέχρις ἂν γνῷς,		
τίνι δῷς.		
Δευτέρα δὲ ἐντολὴ	Πέτρος εἶπεν	
τῆς διδαχῆς· οὐ	· οὐ	Cf. 19.4a-b:
φονεύσεις, οὐ	φονεύσεις, οὐ	οὐ πορνεύσεις, οὐ
μοιχεύσεις, οὐ	μοιχεύσεις, οὐ	μοιχεύσεις, οὐ
	πορνεύσεις, οὐ	
παιδοφθορήσεις, οὐ	παιδοφθορήσεις, οὐ	παιδοφθορήσεις. οὐ
πορνεύσεις, οὐ		μή σου ὁ λόγος τοῦ
κλέψεις, οὐ	κλέψεις, οὐ	θεοῦ ἐξέλθῃ ἐν
μαγεύσεις, οὐ	μαγεύσεις, οὐ	ἀκαθαρσίᾳ τινῶν...
φαρμακεύσεις, οὐ	φαρμακεύσεις, οὐ	Cf. 19.5d: οὐ
φονεύσεις τέκνον	φονεύσεις τέκνον	φονεύσεις τέκνον
ἐν φθορᾷ οὐδὲ	ἐν φθορᾷ οὐδὲ	ἐν φθορᾷ οὐδὲ
γεννηθὲν	γεννηθὲν	πάλιν γεννηθὲν
ἀποκτενεῖς,	ἀποκτενεῖς,	ἀποκτενεῖς...
οὐκ	οὐκ	Cf. 19.6a: οὐ μὴ
ἐπιθυμήσεις τὰ	ἐπιθυμήσεις τὰ	γένῃ ἐπιθυμῶν τὰ
τοῦ πλησίον. οὐκ	τοῦ πλησίον. οὐκ	τοῦ πλησίον σου...
ἐπιορκήσεις, οὐ	ἐπιορκήσεις, οὐ	
ψευδομαρτυρήσεις,	ψευδομαρτυρήσεις,	
οὐ κακολογήσεις,	οὐ κακολογήσεις,	Cf. 19.4d:
οὐδὲ	οὐδὲ	οὐ
μνησικακήσεις,	μνησικακήσεις,	μνησικακήσεις τῷ
		ἀδελφῷ σου...
οὐκ ἔσῃ	οὐκ ἔσῃ	Cf. 19.7a: οὐκ ἔσῃ
διγνώμων οὐδὲ	δίγνωμος οὐδὲ	διγνώμων οὐδὲ
δίγλωσσος·	δίγλωσσος·	γλωσσώδης...
		Cf. 19.8b-c: οὐκ ἔσῃ
παγὶς	παγὶς	πρόγλωσσος· παγὶς
γὰρ θανάτου	γὰρ θανάτου ἐστὶν	γὰρ τὸ στόμα
ἡ διγλωσσία·	ἡ διγλωσσία· οὐκ	θανάτου. ὅσον
οὐκ ἔσται ὁ λόγος	ἔσται ὁ λόγος σου	δύνασαι, ὑπὲρ τῆς
σου ψευδής, οὐ	κενὸς οὐδὲ ψευδής.	ψυχῆς σου
κενός, ἀλλὰ		ἁγνεύσεις...
μεμεστωμένος		
πράξει. οὐκ	οὐκ	Cf. 19.6a: οὐ μὴ

ἔσῃ πλεονέκτης οὐδὲ ἅρπαξ οὐδὲ ὑποκριτὴς οὐδὲ κακοήθης, οὐδὲ ὑπερήφανος· οὐ λήψῃ βουλὴν πονηρὰν κατὰ τοῦ πλησίον σου· οὐ μισήσεις πάντα ἄνθρωπον, ἀλλὰ οὓς μὲν ἐλέγξεις,	ἔσῃ πλεονέκτης οὐδὲ ἅρπαξ οὐδὲ ὑποκριτὴς οὐδὲ κακοήθης, οὐδὲ ὑπερήφανος· οὐ λήψῃ βουλὴν πονηρὰν κατὰ τοῦ πλησίον σου· οὐ μισήσεις πάντα ἄνθρωπον, ἀλλ᾽ οὓς μὲν ἐλέγξεις, οὓς δὲ ἐλεήσεις,	γένῃ πλεονέκτης Cf. 19.3b: οὐ λήμψῃ βουλὴν πονηρὰν κατὰ τοῦ πλησίον σου...
περὶ δὲ ὧν προσεύξῃ, οὓς δὲ ἀγαπήσεις ὑπὲρ τὴν ψυχήν σου.	περὶ ὧν δὲ προσεύξῃ, οὓς δὲ ἀγαπήσεις ὑπὲρ τὴν ψυχήν σου.	Cf. 19.5c: ἀγαπήσεις τὸν πλησίον σου ὑπὲρ τήν ψυχήν σου.
	Ἀνδρέας εἶπεν·	
τέκνον μου, φεῦγε ἀπὸ παντὸς πονηροῦ καὶ ἀπὸ παντὸς ὁμοίου αὐτοῦ· μὴ γίνου ὀργίλος· ὁδηγεῖ γὰρ ἡ ὀργὴ πρὸς τὸν φόνον,	τέκνον μου, φεῦγε ἀπὸ παντὸς πονηροῦ καὶ ἀπὸ παντὸς ὁμοίου αὐτοῦ· μὴ γίνου ὀργίλος· ὁδηγεῖ γὰρ ἡ ὀργὴ πρὸς τὸν φόνον. ἔστι γὰρ δαιμόνιον ἀρρενικὸν ὁ θυμός.	
μηδὲ ζηλωτὴς μήδὲ ἐριστικὸς μηδὲ θυμικός· ἐκ γὰρ τούτων ἁπάντων φόνοι γεννῶνται.	μὴ γίνου ζηλωτὴς μήδὲ ἐριστικὸς μηδὲ θυμαντικός· ἐκ γὰρ τούτων φόνος γεννᾶται.	
	Φίλιππος εἶπεν·	
τέκνον μου, μὴ γίνου ἐπιθυμητής, ὁδηγεῖ γὰρ ἡ ἐπιθυμία πρὸς τὴν πορνείαν,	τέκνον μου, μὴ γίνου ἐπιθυμητής. ὁδηγεῖ γὰρ ἡ ἐπιθυμία πρὸς τὴν πορνείαν και ἕλκει τοὺς ἀνθρώπους	

πρὸς ἑαυτήν. Ἔστι γὰρ θηλυκὸν δαιμόνιον ἡ ἐπιθυμία, καὶ ὃ μὲν μετ᾽ ὀργῆς, ὃ δὲ μεθ᾽ ἡδονῆς ἀπόλλυσι τοὺς εἰσερχομένους αὐτά. Ὁδὸς δὲ πονηροῦ πνεύματος ἁμαρτία ψυχῆς, καὶ ὅταν βραχεῖαν εἴσδυσιν σχῇ ἐν αὐτῷ, πλατύνει αὐτὴν καὶ ἄγει ἐπὶ πάντα τὰ κακὰ τὴν ψυχὴν ἐκείνην καὶ οὐκ ἐᾷ διαβλέψαι τὸν ἄνθρωπον καὶ ἰδεῖν τὴν ἀλήθειαν. Ὁ θυμὸς ὑμῶν μέτρον ἐχέτω καὶ ἐν βραχεῖ διαστήματι αὐτὸν ἡνιοχεῖτε καὶ ἀνακρούετε, ἵνα μὴ ἐμβάλλῃ ὑμᾶς εἰς ἔργον πονηρόν. Θυμὸς γὰρ καὶ ἡδονὴ πονηρὰ ἐπὶ πολὺ παραμένουσα κατὰ ἐπίτασιν δαιμόνια γίνεται, καὶ ὅταν ἐπιτρέψῃ αὐτοῖς ὁ ἄνθρωπος, οἰδαίνουσιν ἐν τῇ ψυχῇ αὐτοῦ καὶ γίνονται μείζονες καὶ ἐπάγουσιν αὐτὸν εἰς ἔργα

	ἄδικα καὶ
	ἐπιγελῶσιν αὐτῷ
	καὶ ἥδονται ἐπὶ τῇ
	ἀπωλείᾳ τοῦ
	ἀνθρώπου.
	Σίμων εἶπεν·
μηδὲ	τέκνον, μὴ γίνου
αἰσχρολόγος μηδὲ	αἰσχρολόγος μηδὲ
ὑψηλόφθαλμος. ἐκ	ὑψηλόφθαλμος. ἐκ
γὰρ τούτων	γὰρ τούτων
ἁπάντων	
μοιχεῖαι	μοιχεῖαι
γεννῶνται..	γίνονται..
	Ἰάκωβος εἶπεν·
τέκνον μου, μὴ	τέκνον μου, μὴ
γίνου οἰωνοσκόπος,	γίνου οἰωνοσκόπος,
ἐπειδὴ ὁδηγεῖ εἰς	ἐπειδὴ ὁδηγεῖ εἰς
τὴν εἰδωλολατρίαν,	τὴν εἰδωλολατρίαν,
μηδὲ ἐπαοιδός,	μηδὲ ἐπαοιδός,
μηδὲ μαθηματικὸς	μηδὲ μαθηματικὸς
μηδὲ	μηδὲ
περικαθαίρων,	περικαθαίρων,
μηδὲ θέλε αὐτὰ	μηδὲ θέλε αὐτὰ
βλέπειν·	ἰδεῖν μηδὲ ἀκούειν·
ἐκ γὰρ τούτων	ἐκ γὰρ τούτων
ἁπάντων	ἁπάντων
εἰδωλολατρία	εἰδωλολατρεῖαι
γεννᾶται.	γεννῶνται.
	Ναθαναὴλ εἶπεν·
τέκνον μου, μὴ	τέκνον μου, μὴ
γίνου ψεύστης,	γίνου ψεύστης,
ἐπειδὴ ὁδηγεῖ τὸ	ἐπειδὴ ὁδηγεῖ τὸ
ψεῦσμα εἰς τὴν	ψεῦσμα ἐπὶ τὴν
κλοπήν, μηδὲ	κλοπήν, μηδὲ
φιλάργυρος, μηδὲ	φιλάργυρος, μηδὲ
κενόδοξος· ἐκ γὰρ	κενόδοξος· ἐκ
τούτων ἁπάντων	τούτων ἁπάντων
κλοπαὶ γεννῶνται.	κλοπαὶ γεννῶνται.
Τέκνον μου, μὴ	Τέκνον μου, μὴ
γίνου γόγγυσος,	γίνου γόγγυσος,
ἐπειδὴ ὁδηγεῖ εἰς	ἐπειδὴ ἄγει πρὸς

τὴν βλασφημίαν,	τὴν βλασφημίαν,	
μηδὲ αὐθάδης,	μηδὲ αὐθάδης,	
μηδὲ πονηρόφρων·	μηδὲ πονηρόφρων·	
ἐκ γὰρ τούτων	ἐκ γὰρ τούτων	
ἁπάντων	ἁπάντων	
βλασφημίαι	βλασφημίαι	
γεννῶνται. Ἴσθι δὲ	γεννῶνται. Ἴσθι δὲ	Cf. 19.4c: ἔσῃ
πραΰς, ἐπεὶ οἱ	πραΰς, ἐπειδὴ	πραΰς,
πραεῖς	πραεῖς	
κληρονομήσουσι	κληρονομήσουσι	
τὴν γῆν.	τὴν βασιλείαν τῶν	
Γίνου	οὐρανῶν. Γίνου	
μακρόθυμος,	μακρόθυμος,	
ἐλεήμων καὶ	ἐλεήμων,	
	εἰρηνοποιός,	
	καθαρὸς τῇ καρδίᾳ	
	ἀπὸ παντὸς κακοῦ,	
ἄκακος καὶ	ἄκακος καὶ	ἔσῃ
ἡσύχιος καὶ	ἡσύχιος,	ἡσύχιος, ἔσῃ
ἀγαθός καὶ	ἀγαθός καὶ	
	φυλάσσων καὶ	
τρέμων τοὺς λόγους	τρέμων τοὺς λόγους	τρέμων τοὺς λόγους
διὰ παντός οὓς	οὓς	οὓς
ἤκουσας.	ἤκουσας.	ἤκουσας... Cf. 19.3:
Οὐχ ὑψώσεις	Οὐχ ὑψώσεις	Οὐχ ὑψώσεις
σεαυτόν,	σεαυτόν,	σεαυτόν, ἔσῃ δὲ
		ταπεινόφρων κατὰ
		πάντα· οὐκ ἀρεῖς
		ἐπὶ σεαυτὸν δόξαν.
		οὐ λήμψῃ βουλὴν
		πονηρὰν κατὰ τοῦ
		πλησίον σου,
οὐδὲ δώσεις	οὐδὲ δώσεις	οὐ δώσεις
τῇ ψυχῇ σου	τὴν ψυχήν σου	τῇ ψυχῇ σου
θράσος.		θράσος... cf. 19.6a-b:
οὐ κολληθήσεται		...οὐδὲ κολληθήσῃ
ἡ ψυχή σου μετὰ	μετὰ	ἐκ ψυχῆς σου μετὰ
ὑψηλῶν, ἀλλὰ μετὰ	ὑψηλῶν ἀλλὰ μετὰ	ὑψηλῶν, ἀλλὰ μετὰ
δικαίων καὶ	δικαίων καὶ	ταπεινῶν καὶ
ταπεινῶν	ταπεινῶν	δικαίων
ἀναστραφήσῃ. Τὰ	ἀναστραφήσῃ. Τὰ	ἀναστραφήσῃ. Τὰ

δὲ συμβαίνοντά σοι	δὲ συμβαίνοντά σοι	συμβαίνοντά σοι
ἐνεργήματα ὡς	ἐνεργήματα ὡς	ἐνεργήματα ὡς
ἀγαθὰ προσδέξῃ,	ἀγαθὰ προσδέξῃ,	ἀγαθὰ προσδέξῃ,
εἰδὼς ὅτι ἄτερ	εἰδὼς ὅτι ἄτερ	εἰδὼς ὅτι ἄνευ
θεοῦ οὐδὲν	θεοῦ οὐδὲν	θεοῦ οὐδὲν
γίνεται.	γίνεται..	γίνεται.
	Θωμᾶς εἶπεν·	
τέκνον μου, τοῦ	τέκνον, τὸν	
λαλοῦντός σοι τὸν	λαλοῦντά σοι τὸν	
λόγον τοῦ θεοῦ	λόγον τοῦ θεοῦ καὶ	
	παραίτιόν σοι	
	γινόμενον τῆς ζωῆς	
	καὶ δόντα σοι τὴν	
	ἐν κυρίῳ σφραγῖδα	Cf. 19.9b-10:
	ἀγαπήσεις ὡς	ἀγαπήσεις ὡς
	κόρην	κόρην τοῦ
	ὀφθαλμοῦ σου,	ὀφθαλμοῦ σου
		πάντα τὸν
		λαλοῦντα σοι τὸν
		λόγον κυρίου.
μνησθήσῃ	μνησθήσῃ αὐτοῦ	μνησθήσῃ ἡμέραν
		κρίσεως
νυκτὸς καὶ ἡμέρας,	νύκτα καὶ ἡμέραν,	νυκτὸς καὶ ἡμέρας,
τιμήσεις δὲ αὐτὸν	τιμήσεις αὐτὸν	καὶ
ὡς κύριον.	ὡς τὸν κύριον.	
Ὅθεν γὰρ ἡ	Ὅθεν γὰρ ἡ	
κυριότης λαλεῖται,	κυριότης λαλεῖται,	
ἐκεῖ κύριός ἐστιν.	ἐκεῖ κύριός ἐστιν.	
Ἐκζητήσεις	Ἐκζητήσεις δὲ	ἐκζητήσεις
δὲ καθ᾽		καθ᾽ ἑκάστην
ἡμέραν τὰ	το	ἡμέραν τὰ
πρόσωπα τῶν	πρόσωπον αὐτοῦ	πρόσωπα τῶν
	καθ᾽ ἡμέραν καὶ	ἁγίων, ἢ διὰ λόγου
	τοὺς λοιποὺς	κοπιῶν καὶ
ἁγίων, ἵνα	ἁγίους, ἵνα	πορευόμενος εἰς τὸ
ἀπαναπαῇς τοῖς	ἐπαναπαύσῃ τοῖς	παρακαλέσαι καὶ
λόγοις αὐτῶν.	λόγοις αὐτῶν·	μελετῶν εἰς τὸ
	κολλώμενος γὰρ	σῶσαι ψυχὴν τῷ
	ἁγίους ἅγιος	λόγῳ...
	ἁγιασθήσῃ.	
	Τιμήσεις δὲ αὐτὸν	

	καθ' ὃ δυνατὸς εἶ ἐκ τοῦ ἱδρῶτός σου καὶ ἐκ τοῦ πόνου τῶν χειρῶν σου. Εἰ γὰρ ὁ κύριος δι' αὐτοῦ ἠξίωσέν σοι δοθῆναι πνευματικὴν τροφὴν καὶ ποτὸν καὶ ζωὴν αἰώνιον, σὺ ὀφείλεις πολὺ μᾶλλον τὴν φθαρτὴν καὶ πρόσκαιρον προσφέρειν τροφήν. ἄξιος γὰρ ὁ ἐργάτης τοῦ μισθοῦ αὐτοῦ, καὶ βοῦν ἀλοῶντα οὐ φιμώσεις καὶ οὐδεὶς φυτεύει ἀμπελῶνα καὶ ἐκ τοῦ καρποῦ αὐτοῦ οὐκ ἐσθίει.	
οὐ ποιήσεις σχίσμα, εἰρηνεύσεις δὲ μαχομένους,	Κηφᾶς εἶπεν· οὐ ποιήσεις σχίσματα, εἰρηνεύσεις δὲ μαχομένους,	Cf. 19.12a: οὐ ποιήσεις σχίσμα, εἰρηνεύσεις δὲ μαχομένους συναγαγών...
κρινεῖς δικαίως,	κρινεῖς δικαίως,	Cf. 19.11d: κρινεῖς δικαίως...
οὐ λήψῃ πρόσωπον ἐλέγξαι ἐπὶ παραπτώμασιν.	οὐ λήψῃ πρόσωπον ἐλέγξαι τινὰ ἐπὶ παραπτώματι, οὐ γὰρ ἰσχύει πλοῦτος παρὰ κυρίῳ· οὐ γὰρ ἀξία προσκρίνει οὐδὲ κάλλος ὠφελεῖ, ἀλλ' ἰσότης ἐστι πάντων	Cf. 19.4b: οὐ λήμψῃ πρόσωπον ἐλέγξαι τινὰ ἐπὶ παραπτώματι...

	παρ᾽ αὐτῷ. ἐν	
οὐ διψυχήσεις πότερον ἔσται ἢ οὔ.	προσευχῇ σου μὴ διψυχήσεις πότερον ἔσται ἢ οὔ.	Cf. 19.5a: οὐ μὴ διψυχήσῃς, πότερον ἔσται ἢ οὔ. οὐ μὴ λάβῃς ἐπὶ ματαίῳ τὸ ὄνομα κυρίου...
Μὴ γίνου πρὸς μὲν τὸ λαβεῖν ἐκτείνων τὰς χεῖρας, πρὸς δὲ τὸ δοῦναι συσπῶν.	Μὴ γίνου πρὸς μὲν τὸ λαβεῖν ἐκτείνων τὰς χεῖρας, πρὸς δὲ τὸ διδόναι συσπῶν.	Cf. 19.9a: Μὴ γίνου πρὸς μὲν τὸ λαβεῖν ἐκτείνων τὰς χεῖρας, πρὸς δὲ τὸ δοῦναι συσπῶν...
Ἐὰν ἔχῃς διὰ τῶν χειρῶν σου, δώσεις λύτρωσιν ἁμαρτιῶν σου. οὐ διστάσεις δοῦναι οὐδὲ διδοὺς γογγύσεις· γνώσῃ γάρ, τίς ἐστιν ὁ τοῦ μισθοῦ καλὸς ἀνταποδότης.	Ἐὰν ἔχῃς διὰ τῶν χειρῶν σου, δώσεις λύτρωσιν τῶν ἁμαρτιῶν σου. οὐ διστάσεις δοῦναι οὐδὲ διδοὺς γογγύσεις· γνώσῃ γάρ, τίς ἐστιν ὁ τοῦ μισθοῦ καλὸς ἀνταποδότης.	Cf. 19.10-11a: ...ἢ διὰ τῶν χειρῶν σου ἐργάσῃ εἰς λύτρωσιν ἁμαρτιῶν σου. οὐ διστάσεις δοῦναι οὐδὲ διδοὺς γογγύσεις· γνώσῃ δέ, τίς ἐστιν ὁ τοῦ μισθοῦ καλὸς ἀνταποδότης...
Οὐκ ἀποστραφήσῃ τὸν ἐνδεούμενον, συγκοινωνήσεις δὲ πάντα τῷ ἀδελφῷ σου καὶ οὐκ ἐρεῖς ἴδια εἶναι· εἰ γὰρ ἐν τῷ ἀθανάτῳ κοινωνοί ἐστε, πόσῳ μᾶλλον ἐν τοῖς θνητοῖς;	Οὐκ ἀποστραφήσῃ ἐνδεούμενον, κοινωνήσεις δὲ ἁπάντων τῷ ἀδελφῷ σου καὶ οὐκ ἐρεῖς ἴδια εἶναι· εἰ γὰρ ἐν τῷ ἀθανάτῳ κοινωνοί ἐστε, πόσῳ μᾶλλον ἐν τοῖς φθαρτοῖς;	Cf. 19.8a: κοινωνήσεις ἐν πᾶσιν τῷ πλησίον σου καὶ οὐκ ἐρεῖς ἴδια εἶναι· εἰ γὰρ ἐν τῷ αφθάρτῳ κοινωνοί ἐστε, πόσῳ μᾶλλον ἐν τοῖς φθαρτοῖς...
οὐκ ἄρῃς τὴν χεῖρά σου ἀπὸ τοῦ υἱοῦ σου ἢ ἀπὸ τῆς θυγατρός σου, αλλὰ ἀπὸ νεότητος διδάξεις αὐτοὺς τὸν φόβον τοῦ θεοῦ.	Βαρθολομαῖος εἶπεν· Ἐρωτῶμεν ὑμᾶς, ἀδελφοί, ὡς ἔτι καιρός ἐστι καὶ ἔχετε εἰς οὓς ἐργάζεσθε μεθ᾽ ἑαυτῶν μὴ ἐκλίπητε ἐν μηδενί, ἐξ οὗ ἂν	Cf. 19.5e: οὐ μὴ ἄρῃς τὴν χεῖρά σου ἀπὸ τοῦ υἱοῦ σου ἢ ἀπὸ τῆς θυγατρός σου, αλλὰ ἀπὸ νεότητος διδάξεις φόβον θεοῦ... Cf. 19.7c:

οὐκ ἐπιτάξεις δούλῳ σου ἢ παιδίσκη, τοῖς ἐπὶ τὸν αὐτὸν θεὸν ἐλπίζουσιν, ἐν πικρίᾳ σου, μήποτε οὐ μὴ φοβηθήσονται τὸν ἐπ᾽ ἀμφοτέροις θεόν· οὐ γὰρ ἔρχεται κατὰ πρόσωπον καλέσαι, ἀλλ᾽ ἐφ᾽ οὓς τὸ πνεῦμα ἡτοίμασεν, ὑμεῖς δὲ οἱ δοῦλοι ὑποταγήσεσθε τοῖς κυρίοις ὑμῶν ὡς τύπῳ θεοῦ ἐν αἰσχύνῃ καὶ φόβῳ.	ἔχητε. Ἐγγυς γὰρ ἡ ἡμέρα κυρίου, ἐν ᾗ συναπολεῖται πάντα σὺν τῷ πονηρῷ· ἥξει γὰρ ὁ κύριος καὶ ὁ μισθὸς αὐτοῦ μετ᾽ αὐτοῦ. Ἑαυτῶν γίνεσθε νομοθέται, ἑαυτῶν γίνεσθε σύμβουλοι ἀγαθοί, θεοδίδακτοι·	οὐ μὴ ἐπιτάξῃς δούλῳ σου ἢ παιδίσκῃ ἐν πικρίᾳ τοῖς ἐπὶ τὸν αὐτὸν θεὸν ἐλπίζουσιν, μή ποτε οὐ μὴ φοβηθήσονται τὸν ἐπ᾽ ἀμφοτέροις θεόν· ὅτι οὐκ ἦλθεν κατὰ πρόσωπον καλέσαι, ἀλλ᾽ ἐφ᾽ οὓς τὸ πνεῦμα ἡτοίμασεν... Cf. 19.7b: ὑποταγήσῃ κυρίοις ὡς τύπῳ θεοῦ ἐν αἰσχύνῃ καὶ φόβῳ Cf. 19.2b: ἔσῃ ἁπλοῦς τῇ καρδίᾳ καὶ πλούσιος τῷ πνεύματι· οὐ κολληθήσῃ μετὰ τῶν πορευομένοων ἐν ὁδῷ θανάτου,
Μισήσεις πᾶσαν ὑπόκρισιν καὶ πᾶν ὃ μὴ ἀρεστὸν τῷ κυρίου.		μισήσεις πᾶν, ὃ οὐκ ἔστιν ἀρεστὸν τῷ θεῷ, μισήσεις πᾶσαν ὑπόκρισιν·
οὐ μὴ ἐγκαταλίπης ἐντολὰς κυρίου,		οὐ μὴ ἐγκαταλίπῃς ἐντολὰς κυρίου... Cf. 19.11b:
φυλάξεις δὲ ἃ παρέλαβες μήτε προστιθεὶς μήτε ἀφαιρῶν.	φυλάξεις ἃ παρέλαβες μήτε προσθεὶς μήτε ὑφαιρῶν.	φυλάξεις δὲ ἃ παρέλαβες μήτε προστιθεὶς μήτε ἀφαιρῶν. εἰς τέλος

μισήσεις τὸ
πονηρόν...
Cf. 19.12b-c:
ἐξομολογήσῃ ἐπὶ
ἁμαρτίαις σου,
οὐ προσήξεις
ἐπὶ προσευχὴν
ἐν συνειδήσει
πονηρᾷ.
αὕτη ἐστὶν ἡ ὁδὸς
τοῦ φωτός.

ἐν ἐκκλησίᾳ
ἐξομολογήσῃ τὰ
παραπτώματά σου,
καὶ οὐ προσελεύσῃ
ἐπὶ προσευχήν σου
ἐν συνειδήσει
πονηρᾷ·
Αὕτη ἐστὶν ἡ ὁδὸς
τῆς ζωῆς.

Select Bibliography

Aland, K., "The problem of anonymity and pseudonymity in Christian literature of the first two centuries", *JTS* 12 (1961) 39-49.

Audet, J.-P., "Affinités littéraires et doctrinales du 'Manuel de discipline'", *Revue Biblique* 59 (1952) 219-238.

Barnard, L.W., "The Dead Sea scrolls, Barnabas, the Didache and the later history of the 'two ways'", in *Studies in the Apostolic Fathers and Their Background* (Oxford 1966) 87-107.

Bartlet, J.V., *Church-life and Church-order during the First Four Centuries* (Oxford 1943).

Baumstark, A., "Alte und neue Spuren eines ausserkanonischen Evangeliums", *ZNW* 14 (1913) 232-247.

Bestmann, C., *Geschichte der christlichen Sitte* II (Nördlinger 1885).

Bovon, F., "Mary Magdalene in the *Acts of Philip*", in F.S. Jones (ed.), *Which Mary: The Marys of Early Christian Tradition* (Atlanta 2002) 75-89.

Bradshaw, P.F., *Ordination Rites of the Ancient Churches of East and West* (New York 1990).

– *The Search for the Origins of Christian Worship: Sources and Methods for the Study of Early Liturgy* (New York 2002[2]).

Brock, A.G., "What's in a name: the competition for authority in early Christian texts", *SBL 1998 seminar papers I* (Atlanta 1998) 106-124.

– "Peter, Paul and Mary: canonical vs non-canonical portrayals of apostolic witnesses", in *SBL 1999 seminar papers* (Atlanta 1999) 173-202.

Butler, B.C., "The 'two ways' in the Didache", *JTS* 12 (1961) 27-38.

Carleton Paget, J., *The Epistle of Barnabas: Outlook and Background* (WUNT 2.64; Tübingen 1994).

Cerrato, J.A., *Hippolytus Between East and West* (Oxford 2002).

Clarke, G.W., *The Letters of St. Cyprian of Carthage*, vol. 4 (New York 1989).

Connolly, R.H., "The use of the *Didache* in the *Didascalia*", *JTS* 24 (1923) 147-157.

– *Didascalia apostolorum* (Oxford 1929).

Daniélou, J., *The Ministry of Women in the Early Church* (London 1961).

Denzey, N., "What did the Montanists read?", *HThR* 94 (2001) 427-448.

Dibelius, M., *Der Hirt des Hermas* (Tübingen 1923).

Draper, J.A., "Barnabas and the riddle of the Didache revisited", *JSNT* 58 (1995) 89-113.

Duchesne, L., Untitled review of Harnack, *Quellen*, *Bulletin Critique* 7 (1886) 361-370.

Faivre, A., "La documentation canonico-liturgique de l'église ancienne", *RevScRel* 54 (1980) 204-219, 273-297.

– "Le texte grec de la Constitution ecclésiastique des apôtres 16-20 et ses sources", *RevScRel* 55 (1981) 31-42.

– "Apostolicité et pseudo-apostolicité dans la 'Constitution ecclésiastique des apôtres': L'art de faire parler les origines", *RevScRel* 66 (1992) 19-67.

– and Faivre, C., "La place des femmes dans le rituel eucharistique des marcosiens. déviance ou archaïsme?", *RevScRel* 71 (1997) 310-328.

Funk, F.X., *Doctrina duodecim apostolorum* (Tübingen 1887).

Gamble, H.Y., *Books and Readers in the Early Church* (New Haven 1995).

Giet, S., "La Didache: enseignement des douze apôtres?", *Melto* 3 (1967) 223-236.

Goodspeed, E.J., "The Didache, Barnabas and the Doctrina", *Anglican Theological Review* 27 (1945) 228-247.

Gryson, R., *The Ministry of Women in the Early Church* (Collegeville 1976).

Hanson, R.P.C., *Eucharistic Offering in the Early Church* (Bramcote 1979).

Harnack, A., *Die Apostellehre und die jüdischen beiden Wege* (Leipzig 1886).

– *Die Lehre der zwölf Apostel nebst Untersuchungen zur ältesten Geschichte der Kirchenverfassung und des Kirchenrechts* (TU 2.1; Leipzig 1886).

The Sources of the Apostolic Canons (Eng. trans; London 1895).

Harris, W.V., *Ancient Literacy* (Cambridge, MA 1989).

Hatch, E., *The Organization of the Early Christian Churches* (London 1881).

Henne, P., *L'unité du Pasteur d'Hermas* (Paris 1992).

Hennecke, E., "Die Grundschrift der Didache und ihre Recensionen", *ZNW* 2 (1901) 58-72.

"Zur apostolischen Kirchenordnung", *ZNW* 20 (1921) 241-248.

Hill, C.E., "The *Epistula apostolorum*: an Asian tract from the time of Polycarp", *JECS* 7 (1999) 1-53.

Jensen, A., *God's Self-confident Daughters* (Kampen 1996).

Kelly, J.N.D., *Early Christian Creeds* (London 1950).

Koester, H., "Überlieferung und Geschichte der frühchristlichen Evangelienliteratur", in W. Haase (ed.), *Aufstieg und Niedergang der Römischen Welt* II.25.2 (Berlin 1984) 1463-1542.

Kraft, R.A., *The Apostolic Fathers 3: Barnabas and the Didache* (New York 1965).

Krawutzcky, A., "Über das altkirchliche Unterrichtsbuch 'Die zwei Wege oder die Entscheidung des Petrus'", *ThQ* 64 (1882) 359-445.

Lemoine, B., "Étude de la notice sur l'évêque dans la 'Constitution ecclésiastique des apôtres (C.E.A.)', *Questions liturgiques* 80 (1999) 5-23.

Maclean, A.J., *The Ancient Church Orders* (Cambridge 1910).

Methuen, C., "Widows, bishops and the struggle for authority in the *Didascalia apostolorum*", *JEH* 46 (1995) 197-213.

Niederwimmer, K., *Die Didache* (Göttingen 1993^2).

Parrott, D.M., "Gnostic and orthodox disciples in the second and third centuries", in C.W. Hedrick and R. Hodgson (eds), *Nag Hammadi, Gnosticism and Early Christianity* (Peabody, MA 1986) 193-219.

Powell, D.L., "Ordo Presbyterii", *JTS* ns 26 (1975) 290-328.

"Tertullianists and Cataphrygians", *VigChr* 29 (1975) 33-54.

Prostmeier, F.R., *Der Barnabasbrief* (Göttingen 1999).

Rordorf, W., and Tuilier, A., *La doctrine des douze apôtres* (Paris 1998).

Rudolph, K., "Der gnostische Dialog als literarisches Genus", in P. Nagel (ed.), *Probleme der koptischen Literatur* (Halle 1968) 85-107.

Schermann, T., *Eine Elfapostelmoral oder die x-Rezension der "beiden Wege"* (Veröffentlichungen aus dem Kirchenhistorischen Seminar München 2.2; Munich 1903).

Schöllgen, G., "Pseudapostolizität und Schriftgebrauch in den ersten Kirchenordnungen", in G. Schöllgen and C. Scholten (eds), *Stimuli: Exegese und ihre Hermeneutik in Antike und Christentum* (Jahrbubch für Antike und Christentum Ergänzungsband 23; Münster 1996) 96-121.

– "Der Abfassungszweck der frühchristlichen Kirchenordnungen", *Jahrbuch für Antike und Christentum* 40 (1997) 55-77.

Schmidt, C., *Gespräche Jesu mit seinen Jüngern nach der Auferstehung* (TU 43; Leipzig 1919).

Sperry-White, G., *The Testamentum Domini: A Text for Students* (Bramcote 1991).

Steimer, B., *Vertex Traditionis* (Berlin 1992).

Stewart-Sykes, A., "The Asian origin of *Epistula apostolorum* and of the new prophecy", *VigChr* 51 (1997) 416-438.

– *Hippolytus: On the Apostolic Tradition* (Crestwood 2001).

– "Bread, fish, water and wine: the Marcionite menu and the maintenance of purity", in G. May and K. Greschat (eds), *Marcion und seine kirchengeschichtliche Wirkung* (TU 150; Berlin 2002) 207-220.

–*The Life of Polycarp: An Anonymous vita from Third-century Smyrna* (Early Christian Studies 4; Sydney 2002).

– "Prophecy and patronage: the relationship between charismatic functionaries and household officers in early Christianity", in C.M. Tuckett and A.F. Gregory (eds), *Trajectories through the New Testament and the Apostolic Fathers* (Oxford 2005) 165-189.

– "The domestic origin of the liturgy of the word", *Studia Patristica*, forthcoming.

Tabbernee, W., "Revelation 21 and the Montanist New Jerusalem", *Austalian Biblical Revue* 37 (1989) 52-60.

Theissen, G., *The Social Setting of Pauline Christianity* (Philadelphia 1982).

Torjeson, K.J., *When Women Were Priests* (San Francisco 1993).

Trevett, C., *Montanism: Gender, Authority and the New Prophecy* (Cambridge 1996).

– "'Angelic visitations and speech she had': Nanas of Kotiaeion", in P. Allen et al. (eds), *Prayer and Spirituality in the Early Church* 2 (Brisbane 1999) 259-277.

– "Spiritual authority and the 'heretical' woman: Firmilian's word to the church in Carthage", in J.W. Drijvers and J.W. Watt (eds), *Portraits of Spiritual Authority: Religious Power in Early Christianity, Byzantium and the Christian Orient* (Leiden 1999) 45-62.

Van de Sandt, H., and Flusser, D., *The Didache: Its Jewish Sources and its Place in Early Judaism and Christianity* (Assen 2002).

Vilela, A., *La condition collégiale des prêtres au IIIe siècle* (Paris 1971).

Wengst, K., *Schriften des Urchristentums* II (Darmstadt 1984).

Wills, L., "The form of the sermon in Hellenistic Judaism and early Christianity", *HThR* 77 (1984) 277-299.

Bibliographical note: the unpublished notes of Pierre Nautin

The reader will find several references to the unpublished work of Pierre Nautin; these citations result from an examination of Nautin's notes which I made in January 2005 in Aix en Provence.

It is clear that Nautin was planning a book on K much like this, having announced his identification of an ancient church order lying behind K in *Annuaire de l'École pratique des hautes Études, V^e section: sciences religieuses* 90 (1981-1982) 335-339.

However, the only part which reached completion was a translation into French; I have compared my own translation to his. For the rest there are notes, frequently re-written, in which we see Nautin struggling to make sense, as may we all, of the contradictions and tensions within the text. However, it is clear that Nautin had reached provisional conclusions at various points since these are repeated frequently in various ways within his notes as sections were re-written, and it is these conclusions to which reference is made.

Indices

1: Ancient authors[•]

1.1: Scripture

[•] References to TWT material in the introduction are not included here, nor are references to K itself.

1.2: Early Jewish literature

1.3: Early Christian literature

1.4: Classical literature

2: Modern authors